MW00776229

Financial Counseling

Dorothy B. Durband • Ryan H. Law
Angela K. Mazzolini

Editors

Financial Counseling

 Springer

Editors
Dorothy B. Durband
School of Family Studies
and Human Services
Kansas State University
Manhattan, KS, USA

Ryan H. Law
Money Management Resource Center
Personal Financial Planning program
Utah Valley University
Orem, UT, USA

Angela K. Mazzolini
Financial Counseling Consultant
Lubbock, TX, USA

ISBN 978-3-319-72585-7   ISBN 978-3-319-72586-4   (eBook)
https://doi.org/10.1007/978-3-319-72586-4

Library of Congress Control Number: 2018956274

© Springer Nature Switzerland AG 2019
This work is subject to copyright. All rights are reserved by the Publisher, whether the whole or part of the material is concerned, specifically the rights of translation, reprinting, reuse of illustrations, recitation, broadcasting, reproduction on microfilms or in any other physical way, and transmission or information storage and retrieval, electronic adaptation, computer software, or by similar or dissimilar methodology now known or hereafter developed.
The use of general descriptive names, registered names, trademarks, service marks, etc. in this publication does not imply, even in the absence of a specific statement, that such names are exempt from the relevant protective laws and regulations and therefore free for general use.
The publisher, the authors, and the editors are safe to assume that the advice and information in this book are believed to be true and accurate at the date of publication. Neither the publisher nor the authors or the editors give a warranty, express or implied, with respect to the material contained herein or for any errors or omissions that may have been made. The publisher remains neutral with regard to jurisdictional claims in published maps and institutional affiliations.

This Springer imprint is published by the registered company Springer Nature Switzerland AG
The registered company address is: Gewerbestrasse 11, 6330 Cham, Switzerland

Foreword

Financial Counseling is a book that is long overdue. And it is a treat! Durband, Law, and Mazzolini have pulled together an excellent collection of readings about the current status of the profession, its competencies, best practices, an overview of effective theories used in financial counseling, and useful resources and tools. It concludes with a provocative chapter on the future.

The book gets the reader off to the right start. This profession is much more than simply financial knowledge or financial literacy. Any practitioner should be competent in educating clients about consumer protection, making major acquisitions (vehicles and homes), managing financial risks, investment basics, and the financial aspects of retirement and estate planning. These topics, and much more, are explored in the initial chapters.

Modern theory used in financial counseling is explored in the middle section of the book. These chapters are well done and introduce the reader to four theoretically rooted postmodern approaches to counseling. This is critical for financial counselors to understand as one assesses a client's readiness for change.

Human behavior, and its impact on our ability to practice financial counseling, is an important focus in the latter third of the book. The psychology behind the physical aspects of office design can help strengthen the counselor–client relationship. Decision-making theories and application of irrational decision-making concepts help counselors make more effective interventions. These chapters include nudges, decision aids, timely education, and conscious perspective changes. Recognizing the signs and symptoms of money disorders—and their accompanying beliefs—enable skilled counselors to help clients who are struggling with these challenges. As these chapters remind us, these disorders are not limited to compulsive buying, overspending, hoarding, gambling, and financial enabling.

The closing chapters are especially helpful for new counselors as they highlight many valuable and proven resources, including tools that may be used to help clients achieve success. If an experienced financial counselor is not already utilizing these resources with clients, it is wise for them to review this list.

The profession of financial counseling is desperate for a unified vision of the future as well as a loyal cadre of followers who are determined to set clear standards and benchmarks about what services they offer and for whom. Helping clients who are financially troubled is important, but guiding those clients through their financial crises and then showing them the tools to remain proactive with their financial future provide them with lasting value. Showing clients the "hows" of achieving lasting success with their personal finances is critical to the sustainability and growth of the profession of financial counseling. It is the old proverb of give someone a fish and you feed them for a day. Teach someone to fish, and you feed them for a lifetime. Building client skills and capabilities is important to both the present and the future of the financial counseling profession.

Professor Emeritus, Virginia Tech   E. Thomas Garman
Blacksburg, VA, USA
Senior author, Personal Finance
Cengage Publications, Boston, MA, USA

Preface

Why This Book?

The ideas that eventually coalesced into this collaborative book came from several distinct, though complementary, places. Multiple thought-provoking hallway discussions at conferences, learning from inspiring colleagues, requests from students, and a shared passion for financial counseling were ultimately what motivated us to consider the need for an updated foundational financial counseling book. A collection gathering essential skills and knowledge is both necessary and timely to continue to introduce people to our profession and to continue to advance our shared goals for the profession.

The editors of this book are all Accredited Financial Counselors who recognize and acknowledge the variety of opportunities and challenges that are encountered during our shared mission to provide for our clients. As financial counseling has grown and expanded into niches that no one could have anticipated even a decade ago, the need for tools that help practitioners serve their varied clientele has grown exponentially. We support the mission of the Association for Financial Planning and Counseling Education, the organization that was formed by professionals from universities, nonprofit organizations, and government and now sets the standard for improving the financial well-being of those whom we serve.

The authors of this book are professionals from a variety of backgrounds who work with clients, teach university students, and conduct research. As financial counseling expands its service to larger and more diverse populations, our ability to draw upon research to inform our practice is imperative. We look to evidence-based approaches used in clinical fields to inform our practice. Our initial idea was to produce a book for financial counseling that sought to marry traditional practices in financial counseling to the growing body of evidence in the field. In our environmental scan and literature review, it is clear that we still have a ways to go, and though this is still a goal, evidence-based was not included as part of the final title.

We are excited to share this book with you and to introduce you to our authors and their perspectives on financial counseling. The current landscape is ever-changing, and as technology is improving, it is becoming more challenging to stay near the curve, let alone ahead of it. A few examples of this hit home during the writing of this book such as the Equifax data breach and Mint.com changing their entire service platform (requiring an entire rewrite of a section that had been completed just the day prior). Imagine how challenging it can be for clients who seek our services. This is why continuing professional development is so important!

How to Use This Book

This edited compilation draws from theoretical foundations using classical and contemporary integrated approaches. This book is intended for readers who are new to the profession and also for more experienced practitioners who want to enhance their professional development. Chapters are authored by financial counseling experts from both academia and practice and cover a series of topics that incorporate the available evidence base for practical and immediate application by both experienced and new financial counselors. These chapters develop a series of themes that include the elements of the financial counseling relationship, the scope and spectrum of financial counseling, self-awareness, delivery models, financial decision-making, problematic financial behaviors, and managing challenging conversations with clients.

We aim to provide the essential components of financial counseling with the intention that the chapters in this book may be used like a ready reference handbook. We chose the various topics for this book based on our training by our mentors, our work with clients, and our interactions with our students in current and previous classes. Our theory selections were driven by the potential for implementation and the authors' experiences teaching or using the theories with students and clients. This book does not need to be read chapter by chapter. Each chapter can stand alone. In most cases, the goal of the authors is to provide as much detail as possible; however, some of the individual chapters cover complex issues that could be expanded to entire books.

Where available, research is cited to advance the use of the evidence base in the practice of financial counseling. It is imperative that we continue to build a bridge between research and practice. Applying research to practice is important, yet historically much of financial counseling has been driven by anecdotal methods and proprietary practices.

It is our hope that this volume will enhance teaching and learning about financial counseling and provide a starting point for the creation of future university courses and training programs in financial counseling. No matter your entry point into the profession, the contents of this book will help you enhance your financial counseling skills.

What's Next

We encourage readers to put the contents of this book to use, share ideas, and provide us with feedback. Together, let's think ahead to the future of financial counseling so that we can advance the profession, help set the future research agenda, and make a difference in the lives of our financial counseling clients.

Manhattan, KS, USA   Dorothy B. Durband
Orem, UT, USA   Ryan H. Law
Lubbock, TX, USA   Angela K. Mazzolini

Acknowledgments

The editors would like to thank Thomas Duffany and Arthur Durband for their work as editorial assistants throughout the idea phase and writing of this book.

The editors express their appreciation to the individuals who provided peer reviews of book chapters.

Michael Abbott, Rosenthal Retirement Planning
Bryan Ashton, Trellis Company
Sonya Britt-Lutter, Kansas State University
Jamie Lynn Byram, Jamie Lynn Byram, LLC
Cristy Cash, Independent Financial Counseling Consultant
Saundra Davis, Sage Financial Solutions
Alycia N. DeGraff, University of Georgia
Daniel Dillon, Program Evaluation Consultant
Thomas A. Duffany, Brightside Benefits
Joseph W. Goetz, University of Georgia
Timothy Griesdorn, University of the Incarnate Word
Clinton Gudmunson, Iowa State University
Ann C. House, University of Utah
Craig Israelsen, Utah Valley University
Vicki Jacobson, Center for Excellence in Financial Counseling
Alena C. Johnson, Utah State University
Emily Koochel, Kansas State University
Derek R. Lawson, Kansas State University
Kari Morgan, Kansas State University
Sarah Newcomb, Morningstar
Niki Pechinski, University of Minnesota Duluth
Sissy R. Osteen, Oklahoma State University
Lance Palmer, University of Georgia
Erika Rasure, Maryville University
Laura C. Ricaldi, Utah Valley University
Oscar J. Solis, Virginia Tech
Rebecca Wiggins, Association for Financial Counseling and Planning Education
Jennifer Wilson, Texas Tech University

Contents

Contributors

Kristy L. Archuleta, Ph.D., LMFT Institute of Personal Financial Planning, Kansas State University, Manhattan, KS, USA

Department of Financial Planning, Housing and Consumer Economics, University of Georgia, Athens, GA, USA

Sarah D. Asebedo, Ph.D., CFP® Department of Personal Financial Planning, Texas Tech University, Lubbock, TX, USA

Bryan Ashton, B.S.B.A. Trellis Company, Austin, TX, USA

Sonya Britt-Lutter, Ph.D., CFP® Institute of Personal Financial Planning, Kansas State University, Manhattan, KS, USA

Mary Bell Carlson, Ph.D., CFP®, AFC® Department of Financial Planning, Housing, and Consumer Economics, College of Family and Consumer Sciences, University of Georgia, Athens, GA, USA

Benjamin F. Cummings, Ph.D., CFP® The American College of Financial Services, Bryn Mawr, PA, USA

Alycia N. DeGraff, M.S., LMFTA University of Georgia, Athens, GA, USA

Lucy M. Delgadillo, Ph.D., CMC School of Applied Sciences, Technology and Education, Utah State University, Logan, UT, USA

Daniel Dillon, M.P.A. Program Evaluation Consultant, Austin, TX, USA

Thomas A. Duffany, M.S., CFP®, AFC® Brightside, Chandler, AZ, USA

Dorothy B. Durband, Ph.D., AFC® School of Family Studies and Human Services, Kansas State University, Manhattan, KS, USA

Megan Ford, M.S., LMFT College of Family & Consumer Sciences, ASPIRE Clinic, University of Georgia, Athens, GA, USA

Joseph W. Goetz, Ph.D. Department of Financial Planning, Housing, and Consumer Economics, University of Georgia, Athens, GA, USA

Camila A. Haselwood, M.S. Institute of Personal Financial Planning, Kansas State University, Manhattan, KS, USA

Ann C. House, M.S. Personal Money Management Center, University of Utah, Salt Lake City, UT, USA

Vicki Jacobson, M.Ed. Center for Excellence in Financial Counseling, University of Missouri-St. Louis, St. Louis, MO, USA

Bradley T. Klontz, Psy.D., CFP® Heider College of Business, Creighton University, Omaha, NE, USA

Ryan H. Law, M.S., CFP®, AFC® Money Management Resource Center, Personal Financial Planning program, Utah Valley University, Orem, UT, USA

Derek R. Lawson, M.S., CFP® Institute of Personal Financial Planning, Kansas State University, Manhattan, KS, USA

Angela K. Mazzolini, M.A., AFC® Financial Counseling Consultant, Lubbock, TX, USA

Sarah Newcomb, Ph.D. Morningstar, Inc., Washington, DC, USA

Sissy R. Osteen, Ph.D., CFP® Department of Human Development and Family Science, Oklahoma State University, Stillwater, OK, USA

Lance Palmer, Ph.D., CFP® Department of Financial Planning, Housing, and Consumer Economics, University of Georgia, Athens, GA, USA

Cherie Stueve, M.B.A., CPA-Inactive, AFC® Institute of Personal Financial Planning, Kansas State University, Manhattan, KS, USA

Rebecca Wiggins, M.S., M.B.A. Association for Financial Counseling and Planning Education®, Westerville, OH, USA

Jennifer Wilson, M.S. Department of Personal Financial Planning, Texas Tech University, Lubbock, TX, USA

About the Authors

Kristy L. Archuleta, Ph.D., LMFT is an Associate Professor of Personal Financial Planning in the School of Family Studies and Human Services at Kansas State University and a Licensed Marriage and Family Therapist. Dr. Archuleta's research interests and therapy work include bridging the fields of financial planning and counseling and marriage and family therapy. She is Co-founder and Co-director of the Institute of Personal Financial Planning Clinic where she conducts research and practices in financial therapy. She is a founding board member of the Financial Therapy Association and is the Coeditor of the *Journal of Financial Therapy*. Dr. Archuleta's research interests are related to the area of financial therapy and include dyadic processes influencing financial satisfaction and marital satisfaction, empirical-based treatment for couples experiencing financial difficulties, and rural and farm families. She has co-edited two books, *Financial Planning and Counseling Scales* and *Financial Therapy: Theory, Research, and Practice* (Springer).

Sarah D. Asebedo, Ph.D., CFP® is an Assistant Professor of Personal Financial Planning with Texas Tech University. With extensive financial planning practitioner experience, her goal is to connect research and financial planning practice. She is spearheading research focused on the intersection between personality, positive psychology, and financial behavior and how mediation and principled negotiation techniques can be employed to resolve money arguments. Her work has been published in the *Journal of Financial Planning*, *Journal of Behavioral Finance*, *Journal of Financial Therapy*, *Journal of Financial Counseling and Planning*, and *Financial Planning Review*. Asebedo's work has been recognized with the 2016 Montgomery-Warschauer Award, 2017 Best Applied Research Award by the Financial Planning Association, 2017 Top 40 Under 40 Award by Investment News, 2017 AARP Public Policy Institute Financial Services and the Older Consumer Award (ACCI), and 2017 Robert O. Herrmann Outstanding Dissertation Award. Asebedo currently serves as President-Elect for the Financial Therapy Association.

Bryan Ashton serves as the Vice-President of Community Investment at Trellis Company (formerly TG). In this capacity, Bryan is responsible for leading the organization's institutional consulting efforts, student support efforts, including student financial coaching services and higher education research, and public policy efforts. Additionally, Bryan is the Co-founder and Co-chair of the Higher Education Financial Wellness Summit. Bryan joined Trellis from Ohio State University, where he led the University's financial wellness efforts (including the nationally recognized Scarlet and Gray Financial Program) and served as the Lead Practitioner and Co-investigator on the Study on Collegiate Financial Wellness.

Sonya Britt-Lutter, Ph.D is an Associate Professor of Personal Financial Planning at Kansas State University and a Certified Financial Planner™ professional. She holds degrees from Kansas State University and Texas Tech University. Her research has been featured in news outlets such as *The New York Times*, *The Wall Street Journal*, Kiplinger, and Yahoo! Finance and has been recognized with the Best Theoretical Paper Award sponsored by the Financial Planning Association and *Journal of Financial Planning* in 2016 and 2017. Sonya recently wrote a love and money curriculum and forthcoming book for couples. Britt-Lutter co-edited *Student Financial Literacy: Campus-Based Program Development*, which leads readers through the process of developing or enhancing financial literacy programs for college students, with Dr. Dorothy Durband. Sonya's work at the financial counseling centers at Texas Tech University and Kansas State University has guided the effectiveness of her financial counseling research agenda.

Mary Bell Carlson, Ph.D is a financial behavior expert. She is a part-time instructor at the University of Georgia and runs her own small business. She has worked with financial counseling clients in various settings including military members, government workers and contractors, and private pay clients. Her Ph.D. is from Kansas State University in Personal Financial Planning with an emphasis in Financial Therapy. She holds the Certified Financial Planner™ and Accredited Financial Counselor® designations. In addition to her academic publications, Dr. Carlson has helped numerous clients and presented various financial topics to a wide variety of audiences. Dr. Carlson has become a sought-after speaker and consultant given her wealth of experience and expertise in the field. She cares deeply about people and is committed to helping others understand more about money, communication, and relationships.

Benjamin F. Cummings, Ph.D., CFP® is an Associate Professor of Behavioral Finance at the American College of Financial Services. He has completed award-winning research on the use and value of financial advice and has been quoted in the media, including in MarketWatch and *USA Today*. Prior to joining the American College, Benjamin was an Assistant Professor at Saint Joseph's University. Previously, he was the Scholar in Residence at CFP Board, and he worked briefly for FJY Financial, a fee-only financial planning firm in Northern Virginia. Benjamin received a B.S. in Psychology from Utah State University and a Ph.D. in Personal Financial Planning from Texas Tech University. When not working, Benjamin enjoys spending time with his family and volunteering for his church.

Alycia N. DeGraff is a Licensed Marriage and Family Therapist Associate in Texas and a Human Development and Family Science doctoral student at the University of Georgia. Ally holds a Master of Science in Marriage and Family Therapy and a Bachelor of Science in Community, Family, and Addiction Services from Texas Tech University. Her interests include topics of military families, addiction and recovery, family finances, and human diversity. She lives in Austin, Texas, with her partner and three animal companions.

Lucy M. Delgadillo, Ph.D. is a Professor and Certified Master Coach in the School of Applied Sciences, Technology and Education, Utah State University. She holds two bachelor's degrees, one in Journalism and one in Broadcasting and Sociology, a Master of Science in Political Sciences, and a Ph.D. in Family Life. Her research interests focus on financial intervention programs to improve individual and family well-being, specifically financial education, financial and housing counseling, financial coaching, and financial therapy. She is also interested in consumer protection and in the synergy between family relations and family finance.

Daniel Dillon is a Program Evaluation Consultant in Texas, where he evaluates health programs and social policy initiatives for state and federal agencies. Daniel holds a Master of Public Affairs and a Bachelor of Arts in Sociology from the University of Texas at Austin. His research includes topics related to income inequality, criminal justice, child support, health care, financial education, and asset-building programs. Daniel's work has been published in academic journals, government reports, and national news outlets. He lives in Austin, Texas, with a human, a dog, and two cats.

Thomas A. Duffany, M.S., CFP®, AFC® is a Financial Assistant at Brightside Benefits where he works with clients to get a handle on their financial situation, improve their financial health, and reduce the stress that results from financial concerns. Previously, he worked for AFCPE® as the Certification Special Programs Director. In that role, he coordinated training and professional development for 60 financial coaches in conjunction with the CFPB Financial Coaching Initiative and worked with universities to establish and maintain programs to support students obtaining AFC® certification and pursuing careers in personal finance. Thomas serves on the AFCPE Career and Student Task Forces to support student programs and raise awareness of career opportunities in financial counseling and education. Thomas earned a bachelor's degree in Personal Financial Planning from the University of Missouri and a master's degree in Personal Financial Planning from Texas Tech University. He has experience working in and with student money management centers on university campuses, has worked with two financial planning firms, and taught undergraduate personal finance courses.

Dorothy B. Durband is Director of the School of Family Studies and Human Services and Professor at Kansas State University. She taught counseling and communication skills courses for students in personal financial planning and was

Founding Director of the nationally recognized Red to Black® program at Texas Tech University. Durband earned a Ph.D. in Resource Management with a specialization in Family Financial Management from Virginia Tech, a master's degree in Family Studies from Texas Woman's University, and a bachelor's degree in Family Life and Environment with an emphasis in Human Services from Louisiana State University. She has been the recipient of three university teaching awards. Dottie is an Accredited Financial Counselor® and is Co-editor of *Student Financial Literacy: Campus-Based Program Development* (Springer).

Megan Ford, M.S., LMFT is the Director of the University of Georgia's ASPIRE Clinic. She served as the President of the Financial Therapy Association from 2016 to 2018. She is a licensed Marriage and Family Therapist in the state of Georgia and is currently pursuing a Ph.D. in Financial Planning at the University of Georgia. Megan earned a master's degree in Family Studies and Human Services from Kansas State University and holds a bachelor's degree in Psychology from the University of South Dakota. She is the former copy editor for *The Journal of Financial Therapy*, and her research interests include linking the areas of mental health and finances, financial conflict in couples, and enhancing therapeutic and communication skill development in the financial services field.

Joseph W. Goetz, Ph.D. teaches in the undergraduate and graduate degree programs in financial planning at the University of Georgia. He is a Co-founder of Elwood & Goetz Wealth Advisory Group, an independent, SEC-registered RIA firm providing comprehensive financial planning services, and the ASPIRE Clinic, which offers pro bono financial planning services to low-income families. He has co-authored more than 50 peer-reviewed publications in the financial planning and counseling field and received the Richard B. Russell Excellence in Teaching Award. Dr. Goetz served as the 2013 President of the Financial Therapy Association and was recognized as the Financial Counselor of the Year by the Association for Financial Counseling and Planning Education. He serves on multiple journal editorial boards. Dr. Goetz completed his studies at the University of Missouri–Columbia, the University of North Carolina at Chapel Hill, and Texas Tech University. He resides in Athens, Georgia, with his wife and son.

Camila A. Haselwood, M.S. is a doctoral student in the personal financial planning program at Kansas State University. She has been an Instructor and Co-instructor for Personal Financial Planning 105 and taught a Love and Money intersession course at Kansas State University. She is a Co-author of *A Descriptive Analysis of Physiological Stress and Readiness to Change*. Camila has been a Powercat Financial Counselor for Kansas State University and Co-chair of the Student Advisory Board and of the Student Affairs Committee for the Graduate School Council.

Ann C. House, M.S. is an Accredited Financial Counselor® and Educator. She established the Personal Money Management Center, a resource for students at the

University of Utah. Before building the center, Ann worked with the state legislature and the state office of education to implement a required financial course in high school. A recently issued "national report card" on state efforts to improve financial literacy gave Utah the only A+. She has managed project grants associated with public education of adults and youth in the areas of personal financial management and microeconomics. She is a published author, adjunct instructor, and professional speaker. She wants her university students to learn to become savvy consumers as they will be making dozens of consumer financial decisions each day throughout their lives.

Vicki Jacobson is the Director of the Center for Excellence in Financial Counseling at the University of Missouri–St. Louis. She recently directed the Center's demonstration project in the development, implementation, monitoring, and evaluation of an evidence-based Student Loan Borrower Repayment Counseling Pilot Program. Vicki previously served as the President of the Foundation for Credit Education prior to its transition as a center at the university. Vicki served in various management roles for the former regional nonprofit Consumer Credit Counseling Service of St. Louis directing the development of numerous award-winning counseling and education programs, including the development of the Council for Economic Education's K-12 Personal Finance Economics curriculum, now known as Financial Fitness for Life. Vicki earned a Bachelor of Science degree from the University of Nebraska–Lincoln and an M.Ed. from Lehigh University in Bethlehem, PA.

Bradley T. Klontz, Psy.D., CFP® is an expert in the field of financial psychology. He is an Associate Professor of Practice at Creighton University–Heider College of Business, Co-founder with Dr. Ted Klontz of the Financial Psychology Institute™, and a Managing Principal at Your Mental Wealth Advisors™. Dr. Klontz is Co-editor of *Financial Therapy: Theory, Research, and Practice* (Springer, 2015) and Co-author of *Mind Over Money: Overcoming the Money Disorders that Threaten Our Financial Health* (Broadway Business, 2009), *Wired for Wealth* (HCI, 2008), *Facilitating Financial Health* (NUCO, 2008; 2016), and *The Financial Wisdom of Ebenezer Scrooge* (HCI, 2005; 2008).

Derek R. Lawson, M.S., CFP® is a doctoral candidate in personal financial planning at Kansas State University where he has served as a Graduate Research Assistant. Derek's research focuses on relationship dynamics, financial therapy, physiological stressors, and behavioral finance. His works have been published in the *Journal of Financial Planning*, *Journal of Financial Therapy*, and *Financial Services Review*. Derek is a Financial Planner at Priority Financial Partners based out of Durango, CO., and serves as the Treasurer of the Financial Therapy Association.

Sarah Newcomb, Ph.D. is a Behavioral Economist at Morningstar where she works to integrate findings from psychological research into financial advice products and services. Prior to joining Morningstar, Sarah earned her Ph.D. in Behavioral

Economics at the University of Maine. Sarah also holds a master's degree in Financial Economics from the University of Maine, a master's certification in Personal Financial Planning from Bentley University, and a bachelor's degree in Mathematics from Salem State University. As an authority on the psychology of financial decisions, Sarah is widely quoted in trade and business publications including *The Wall Street Journal*, *The New York Times*, *Forbes*, *Bloomberg*, and *Money*. She is a regular blogger for *Psychology Today*. She lives with her daughter in Washington, DC.

Sissy R. Osteen is Associate Professor and Department Head in the Department of Human Development and Family Science at Oklahoma State University. Dr. Osteen received her B.S. degree and M.S. degree from the University of Arkansas in Fayetteville, a specialist in education degree in counselor education from the University of South Carolina in Columbia, and received her Ph.D. in Human Sciences from Oklahoma State University. She is a faculty member for the master's program in Family Financial Planning with the Great Plains Interactive Distance Education Alliance (GPIDEA). She is a Certified Financial Planner™ professional. Previously she held positions as a Financial Counselor (Certified Consumer Credit Counselor) and Director of Consumer Credit Counseling Service in Columbia, South Carolina.

Lance Palmer, Ph.D., CFP® is a Professor of financial planning at the University of Georgia. He serves as a clinical faculty supervisor for the ASPIRE Clinic outreach programs, including the Volunteer Income Tax Assistance (VITA) program and financial coaching. He is currently focused on developing brief interventions that are informative and scalable and can easily be integrated into the income tax preparation process. The design and format of the brief interventions are informed by research findings from behavioral economics and behavior change theory, as well as evidenced-based counseling practices such as Solution-Focused Brief Coaching. Dr. Palmer received his bachelor's and M.B.A. degrees from the University of Utah and his doctorate degree from Utah State University. He is a recipient of the University's Richard B. Russell Award for Excellence in Teaching and Engaged Scholar Award.

Cherie Stueve, M.B.A., CPA-Inactive, AFC® is currently completing her doctorate in personal financial planning at Kansas State University. Her research interests include childhood financial socialization and factors that influence financial help-seeking. She has earned a Certificate in Financial Planning and a Financial Therapy Certificate from Kansas State University. Cherie has taught online undergraduate courses in personal finance and created a new course on understanding debt and credit. Cherie has been providing personalized private financial counseling since 2009, helping working families and seniors on money management, savings, and debt payoff goals. In Northeast Kansas, Cherie volunteers her time with various groups to provide financial literacy workshops and financial mentoring.

Rebecca Wiggins is Executive Director of the Association for Financial Counseling and Planning Education® (AFCPE®), where she leads the professional membership and certification organization for the field of financial counseling and education and provides an annual research and training symposium. She has over 10 years of experience in nonprofit organizational management. Previously, Rebecca managed financial education grant-funded programs for military financial counselors and educators, in partnership with FINRA Investor Education Foundation and Department of Defense. As Director of Certification Programs, Ms. Wiggins expanded the Accredited Financial Counselor® (AFC®) University partnership program and implemented policies and procedures for certification candidates. Additionally, she worked to elevate standards and support for the post certification requirements to maintain AFCPE designations. Ms. Wiggins holds a master's degree in Family Financial Planning and a master's degree in Business Administration.

Jennifer Wilson, M.S. is an Instructor in the Department of Personal Financial Planning at Texas Tech University and the Assistant Director of the Personal Finance (PFI) Program. Prior to Texas Tech, she served 3 years in AmeriCorps throughout the country with a focus in financial education, counseling, and resource development. Jennifer earned a master's degree in Personal Financial Planning with a Certificate in Charitable Planning from Texas Tech in 2016. She also has a bachelor's degree in Finance from East Carolina University and an associate's degree from Centralia College. Jennifer serves on the board of the local VITA Program, volunteers with the Lubbock Area United Way, and connects her students through service learning to raise financial awareness throughout Lubbock.

About the Editors

Dorothy B. Durband is Professor and Director of the School of Family Studies and Human Services at Kansas State University. She has spent much of her academic career teaching counseling concepts and communication skills for use in financial planning and counseling settings. Dr. Durband was the Founding Director of the nationally recognized Red to Black® program at Texas Tech University. Her experience includes providing financial counseling and financial education, employee training, and special events planning. She has been the recipient of three university teaching awards. Durband received a Ph.D. in Resource Management with a specialization in Family Financial Management from Virginia Tech, a Master of Science in Family Studies from Texas Woman's University, and a Bachelor of Science in Family Life and Environment from Louisiana State University. She is an Accredited Financial Counselor® and Co-editor of the book *Student Financial Literacy: Campus-Based Program Development* with Dr. Sonya Britt-Lutter.

Ryan H. Law is the Director of the Utah Valley University Money Management Resource Center and an award-winning educator who teaches financial counseling courses as part of the Personal Financial Planning program at Utah Valley University. He teaches Financial Counseling and CFP® and AFC® test preparation. Ryan graduated with a bachelor's degree in Family and Consumer Sciences from Utah State University and a master's degree in Personal Financial Planning from Texas Tech University. He is a Certified Financial Planner™ professional and an Accredited Financial Counselor®.

Angela K. Mazzolini is an Accredited Financial Counselor® and financial counseling consultant living in Lubbock, Texas. She is the former Program Director for Red to Black® Peer Financial Coaching at Texas Tech University, which received campus, state, and national recognition under her leadership. Angela received her Bachelor of Science in Personal Financial Planning and her master's degree in Interdisciplinary Studies with a focus in Personal Financial Planning, Counselor Education, and Management, both from Texas Tech University. She is honored to serve on the Advisory Committee for the

Higher Education Financial Wellness Summit and the Symposium Task Force for the Association for Financial Counseling and Planning Education. She also served on the inaugural Board of Directors for the Texas Association of Collegiate Financial Education Professionals.

Chapter 1
The Financial Counseling Profession

Dorothy B. Durband, Mary Bell Carlson, and Cherie Stueve

Introduction

With a purpose of influencing and motivating clients toward acceptable goals (Pulvino & Pulvino, 2010), financial counseling is "the creative use of all resources to obtain economic well-being for individuals and families" (Williams, 2002). An underlying foundation of the profession is that counseling empowers individuals to resolve financial problems, meet financial goals, and improve their quality of life (Schuchardt et al., 2007). Financial counselors, generally through one-on-one consulting or advice (Collins & O'Rourke, 2010), help clients resolve immediate problems and help them change ingrained problem behaviors (Mason, 1986). Financial counselors are change experts who aid their clients in changing income, expenses, behaviors, and patterns of communication about money or problem-solving methods (Williams, 1997). This collaborative effort between a counselor and client (Carlson, 2014) is about understanding the complex relationship between (a) values, attitudes, emotions, beliefs, self-esteem and (b) spending, saving, borrowing and investing (Hira, 2009).

D. B. Durband (✉)
School of Family Studies and Human Services, Kansas State University,
Manhattan, KS, USA
e-mail: dottie.durband@gmail.com

M. B. Carlson
Department of Financial Planning, Housing, and Consumer Economics, College of Family
and Consumer Sciences, University of Georgia, Athens, GA, USA
e-mail: mary.carlson@uga.edu

C. Stueve
Institute of Personal Financial Planning, Kansas State University, Manhattan, KS, USA

© Springer Nature Switzerland AG 2019   1
D. B. Durband et al. (eds.), *Financial Counseling*,
https://doi.org/10.1007/978-3-319-72586-4_1

Financial Counseling: The Profession

The financial counseling profession emerged as a development from traditional family and consumer economics programs during the late 1970s and early 1980s (Archuleta & Grable, 2011). Universities began providing courses in family financial counseling in the early 1970s and added family financial counseling courses for majors in family economics and family financial counseling in the 1980s (Langrehr & Langrehr, 1986). Such financial counseling programs were created by faculty who recognized the need to create a college major that provided students with the ability to apply family financial management knowledge as a career focus (Langrehr & Langrehr, 1986).

Faculty and Cooperative Extension professionals at Virginia Polytechnic Institute and State University held a national conference on financial counseling in 1979 to bring together a diverse group of financial counselors from the USA and Canada. A review of the conference proceedings roster revealed the conference attendance included individuals representing academia, industry, credit counseling, credit unions, family services, the legal profession, and government (Myhre, 1979). The proceedings also referenced two prior conferences of a similar nature at the University of Wisconsin in 1967 and the University of Maryland in 1975 (Myhre, 1979). A few years later, in 1983 at Brigham Young University, a national financial planning and counseling consortium led to the formation of the Association for Financial Counseling and Planning Education® [AFCPE®] (Hira, 2009). The AFCPE was formally established a year later during a subsequent conference in 1984 at Iowa State University (Burns, 2008; Hira, 2009).

As of 1991, no clear definition of the professional financial counselor existed nor did a set of standards or board of examiners for accreditation (Langrehr, 1991). AFCPE led the efforts to create a certification program with established standards for education requirements for individuals in practice to refer to themselves as financial counselors (Langrehr). A financial counseling certification program was launched by AFCPE® in 1993 (Burns, 2008) and today, the association offers the Accredited Financial Counselor® and Certified Housing Counselor® (CHC®) certification and training programs. To bring further validity to the high quality of the AFC® credential, AFCPE sought and received accreditation by the National Commission for Certifying Agencies (AFCPE, n.d.-b) in 2015.

Financial counseling, as contrasted with financial planning, is seen as a distinct approach to help consumers change their financial behavior and resulting outcomes (Archuleta & Grable, 2011). "During the formative years of the profession, financial counselors sometimes explored the same client issues as financial planners, but in most cases the focus was on helping consumers utilize skills and family resources to help meet financial objectives" (Archuleta & Grable, 2011, p. 36). Both financial counselors and planners must have some depth of knowledge in all areas of personal finance (Langrehr, 1991). The chapter that immediately follows addresses core competencies for financial counselors.

Although financial counseling may be thought of as only helping with remedial issues, more often, financial counselors can assist their clients with proactive financial decisions (Carlson, 2014). Individuals and couples have a variety of reasons for seeking financial counseling, though no comprehensive studies exist that provide in-depth insight into this area. In a survey of credit counseling clients who participated in a nationwide initiative over 18 months ($n = 14,072$), over half of the clients (63%) reported seeking the services of a credit counselor because of a reduction in income, driven by a change in employment. Nearly 30% of the clients reported increased expenses as the reason for credit counseling due to medical/disability expenses and increases in debt payments because of increased interest rates. The remainder of clients (31%) reported other reasons, with most reporting poor credit standing (Roll & Moulton, 2016). A survey of credit unions representing 45 states and 27% of credit union memberships in the USA revealed five common reasons members sought financial counseling services: money management, credit report reviews, debt management, savings accumulation, and retirement/ estate planning (National Credit Union Foundation [NCUF], 2012). A national survey of community-based organizations (CBOs) in the Consumer Action network, inclusive of credit counseling agencies, immigrant/refugee services, government agencies, Cooperative Extension, libraries, social services, churches, and other local nonprofits, revealed that 36.8% of individuals who sought their services were primarily for financial counseling. Other frequent responses were mortgage/housing counseling (50%), utility bill counseling (29%), and public benefit counseling (28.2%) (Consumer Action, 2009). Of note is the teachable moment; CBOs reported that while an urgent issue such as a late utility bill brings clients to them, "It is then that the counselor has an opportunity to address the larger financial issue that most likely exists but is not acknowledged…. he or she can educate the client on personal finance at the very point in time when he or she is most receptive to the information and advice" (Consumer Action, 2009, p. 6). In a decade of annual surveys on the state of general stress in the USA, Americans have consistently reported money, work, and the economy as very significant or somewhat significant sources of stress in their lives (American Psychological Association, 2017). The increasing complexity and number of financial decisions households make may also increase the need for professional assistance (Robb, Babiarz, & Woodyard, 2012). Thus, the number of individuals and families seeking financial counseling is expected to continue to be robust.

Approaches to Financial Counseling

Approaches to providing financial counseling have generally followed a series of steps and been process driven, rather than determined by a theory or a model (Archuleta & Grable, 2011). However, no one single approach to financial counseling is recommended over another one. Toward a goal of enhancing the practice of financial counseling, this book presents theories, frameworks, and tools that may be applied in an integrated or blended approach to financial counseling. A financial counselor's role or approach to working with clients is inclusive of several factors, such as (a) how and why the client(s) were referred to the counselor, (b) the needs and goals of the client(s), (c) the motivation level of the client(s), and (d) the training, educational background, and expertise of the counselor. Each practice environment and approach are also influenced by the aforementioned factors, the preferences of the individual financial counselor, and the mission and values of one's employer and umbrella professional organizations.

Career paths are still evolving in this relatively young profession and are becoming more varied over time; therefore, no single role can be dubbed "financial counselor." A search of the *Occupational Outlook Handbook* of the U.S. Bureau of Labor Statistics (BLS) for the term financial counselor offers a description for personal financial advisor (2017, October). The BLS provides an optimistic overview for expected occupational growth in financial specialists who work with money and help clients achieve their goals. Though financial counselors are not explicitly referenced in the search, BLS provides a list of varied titles for financial specialists such as credit counselors and personal financial advisors (Royster, 2014). The BLS estimates a 15% growth in the financial advising field between 2016 and 2026, more than twice the average growth rate of other professions. This highlights the diversification and growth potential of financial services professions, most of which will engage in some form of financial counseling.

Where Do Financial Counselors Work?

Financial counselors engage in a variety of different occupations and delivery methods when working with their clients. A review from some earlier discussions of financial counseling provides some context on the progression of the profession into a variety of services and delivery styles. For many years, financial counseling has been provided as a stand-alone service or as a portion of the offerings of many programs and organizations including: consumer credit counseling agencies, commercial credit counseling agencies, credit unions, extension, family services, community action programs, housing counseling, mental health agencies and by clergy and private therapists (AFCPE, n.d.-a; Myhre, 1979; Williams, 1979). In a 1980 review, Bagarozzi and Bagarozzi identified three major areas for financial counseling: credit counseling organizations, credit union programs, and corporate credit counseling programs. Since that time, financial counselors have expanded to practice in several additional settings. Today, many different career pathways and occupational opportunities exist for financial counselors, but estimating the size of the profession is difficult, as there have been no known comprehensive studies of individuals that specifically refer to themselves as financial counselors. The following sections provide an overview of current known career pathways.

Financial Counselors as a Part of a Program or Organization

Financial counselors are employed in nonprofit social service organizations, health-care organizations, and financial services organizations. Because the missions of these organizations vary, the role of the financial counselor will also vary depending on the agency and the needs of the target audiences they serve. Financial counselors are typically tasked with teaching financial literacy and techniques for increasing financial capability. Such programs may be aligned with the organization's mission, or they could be offered as a part of an employee's benefits or wellness initiative.

Workplace programs. Employers may offer financial counseling to employees as an employer-provided benefit to help them with personal financial matters (Kim, 2016). Employee Assistance Programs (EAPs) or workplace wellness programs are intended to help employees correct or prevent problems that pose issues for performance productivity (Hutchison & Vickerstaff, 2009). Many employers have moved their EAP efforts into health wellness programs, whereas some employers have added a financial counseling component (Consumer Financial Protection Bureau [CFPB], 2014). Financial wellness programs embedded within EAPs can complement the retirement and employee benefits seminars arranged by human resource departments (Kim). Workplace financial wellness programs have gained interest, both from the perspective of the employer (CFPB) and from the employee (International Foundation of Employee Benefit Plans, 2016). According to the Society for Human Resource Management [SHRM] (2015), requests for financial counseling through EAPs are rising at a rate twice that of requests for other EAP services. These financial counseling services may be delivered on site, via telephone, or in an online meeting. Some workplaces maintain financial counselors on site, whereas others outsource counseling services to externally contracted providers.

Credit counseling organizations. Nonprofit consumer credit counseling organizations employ financial counselors to work with individuals or couples to provide three core services: (a) individualized budget and money management counseling, (b) debt management plans to consolidate payments, waive fees, and improve interest rates, and (c) financial education (Roll & Moulton, 2016). Other services provided, contingent on the agency, include credit report reviews, reverse mortgage counseling, first-time homebuyer counseling, housing and mortgage counseling, and student loan debt counseling (National Foundation for Credit Counseling, n.d.). Credit counseling agencies that are approved by the United States Trustee Program provide pre-bankruptcy budget and credit counseling to individuals planning to file bankruptcy (National Consumer Law Center, 2013; United States Department of Justice, n.d.).

Credit unions. Credit unions offer financial counseling to their members through individual sessions or educational programs (NCUF, 2012; National Federation of Community Development Credit Unions [NFCDCU], 2015). Topics for individual sessions can include money management and budgeting, credit report reviews, debt management, and savings accumulations (NCUF). Referrals to a financial counselor can result from situations such as a member being denied a loan, having an overdrawn account, or being delinquent on an account (NFCDCU). Financial counseling services can be provided onsite, via telephone, online, or through a referral to an off-site credit counseling agency (NCUF).

Community-based organizations. Community-based organizations (CBOs) support a wide spectrum of financial counseling and financial literacy services, including free income tax preparation services (e.g., Volunteer Income Tax Assistance [VITA]), housing transition, workforce development, home buying, financial aid, health insurance enrollment, and family services. Individuals may be offered financial counseling services directly from charitable and nonprofit social service agencies, or such services may be offered in conjunction with community-based organizations.

Faith-based programs. Places of worship may supplement their spiritual counseling with financial counseling, offering educational programs developed by other organizations (Leland, 2007), or allowing organizations to present to their parishioners (Fondation, Tufano, & Walker, 1999). Pastors and lay leaders serve as caregivers to their congregations and their communities, which includes helping families experiencing financial crises (Sneed, Wise, Berry, & Gault, 2011). An exploratory study of clergy members revealed that they often include a financial component as a part of premarital counseling programs (Halley, Durband, Gustafson, & Bailey, 2011).

Healthcare-based programs. Financial counselors work in healthcare settings such as hospitals, clinics, and private practice physician offices. Responsibilities may include educating patients about their insurance benefits and coverage, assisting with paperwork, answering questions about billing, and evaluating the availability of financial resources for patients (Gesme & Wiseman, 2011). Hospitals may refer patients who require expensive forms of care (e.g., neurology, rheumatology, or cancer) to financial counselors to review the patient's treatment plans and restrictions on coverage (Associated Press, 2017).

University-based programs. Financial counseling programs that provide education and skills to students are expanding across colleges and universities in the United States (Durband & Britt, 2012). Financial counseling services may be delivered by an employee of the university or by peer student counselors (Grable, Law, & Kaus, 2012). A university-employed financial counselor may work in student affairs or financial aid, with responsibilities that include individual counseling sessions with students or presentations to parents, academic classes, and student groups. Some financial counselors also help with financial aid counseling and other services to meet the needs of the students. In a peer-to-peer program, the university-employed financial counselor's responsibilities are typically centered on their role as program coordinator or director, which includes oversight of policy and procedures, training and supervision of peer counselors, and evaluation of program services.

Extension. Another university-affiliated delivery system for financial counseling is the Cooperative Extension system offered through land-grant colleges or universities (Land grant impacts, n.d.). As part of their missions, land-grant institutions have a third role, beyond teaching and research, to extend programming to adults, youth, and children in their communities throughout their states (AFCPE, n.d.-a). Extension professionals provide financial counseling and financial education to citizens in their assigned location, usually a specific county or region. A county extension professional may offer financial counseling as part of a workshop, or they may provide individual financial counseling sessions. In addition, both extension specialists and extension agents create and publish research-based materials on money management, insurance, retirement, and other financial topics to distribute to consumers (eXtension, n.d.).

Government programs. Governments are increasingly hiring financial counselors to provide services to work with various audiences within the civil service workforce. The Office of Personnel Management (OPM) encourages agencies to enlist financial counseling services to provide information and training to the workforce on federal government benefits (OPM, n.d.). These counselors can help educate government employees to prepare for financial health in retirement, increase financial literacy, and improve financial security. Both OPM and the Thrift Savings Plan employ retirement counselors to help government employees transition into retirement. Many of these retirement consultants also serve as financial counselors and help individuals understand basic financial matters that could impact their retirement capability. Several government agencies have enlisted the services of financial counselors to help their employees who maintain a security clearance. Both the military and intelligence communities hire financial counselors to help mitigate this risk. Financial reasons are documented as the primary motive for espionage (Fischer, 2000). Therefore, a person's financial matters are reviewed before a security clearance is issued.

The Department of Defense (2003) created a financial readiness campaign that includes financial education for all service members. Each of the military branches has its own financial readiness program and employs numerous financial counselors around the world. Some work on military installations within service-funded programs, whereas others work for military contractors who provide resources and counseling to service members as needed. The Consumer Financial Protection Bureau (CFPB) and the Department of Veterans Affairs (DVA) also employ financial counselors to help improve the financial literacy of military personnel and veterans.

Local governments hire financial counselors to help citizens become more financially aware. A city-based initiative, called Cities for Financial Empowerment Fund (n.d.), provides funding to offer financial empowerment services and programs for local citizens. Pilot programs started in large cities have demonstrated success in helping citizens improve their financial capability. Now some cities offer financial counseling programming to help improve the financial stability of residents. Other services, such as local housing authorities, also offer financial education seminars and sessions to help citizens with their housing needs.

Private practice. As the profession of financial counseling expands and more households recognize the need for financial counseling assistance, financial counselors are establishing private fee-based practices to serve the growing demand for financial professionals (Robb et al., 2012; Schuchardt et al., 2007). The private practice financial counseling model is a self-employment, entrepreneurial opportunity for experienced financial counselors to provide services directly to consumers for a fee. Some financial counselors work with individuals, couples, or families in private sessions. Others may teach stand-alone classes or a series of financial education workshops on specific topics such as credit scores, home buying, budgeting, or debt-payoff strategies. Many private practice professionals combine both presentations and private sessions to reach broader audiences. Financial counselors in private practice attract clients based on the services they offer; this can be a narrow focus of counseling in a subject specialty, a problem orientation, or a broader focus of counseling services (Wall, 2002).

Financial counseling in private practice can be structured in many ways. Some practitioners work solely with individual clients, whereas others work as independent contractors within larger organizations. Private practice financial counselors may also create a niche for working in specific areas of need or with targeted groups to help carve out a specific client population to help. Some common niche specialties include: collaborative practice financial specialist for family disputes, consultant to other financial professionals, or keynote speakers. These niches help in marketing the private practice financial counselor's business.

How Is Financial Counseling Delivered?

Financial counseling services can be delivered in person, via telephone, or via video conferencing. In-person counseling is typically delivered in office settings or meeting rooms but also may require a mixed-use or multifunctional space to accommodate the various activities that a financial counselor performs within the organization. In university-based settings, multifunctional office space can be used by clinical programs (e.g., marriage and family therapy or psychology) or student services (e.g., student legal services, student counseling, or career services) (Durband & Gustafson, 2012). For private practitioners who work with clients in private sessions, their work location is typically a permanent office, home office, the client's home, or a neutral location, such as a coffee shop. Some financial counselors rent temporary office space such as by-the-hour office suites or co-op arrangements to meet clients.

How Do Financial Counselors Use Technology?

Financial counselors are increasingly adopting technology to interact with clients, assess client situations, and follow up with clients. Though this has not been a topic of research, the use of technology may influence a client's selection of a financial counselor. A client's schedule, or preference for interaction, may also be determining factors in a financial counselor's use of technology. Frequent business travelers, or clients who telecommute, may prefer the scheduling flexibility offered by a counselor who can offer sessions via video conferencing.

Financial counselors may use computer software to assist clients with budgeting and goal tracking. Some common choices of financial counseling software include Excel, application platforms (e.g., Mint, You Need a Budget, Quicken), or online tools for loan amortization and debt-payoff schedules (e.g., PowerPay). Other uses of technology may include creating financial education videos that a client can access via the counselor or organization's website to help teach financial concepts or reinforce learning. The financial counselor may have additional resources for clients on assorted topics available for reading or downloading. Some counselors maintain a blog to write articles and provide financial education to their clients and readers. (Chapter 12 provides a review of tools and resources that are available for use.)

Larger organizations may subscribe to a software program that is used with the client in both the financial counseling office and at home. With an online program, the financial counselor can review the client's action plan or progress between sessions. Some online programs used by financial counselors include short financial education modules and assessment tools designed to gauge financial behaviors and attitudes. Financial counselors can ask clients to complete specific modules as homework between sessions.

Internet and mobile technology allow financial counselors to serve clients regardless of geographic location. Financial counseling sessions can be conducted by phone or online. Email and text messages allow communication between counseling sessions for follow-up summaries, questions, appointment reminders, or encouragement. Chat sessions and online bulletin boards can provide a means for clients to engage with peers or counselors in a relatively anonymous relationship to help them test and express their ideas (Pulvino & Pulvino, 2010). As noted by Ross, Gale, and Goetz (2016), although financial practitioners maintain the confidential nature of their clients' information, the use of electronic communications is somewhat of a gray area in the ethical codes of two national organizations that certify financial professionals (i.e., CFP® and AFC®). Rapidly changing technology will expand counseling opportunities and ultimately result in innovations for working with financial counseling clients, but counselors should be aware of their ethical obligations to their clients when using such media.

What Are the Terms of the Financial Counseling Engagement?

Regardless of the number of sessions, the goal of financial counseling is to build the client's financial skills and capabilities to make ongoing and future financial decisions independently. Financial counselors should be aware of the potential for client dependency and work to build the confidence and skills needed to eliminate reliance on the professional. Some financial counselors state upfront that their goal with clients is to work themselves out of a job—to build up financial capabilities and confidence to the point where the client no longer needs assistance for ongoing financial management. Mason (1986) noted that financial counselors, as contrasted with financial planners, tend to view their work with clients as successful when clients become more effective at functioning without their counselor's assistance. However, the client may return to the financial counselor in the future with new questions or a life event (e.g., loss of income, changes in relationships) that creates new concerns. A client's financial issue or goal may take time to complete, such as raising a credit score or saving enough for a down payment on a home. In these cases, financial counselors should not overlook the incremental progress a client makes while actively working to resolve a crisis or learning more about money management strategies. This positive feedback can provide ongoing motivation that clients need while working on long-term financial goals or behaviors. A comprehensive financial counseling relationship may involve multiple sessions over time to address issues like savings goals, increasing net worth, investment education, decisions about employer benefits, and retirement plan participation.

How Are Financial Counselors Compensated?

Compensation models for financial counselors vary from salaried positions to hourly rates depending upon the delivery model, the agency, or private practice. A private practice financial counselor may offer individual sessions on an hourly as-needed basis, with a discount for a specific number of sessions. Some private practice financial counselors require a set fee upfront for a specific number of sessions. Others may request an upfront deposit for a specific number of sessions with the remainder due in the future. Some private practice financial counselors work with clients referred from other professionals, such as attorneys, financial planners, or therapists, who pay for a set number of sessions to work with their client. As the field of financial planning explores the effective use of monthly retainer fees (Moore, 2017), financial counseling practices may follow with a set fee for access for a specific period of time.

A private practice financial counselor may choose to work with clients who currently do not have the ability to pay the established fees. In this situation, the financial counselor may elect to reduce the fee, work on a sliding scale based on the client's income, or agree to an increasing-fee schedule. Some private practice financial counselors believe that the client should have some investment in the process regardless of financial circumstances and should pay a nominal amount to work with the counselor. As with financial counselors working in larger organizations, the private practice financial counselor may provide short-term consultation for a specific issue or long-term collaboration with multiple sessions to address different areas of the client's financial life.

Private practice financial counselors who work independently or as part of a financial counseling team may deliver financial education through conducting workshops, and charge attendees an admission fee. Workshops may also be paid for by a sponsor and provided free to attendees. Some financial counselors find that well-advertised classes help introduce consumers to the financial counseling process in a comfortable learning environment. After the session, attendees may then decide to work privately with the financial counselor and pay for future sessions.

Financial counselors may also elect to volunteer their expertise as part of a community program, peer network, ministry, support program, or directly to consumers. Pro bono work may be in addition to their paid work. Sometimes professionals first entering the financial counseling profession find that volunteer work is the most readily available way to earn required practicum hours and gain experience and skills for a certification.

Training and Certification of Financial Counselors

College and university programs offer courses or certificate and degree programs specializing in financial counseling and financial planning (e.g., AFCPE® Approved Education Programs or Certified Financial Planner Board Registered Programs). As part of their curriculum, academic programs provide internships, practicums, or service-learning opportunities for students to gain experience through volunteering as supervised financial counselors.

Historically, nonprofit organizations hired associates as financial counselors with the understanding that training would be provided, and certification achieved within a defined term of employment. Certification program enrollment was contingent upon employment by a financial counseling organization and number of counseling hours delivered before sitting for the certification exam. Obtaining certification credentials is required for continued employment by the nonprofit financial counseling provider. Typically, a nonprofit financial counseling organization offers a variety of services that requires the financial counselor to achieve and maintain certification, such as Housing and Urban Development (HUD) housing counseling certification or the certification for counselors working in National Foundation for Credit Counseling member agencies (NFCC, n.d.), to name a few.

Important to note is that financial counselors employed by nonprofit agencies gain experience through their employment, but upon leaving the organization any certification achieved is no longer valid as it is contingent upon employment by the agency. The employer covers any certification expenses to the financial counselor as a benefit of employment. Some financial counselors may seek certification independently through programs that are not contingent upon employment by a specific provider.

Partnerships and Referrals

In certain situations, a financial counselor will need to refer clients to other professionals, partnerships, or other resources. For example, a client may need a referral to a food bank or to asset building tools toward a goal of home ownership. Another example would be a client that has concerns about their investments and wants further advice that is outside the knowledge base of the counselor. In this case it would be appropriate for the financial counselor to refer the client to a financial planner. Therefore, a financial counselor should not give tax, legal, investment, or mental health advice without being properly trained, registered, and credentialed. Financial counselors should be vigilant and guard against giving advice or working beyond their expertise.

Likewise, situations may arise when financial professionals, such as accountants, attorneys, or financial planners, will defer to the expertise of a financial counselor on a specific client situation. Some financial professionals work with the financial counselor as a consultant on the situation or, more commonly, the financial professional will refer the client to the financial counselor to receive help with the specific concern. One example of how a financial counselor works with other financial professionals is in couples counseling, where both financial and marital counseling services are combined to assist couples decrease both financial and relationship strain (Green-Pimentel, Goetz, Gale, & Bermudez, 2009). A client that struggles with an underlying addiction and has financial concerns could work with both an addiction specialist and a financial counselor. The addiction specialist may require that the client become stable with their treatment plan before receiving financial counseling help. This tiered approach helps target the greatest need while also being sensitive to the complexity of the situation.

In some instances, a client referral made to a financial counselor is not voluntary. The counseling may be mandated by a court order, required to receive a loan, required to file for bankruptcy, or required by an employer through an EAP for disciplinary reasons or performance (SHRM, 2015). Most likely, a financial counselor working with a client under these circumstances would be asked to provide verification to the referring organization that the client attended the session, that the services were delivered, and whether the client participation was satisfactory. Care must be taken to protect client confidentiality. Client information must only be shared with the referral source, and often requires a client-signed release of information form similar to the mental health field.

Sometimes financial counselors must make a referral to another financial counselor due to the need of the counselor to recuse themselves from a given client situation due to a conflict of interest or personality differences. For example, in a divorce case, a financial counselor should refer one party to another counselor if both spouses want financial counseling services from the same professional. In other situations, if a financial counselor feels that they will be biased or unable to work with a client with a specific type of personality, then a referral may be appropriate to offer the best assistance to the client.

Other service providers, such as Certified Public Accountants (CPAs), CERTIFIED FINANCIAL PLANNER™ (CFP®) professionals, legal professionals, and mental health professionals, are expanding their teams to include financial counselors or are referring clients to qualified financial counselors. For example, a client may feel more comfortable meeting with a financial counselor than another financial professional for help with financial issues related to relationships or behaviors. A financial counselor may bring in their expertise about day-to-day money management, saving and spending behaviors, relationship dynamics, or employee benefits that complements the help provided by a legal, mental health, or other financial professional. The presence of a financial counselor as part of a larger financial service practice or as a referred service provider aligns with the concept of a continuum of care that helps individuals with all aspects of their financial health (AFCPE, 2017; Wiggins, 2016). Working together with other professionals in a continuum of care will yield benefits to both clients and professionals.

Conclusion

Financial counselors practice, educate, and volunteer in a variety of settings, including nonprofit organizations, government agencies, higher education, and private practice. Financial counseling is a growing profession that is evolving to address the needs and challenges that individuals and families face in managing their financial resources. Counseling is a tool for constructive change that can equip individuals to help make wise decisions and achieve financial security (Schuchardt et al., 2007). Financial counselors work in education, government agencies, the private sector, and nonprofit organizations (AFCPE, n.d.-a). Services are provided by credit counselors, housing counselors, social workers, university educators, clergy, employers, employee assistance programs, healthcare employees, banking and credit union professionals, and military support services. Other financial counselors work in more independent roles, such as contractors, consultants, self-employed practitioners, and volunteers. Trusted referral sources are essential when additional client services are needed beyond the scope of a financial counseling practice or program. These partnerships with other resources and professionals are a necessary component of holistic services that help clients navigate their financial needs and make decisions throughout the life cycle.

References

American Psychological Association. (2017). *Stress in America: Coping with change.* Retrieved from https://www.apa.org/news/press/releases/stress/2016/coping-with-change.pdf

Archuleta, K., & Grable, J. E. (2011). The future of financial planning and counseling: An introduction to financial therapy. In J. E. Grable, K. Archuleta, & R. R. Nazarinia (Eds.), *Financial planning and counseling scales* (pp. 33–59). New York: Springer. https://doi.org/10.1007/978-1-4419-6908-8

Associated Press. (2017, June 7). *Financial counselors help patients navigate costly care.* Retrieved from https://www.statnews.com/2017/06/07/financial-counselors-hospitals/

Association for Financial Counseling and Planning Education®. (2017). *2017 year in review.* Retrieved from http://www.afcpe.org/uploads/docs/AFCPE%20Annual%20Report-2017%20Year%20In%20Review%20FINAL.pdf

Association for Financial Counseling and Planning Education®. (n.d.-a). *AFCPE® career paths.* Retrieved from https://afcpe.org/career-center

Association for Financial Counseling and Planning Education®.(n.d.-b). *AFCPE® certification & training.* Retrieved from https://www.afcpe.org/certification-and-training

Bagarozzi, J. I., & Bagarozzi, D. A. (1980). Financial counseling: A self control model for the family. *Family Relations, 29*(3), 396–403.

Bureau of Labor Statistics, U.S. Department of Labor (2017, October 17). *Occupational outlook handbook*, Personal financial advisors. Retrieved from https://www.bls.gov/ooh/business-and-financial/personal-financial-advisors.htm

Burns, S. A. (2008). Promoting applied research in personal finance. In J. J. Xiao (Ed.), *Handbook of consumer finance* (pp. 411–418). New York, NY: Springer.

Carlson, M. (2014). Financial counselor versus financial coach: What's the difference anyway? *AFCPE® the Standard, 32*(4), 1 12. Retrieved from http://afcpe.org/assets/publications/newsletter/Q4-2014.pdf

Cities for Financial Empowerment. (n.d.). *Projects*. Retrieved from http://cfefund.org/

Collins, J. M., & O'Rourke, C. (2010, Fall). Financial education and counseling-still holding promise. *Journal of Consumer Affairs, 44*(3), 483–498.

Consumer Action. (2009). *Implementation of community-based financial literacy programs in the US: Results of a national survey.* San Francisco, CA: Author Retrieved from https://www.consumer-action.org/downloads/english/CBO_Survey_Report.pdf

Consumer Financial Protection Bureau. (2014). *Financial wellness at work: A review of promising practices and policies.* Retrieved from http://files.consumerfinance.gov/f/201408_cfpb_report_financial-wellness-at-work.pdf

Department of Defense. (2003, June 3). *DoD campaign to improve financial readiness.* [Press release]. Retrieved from http://archive.defense.gov/news/newsarticle.aspx?id=28917

Durband, D. B., & Britt, S. L. (2012). The case for financial education programs. In D. B. Durband & S. L. Britt (Eds.), *Student financial literacy: Campus-based program development* (pp. 1–8). New York: Springer. https://doi.org/10.1007/978-1-4614-3505-1

Durband, D. B., & Gustafson, W. A. (2012). Obtaining financial education program support. In D. B. Durband & S. L. Britt (Eds.), *Student financial literacy: Campus-based program development* (pp. 57–64). New York: Springer. https://doi.org/10.1007/978-1-4614-3505-1

eXtension. (n.d.). *Personal finance.* Retrieved from http://articles.extension.org/personal_finance

Fischer, L. F. (2000). *Espionage: Why does it happen?* DoD Security Institute. Retrieved from www.au.af.mil/au/awc/awcgate/dod/espionage_whyhappens.pdf

Fondation, L., Tufano, P., & Walker, P. H. (1999, July/August). Collaborating with congregations: Opportunities for financial services in the inner city. *Harvard Business Review.* Retrieved from https://hbr.org/1999/07/collaborating-with-congregations-opportunities-for-financial-services-in-the-inner-city

Gesme, D. H., & Wiseman, M. (2011). A financial counselor on the practice staff: A win-win. *Journal of Oncology Practice, 7*(4), 273–275. https://doi.org/10.1200/JOP.2011.000341

Grable, J. E., Law, R., & Kaus, J. (2012). An overview of university financial education programs. In D. B. Durband & S. L. Britt (Eds.), *Student financial literacy: Campus-based program development* (pp. 9–26). New York: Springer.

Green-Pimentel, L., Goetz, J., Gale, J., & Bermudez, M. (2009). Providing collaborative financial and couples counseling: Experiences of the financial counselors and couple's therapists. *The Forum for Family and Consumer Issues, 14*(2). Retrieved from https://ncsu.edu/ffci/publications/2009/v14-n2-2009-summer-fall/Pimentel-Goetz-Gale-Bermudez.php

Halley, R., Durband, D. B., Gustafson, W., & Bailey, W. (2011, December). A survey of clergy practices associated with premarital financial counseling. *Journal of Pastoral Care and Counseling, 65*(4), 1–14. https://doi.org/10.1177/154230501106500404

Hira, T. K. (2009, December). *Personal finance: Past, present and future.* Networks Financial Institute Policy Brief 2009-PB-10. Retrieved from https://papers.ssrn.com/sol3/papers.cfm?abstract_id=1522299

Hutchison, W. S., & Vickerstaff, S. (2009). The need and rationale for employee assistance programs. In M. A. Richard, W. G. Emener, & W. S. Hutchison (Eds.), *Employee assistance programs* (4th ed.). Springfield: Charles C. Thomas.

International Foundation of Employee Benefit Plans. (2016). *Financial education for today's workforce.* Retrieved from https://www.ifebp.org/pdf/financial-education-2016-survey-results.pdf

Kim, J. (2016). Financial issues of workers. In J. J. Xiao (Ed.), *Handbook of consumer finance research* (2nd ed.). New York: Springer.

Land-grant impacts. (n.d.) *Introduction.* Retrieved from https://landgrantimpacts.tamu.edu/about

Langrehr, V. B. (1991). Financial counseling and planning: Similarities and distinctions. *Financial Counseling and Planning, 2,* 155–167.

Langrehr, V. B., & Langrehr, F. W. (1986). Course requirements, job responsibilities, and compensation for financial counselors: The not-for-profit industry view. *Journal of Consumer Affairs, 20*(1), 131–141.

Leland, J. (2007, April 29). Turning to churches or scripture to cope with debt. *The New York Times.* Retrieved from http://www.nytimes.com/2007/04/29/us/29debt.html?smid=pl-share

Mason, J. (1986, Summer). Financial planner or counselor: The differences are significant. *Journal of Consumer Affairs, 1*(20), 142–147.

Moore, A. (2017, November). *Serving the other 95%: Bridging the gap between financial counseling, coaching and planning.* Presented at the 2017 AFCPE annual research & training symposium, San Diego, CA.

Myhre, D. C. (1979). Assessing the state of the art. In D. C. Myhre (Ed.), *Financial counseling: Assessing the state of the art. Proceedings of a national conference sponsored by the Financial Counseling Project* (pp. 197–201). Blacksburg, VA: Virginia Polytechnic Institute and State University.

National Consumer Law Center. (2013). *Guide to surviving debt.* Boston: NCLC Publications.

National Credit Union Foundation. (2012). *Credit unions: Focused on financial capability across the nation.* Retrieved from https://www.ncuf.coop/media. acux/322bcbad-831d-475d-bec4-5dca4c3da4a9

National Federation of Community Development Credit Unions and Neighborhood Trust Financial Partner. (2015, April). *Financial counseling in credit unions: A survey of the field.* Retrieved from http://www.cdcu.coop/wp-content/uploads/2015/04/Financial-Counseling-in-Credit-Unions-Issue-Brief-April-2015.pdf

National Foundation for Credit Counseling. (n.d.). *About us.* Retrieved from https://www.nfcc.org/about-us/

Office of Personnel Management. (n.d.). *Benefits officers center training: Retirement financial literacy and education strategy.* Retrieved from https://www.opm.gov/retirement-services/benefits-officers-center/training/#model

Pulvino, C. J., & Pulvino, C. A. (2010). *Financial counseling: A strategic approach* (3rd ed.). Sarasota, FL: Instructional Enterprises.

Robb, C. A., Babiarz, P., & Woodyard, A. (2012). The demand for financial professionals' advice: The role of financial knowledge, satisfaction, and confidence. *Financial Services Review, 21*(4), 291–305.

Roll, S., & Moulton, S. (2016). The impact of credit counseling on consumer outcomes: Evidence from a national demonstration program. In *FDIC 6th annual consumer research symposium.* Retrieved from https://www.fdic.gov/news/conferences/consumersymposium/2016/documents/roll_paper.pdf

Ross, D. B., Gale, J., & Goetz, J. (2016, September). Ethical issues and decision making in collaborative financial therapy. *Journal of Financial Therapy, 7*(1), 17–37. Retrieved from http://newprairiepress.org/jft/vol7/iss1/3/

Royster, S. (2014). *Financial specialists: Working with money.* Retrieved from https://www.bls.gov/careeroutlook/2014/article/financial-specialists.htm

Schuchardt, J., Bagwell, D. C., Bailey, W. C., DeVaney, S. A., Grable, J. E., Leech, I. E., et al. (2007). Personal finance: An interdisciplinary profession. *Financial Counseling and Planning, 18*(1), 61–69.

Sneed, C., Wise, D., Berry, A. A., & Gault, J. (2011, Winter). Faith and finance: Empowering faith leaders to care for congregants in financial crisis. *The Forum for Family and Consumer Issues, 16*(2). Retrieved from https://projects.ncsu.edu/ffci/publications/2011/v16-n2-2011-winter/sneed-wise-berry-gault.php

Society for Human Resource Management. (2015, August 23). *Managing employee assistance programs*. Retrieved from https://www.shrm.org/resourcesandtools/tools-and-samples/tool-kits/pages/managingemployeeassistanceprograms.aspx

United States Department of Justice. (n.d.) *Credit counseling and debtor education information*. Retrieved from www.justice.gov/ust/credit-counseling-debtor-education-information

Wall, R. W. (2002). *Financial counseling in practice: A practical guide for leading others to financial wellness*. Honolulu: Financial Wellness Associates.

Wiggins, R. (2016). Setting the standard through communities of practice. *The Professionalizing Field of Financial Counseling and Coaching Journal, 69–70*. Retrieved from http://www.professionalfincounselingjournal.org/assets/cfe-fund-professionalizing-field-of-financial-counseling-and-coaching-journal2.pdf

Williams, F. L. (1997, Winter). Financial counseling: A model for family and consumer sciences professionals. *Journal of Family and Consumer Sciences, 89*(4), 41–48.

Williams, F. L. (2002). Financial counseling: Best practices. In *Financial stress and workplace performance: Developing employer-credit union partnerships*. Retrieved from https://filene.org/assets/pdf-reports/1752-82CCUIFinancial_Stress.pdf

Williams, F. L. (1979). Current issues in financial counseling. In D. C. Myhre (Ed.), *Financial counseling: Assessing the state of the art. Proceedings of a national conference sponsored by the Financial Counseling Project* (pp. 11–22). Virginia Polytechnic Institute and State University, Blacksburg, Virginia.

Chapter 2
Personal Finance Competencies in the Practice of Financial Counseling

Lucy M. Delgadillo and Ryan H. Law

Financial knowledge, financial literacy, and financial capability are terms that are often used interchangeably; however, each term has a specific meaning in the context of working with clients to improve their financial behaviors. One of the goals of financial counseling should be to help clients increase their financial knowledge and financial literacy and ultimately improve their financial capability. To help clients improve in all of these areas, financial counselors need to understand how to use research to enhance their practice and need to have a solid understanding of financial counseling and planning competencies, such as budgeting, credit score improvement, estate planning, and other areas.

In this chapter, we will begin by defining the terms financial knowledge, financial literacy, and financial capability. Then, we will outline core competencies financial counselors need to understand as a baseline, which will be followed up by a discussion about research and how financial counselors can become consumers of financial research.

Electronic supplementary material: The online version of this chapter (https://doi.org/10.1007/978-3-319-72586-4_2) contains supplementary material, which is available to authorized users.

L. M. Delgadillo (✉)
School of Applied Sciences, Technology and Education, Utah State University,
Logan, UT, USA
e-mail: Lucy.delgadillo@usu.edu

R. H. Law
Money Management Resource Center, Personal Financial Planning program, Utah Valley University, Orem, UT, USA

© Springer Nature Switzerland AG 2019
D. B. Durband et al. (eds.), *Financial Counseling*,
https://doi.org/10.1007/978-3-319-72586-4_2

Defining the Terms

Financial Knowledge

Even though financial knowledge and financial literacy are similar in nature, there are differences between the two terms. In practice, these notions frequently overlap. The Oxford Dictionary (n.d.) defines knowledge as a familiarity, awareness of something such as facts, information, description, or skills that are acquired through experience, education, or by perceiving, discovering, or learning. Financial knowledge, in this sense, refers to a basic understanding of financial concepts and procedures as well as the use of this knowledge to solve financial problems. Financial knowledge encompasses conceptual financial knowledge (e.g., define what money is) and procedural financial knowledge (know how to write a check).

Financial knowledge serves a function to society because it informs consumers, but in an increasingly financialized world, financial knowledge per se is lacking. When compared to several decades ago, consumers are now inserted into a global economy, and, therefore, to an unprecedented access of sophisticated financial products and services. At the same time, there has been a transfer of financial responsibilities away from states and firms towards households (e.g., from defined benefit pension plans to defined contribution plans), declines of health care coverages and growing life expectancy. Having sufficient financial knowledge will help clients navigate these changes.

Financial Literacy

Currently, there is not a standard definition of financial literacy. An international group, the Organisation for Economic Co-operation and Development (OECD), proposed a conceptual definition of financial literacy. OECD is an intergovernmental economic organization with 35 member countries founded in 1960 to stimulate economic progress and world trade. OECD provides a forum in which governments can work together to share experiences and seek solutions to common problems (OECD, n.d.). For more than a decade, the OECD has encouraged dialogue among its country members to agree on a definition of financial literacy. In one of their latest studies, specifically the PISA study (Programme for International Student Assessment) (2014), the OECD broadens the definition of financial literacy beyond just personal finance to include attitudes related to societal requirements:

> Financial literacy is knowledge and understanding of financial concepts and risks, and the skills, motivation, and confidence to apply such knowledge and understanding in order to make efficient decisions across a range of financial contexts, to improve the financial well-being of individuals and society and to enable participation in economic life (p. 33).

Notice that the OECD's definition includes the assumption that financial literacy requires not only *financial knowledge* but also *financial understanding* of financial concepts and risks. This is in itself an important shift from the days when financial knowledge was thought to be sufficient. It is a subtle but critical change. So, the question is, what is "knowledge"? And what is "understanding"? Knowledge is a fact or a piece of information, while understanding is the ability to explain, interpret, and apply knowledge (Wiggins & McTighe, 2012). Consider the following example that shows a competency in financial knowledge versus a competency in financial literacy:

Financial knowledge	Financial literacy: knowledge plus understanding
Know how to pay for a purchase by writing a check, using a debit card, or a credit card	Explain the costs and benefits of choosing different payment options for a particular situation

The conclusion, then, can be drawn that one is financially literate when one has the skills to explain and predict the relationships between concepts, e.g., the relation between savings and investments, between risks and returns, between average annual return and inflation, etc..

The OECD definition of financial literacy also implies that consumers have the *motivation* and *confidence* to apply financial knowledge. Motivation and confidence can be used as commitment devices to sustain behavior change. Financial literacy aims to change behavior in the sense that knowledge of financial issues ought to be applied into daily life (Huston, 2010). Although motivation and confidence seem to converge towards the same direction, namely, financial well-being, there are as many different confidence and motivation levels as individuals. Financial counselors should be aware that people can be oblivious of their confidence and motivation, and these unbeknownst qualities will certainly impact their outcomes. For example, a financially over-confident person may overestimate resources and underestimate financial risks (resulting in significant losses). An under-confident person may be too conservative in their risk tolerance (resulting in significant decreases in their rate of return).

To be financially literate means to make *effective decisions* across a range of *life and financial contexts*. Financial knowledge alone will neglect this topic. Consumers move through different life situations, and with each stage, their financial needs change. They will experience and go through different life contexts. Depending on their life context and stage, their role as consumers might change. A client may be a buyer (e.g., buying insurance), or a seller (e.g., selling a home), an investor (e.g., holding an IRA), a debtor (e.g., having a car loan), or a lender (e.g., holding an income mutual fund). Differentiating the distinct roles and settings of a client in a counseling engagement is useful for financial counselors because their clients' roles and settings require different approaches. For example, as loan applicants, clients seek for the lowest APR; as investors, they want the highest returns.

The OECD also names *societal well-being* and *participation in economic life* as part of their financial literacy definition. Financial literacy recognizes that consumers are economic citizens. Financially literate individuals understand that the political framework shapes financial systems. They understand the intertwined relationship between government and markets. As economic citizens and voters, consumers make choices to protect themselves from financial risks, and devise collective action to nurture financial security.

The Emergence of Financial Capability

As outlined in the previous paragraphs, financial literacy expands the definition of financial knowledge by including the skills to achieve *financial understanding* of *conceptual relationships* (e.g., time value of money and rate of returns), and *contextual factors* (financial life cycle as well as different consumer's market roles and sides within financial markets). In addition, there are internal factors (*motivation and confidence*) that mediate and determine the financial outcomes for the individual. Lastly, financial literacy assumes consumers are active participants in the macro-economic life.

Rather than adopting the OECD definition of financial literacy, the United States devised a new term, *financial capability*. The term financial capability was first used in the 2013 President's Advisory Council on Financial Capability (PACFC) report. Subsequently, many family finance professionals started equating *financial literacy* with *financial capability*, but this conceptual association is inaccurate.

The term financial capability connects financial literacy with specific financial products and services that facilitate asset-building and asset-protection. The primary goal of financial capability is accumulation and protection of assets. Financial capability is a framework in which financial literacy is only one part of the model; the other two are choice architecture and consumer protection. The choice architecture term was originally coined by Thaler and Sunstein (2008), in their book, *Nudge: Improving Decisions about Health, Wealth, and Happiness*. Choice architecture aims to nudge individuals towards choices that are in their best interest without limiting their financial choices. They are thoughtfully designed to minimize financial biases and errors that arise as the result of bounded rationality. Bounded rationality is the idea that when individuals make decisions, their rationality is constrained by the cognitive limitations of their minds and the time available to make the decision. For example, Thaler and Sunstein (2008) point out that many Americans are not saving enough for retirement. One solution they offered was creating default retirement plans for employees. Employees would be able to adopt any plan they like, but, if no action is taken, they would automatically be enrolled in a retirement program such as a 401(k). Choice architecture also refers to *access* to financial products and services. Choice architecture appears to work best when financial products and services exist within a regulatory framework that provides consumer protection (the third leg of the financial capability model). The existence of a legal consumer protection framework ensures that such products are in the best interests of the consumer (through regulation, transparency, and disclosures). For more information about bounded rationality and choice architecture, see Chaps. 9 and 10.

Below there is an example of a financial knowledge, financial literacy, and financial capability:

Financial knowledge	Financial literacy	Financial capability
	Knowledge plus understanding	Knowledge, understanding plus direct access to financial products and services that exists within a regulatory framework
Identify and list different types of credit cards	Explain how choosing a credit card entails weighing the costs and benefits of the different options	Connect the client with a credit card that is more likely to bring the desired consumer outcome

Fig. 2.1 Principles of connection and hierarchy among the terms financial knowledge, financial literacy, and financial capability

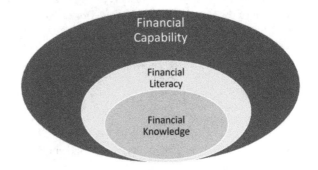

In summary, financial knowledge is an awareness of facts or a transfer of information. It is learning the how-to skills. Financial knowledge in itself promotes the lowest levels of thinking such as listing, describing, and identifying. Financial literacy includes financial knowledge plus the financial understanding of conceptual relationships and contextual factors (financial life cycle as well as different consumer's market roles within financial markets). In addition, there are internal factors (motivation and confidence) that mediate and determine the financial outcomes for the individual. Financial literacy assumes consumers as active participants in the macro-economic life. Lastly, financial capability is a new theoretical paradigm that includes two dimensions unaccounted for in financial literacy, namely, choice architecture and consumer protection. Choice architecture refers to financial products and services designed to minimize financial biases and errors in financial decision-making and to maximize financially desirable behaviors. Consumer protection refers to regulation and legal framework to protect consumers' choices.

Figure 2.1 represents the principles of connection and hierarchy among the concepts. These three definitions are interconnected in a nested relationship, with financial knowledge (the lowest level) embedded into financial literacy and financial literacy embedded into financial capability. Also, complexity of the definitions as well as higher levels of thinking increase from the bottom-up. Hence, an important objective of financial counseling is to include competencies in personal finance that go beyond the delivery of information. Financial counseling competencies should include an understanding of the relationships and contextual factors as well as the access to financial products and services that will help individuals and families in their financial decisions.

Financial Counseling Core Competencies

Effective financial counselors move beyond financial knowledge to facilitating the process by which a client becomes financially literate and financially capable. Financial counselors need to be competent in all areas of personal finance—from budgeting to estate planning, so clients can be helped at every level. This section provides an overview of the core set of competencies that should be studied by financial counselors. For further information about these topics, financial counselors are encouraged to study other sources, including personal finance textbooks and credit and debt management resources such as *Guide to Surviving Debt* (National Consumer Law Center, 2016) and *Solve Your Money Troubles: Strategies to Get Out of Debt and Stay That Way* (Loftsgordon & O'Neill, 2017). To present the competencies, financial counselors need to understand to be effective counselors, we turn to the AFCPE® Accredited Financial Counselor® Core Competencies (AFC Core Competencies, n.d.). These core competencies, which are listed in full in the appendix, are comprised of ten areas:

1. Set the stage and gather client information
2. Assist a client in creating an action plan
3. Develop financial statements, ratios, and spending plans
4. Manage money
5. Manage credit and debt
6. Educate a client about consumer protection
7. Educate a client about major acquisitions
8. Manage financial risks
9. Discuss investment basics with a client
10. Educate a client about the financial aspects of retirement and estate planning

The first two competencies, set the stage and gather client information and assist a client in creating an action plan, are covered in Chap. 3. This chapter will include a brief overview of the other eight areas.

Develop Financial Statements, Ratios, and Spending Plans

Developing financial statements, spending plans, and calculating ratios will be at the heart of most financial counseling appointments. In order for clients to achieve financial goals, they need to assess their financial health and where they currently stand. The two most common statements that financial counselors work with are the cash flow statement and net worth statement (also known as a balance sheet). The cash flow statement is a report showing where money was spent in the past month or year while the net worth statement shows assets, liabilities, and total net worth at a specific point in time. Clients can improve their financial health by spending less than they earn and increasing their net worth through saving and paying off debt. A spending plan (also known as a budget) is a tool that will help clients plan how to spend their total income to achieve their financial goals, including paying off debt and saving for future goals.

Personal financial ratios measure financial strength in a number of different areas. According to Lytton, Garman, and Porter (1991), "Financial ratios are objective measures designed to simplify the process of making judgmental analytical assessments of individual or family financial status" (p. 3). Ratios provide feedback about a client's current financial situation, measure progress over time, and serve as an objective way for financial counselors to make recommendations (Lytton et al., 1991). Research by Greninger, Hampton, Kitt, and Achacosa (1996) identified 13 ratios in 7 categories (liquidity, savings, asset allocation, inflation protection, tax burden, housing expenses, and insolvency/credit) that financial planners and counselors can utilize to measure a client's financial well-being. While all of these serve a purpose, the two that financial counselors will likely use most often with clients are the debt-to-income ratio and the liquidity ratio. In addition, the credit utilization ratio is becoming an important ratio due to its effect on a client's credit score.

The debt-to-income ratio is determined by dividing monthly debt payments by monthly gross income. There are three types of debt-to-income ratios:

- Consumer debt ratio, which is calculated by dividing non-housing debt by monthly gross income. Consumer debt should be 15% or less of monthly gross income.
- Front-end ratio, also called housing expense ratio, is calculated by dividing all housing debt (including total mortgage payment with insurance and taxes and homeowner's association fees) by monthly gross income. Housing expenses should not exceed 28% of a client's monthly gross income.
- Back-end ratio is measured by dividing total debt payments by monthly gross income. This ratio should be at or below 36%.

It is important to remember that the front and back-end ratios represent maximums that a lending institution will lend for a mortgage and not necessarily what is best for an individual. Financial counselors should help their clients evaluate the impact of debt on a client's overall budget.

Let's consider an example of these ratios using a hypothetical family, the Jones family. The Jones' have monthly gross income of $3,500, with total housing debt of $1,400 per month and other debt payments of $500 per month, including credit card payments and an auto loan. The Jones' consumer debt ratio is just over 14% ($500/$3,500), which would be considered to be in the safe range. Their front-end ratio is 40% ($1,400/$3,500), and their back-end ratio is about 54% ($1,900/$3,500), which are both above recommended limits. A financial counselor could work with the Jones family to increase their income and decrease expenses to pay their debt off sooner and lower these ratios.

The liquidity ratio is a way to measure the size of a client's emergency fund. To calculate liquidity, add all liquid assets together, then divide by monthly expenses. Liquid assets include any asset that can easily be converted to cash such as cash, checking and savings accounts, and money market accounts. If a client has $10,000 in liquid assets and their monthly expenses are $2,500, their liquidity ratio is four, or 4 months. Many financial counselors and planners recommend an emergency fund of 3–6 months.

The credit utilization ratio is calculated by dividing total balances on all revolving credit by the total amount of revolving credit available. For example, if a client has three credit cards with $1,000, $1,500, and $500 balances with credit limits of $2,000, $3,000, and $1,000, their credit utilization ratio is 50% ($3,000/$6,000). This ratio accounts for 30% of a client's FICO® score (MyFICO, n.d.). Experian (2017), VantageScore (2016), and Motley Fool (n.d.) recommend this ratio stay at or below 30%. Paperno (2017) at CreditCards.com points out that a credit score isn't going to drop dramatically if a utilization ratio goes above 30%, and that this ratio is more like a sliding scale than a hard-and-fast rule. He also points out that, while the lower the ratio the better, it is better to have something than nothing (i.e., more than a 0% ratio) because a 0% ratio indicates that the consumer is not using credit regularly, which the credit bureaus see as a higher risk. However, many credit card companies simply report the statement balance each month, which means that one can still pay off the card in full each month and the report and score will reflect that the individual is using credit.

Manage Money

While there are many components to managing money, for purposes of this chapter the discussion will be limited to understanding financial services, tax management, and employment considerations.

Financial counselors need to help their clients understand the various forms of financial services that they have access to, including banks and credit unions, and the various types of accounts, such as a checking, savings, certificate of deposit, or money market account. Clients need to understand that different accounts serve different purposes, such as saving for a short-term goal in a money market account or using a checking account for day-to-day expenses. They should also be familiar with Federal Deposit Insurance Corporation (FDIC, 2014) and National Credit Union Administration (NCUA, 2014) protection, including limits to how much is protected.

Clients should also take steps to understand and reduce their taxes. It is important to note that unless one is properly licensed, financial counselors do not provide investment, tax, or legal advice. Financial counselors can educate a client and help them understand taxes, but should not prepare returns or give them specific advice about taxes. Financial counselors should also be familiar with the Volunteer Income Tax Assistance (VITA) program so they can refer clients who could utilize this service. Through the VITA program IRS-certified volunteers provide free tax preparation services for lower-income individuals, persons with disabilities and those who speak limited English (IRS, 2016). Financial counselors can provide tax education, such as helping a client understand what their adjusted gross income is, how a standard deduction is different from itemizing expenses, and how tax credits work.

Employment considerations includes how to compare job offers, how employee benefits work and affect overall pay, and unemployment resources. These are all important aspects to have a working knowledge of so clients can be helped in any employment circumstances.

Manage Credit and Debt

Grist (2016) identifies credit and debt skills as two of the most important competencies for financial counselors. Helping a client set up a spending plan that addresses rapid debt repayment may be the most common type of appointment. Financial counselors should be aware of debt repayment plans, be able to convey strategies to minimize debt, be aware of debt solutions for clients, and have a working knowledge of wage garnishments, repossessions, foreclosures, and bankruptcy. Financial counselors also need to be able to understand and communicate with clients about different types of credit and products, how to best use credit, and how credit reports and scores are calculated.

Some clients seeking assistance from a financial counselor will carry more debt than they are able to repay. In these instances, it is important for the financial counselor to help the client consider the potential for increasing income or decreasing expenses, explore alternatives (such as trading in a vehicle with a high payment for a lower cost one), recognize the consequences associated with failing to repay different loan types (garnishment, repossession, etc.), and prioritize which debts to repay. A financial counselor should also understand and be comfortable discussing the value and merit of options available to clients deep in debt such as foreclosure and bankruptcy along with the processes involved.

Educate a Client About Consumer Protection

Financial counselors may have clients who are facing credit discrimination, or are going through debt collection nightmares, or who have had their identity stolen. Understanding the various laws and safeguards in place, as well as where to turn for help when needed, is an important aspect of a financial counselor's services.

Credit laws include the Fair Debt Collection Practices Act, Truth in Lending Act, Fair Credit Reporting Act, Equal Credit Opportunity Act, Electronic Funds Transfer Act, and the Credit CARD Act. Financial counselors need to understand the basics of each of these laws, how they are enforced and where to get help if needed. Two useful resources for financial counselors to be aware of and utilize are the Consumer Financial Protection Bureau (CFPB), that provides educational resources, and the Federal Trade Commission (FTC), that enforces credit laws.

Regarding identity theft, financial counselors need to understand how to help a client protect themselves from being victims of identity theft and how to fix the problem if they are victims. This would include checking credit reports, credit freezes, consumer statements, and how to file an identity theft affidavit. Financial counselors should be familiar with the identity theft resources the Federal Trade Commission (FTC) offers clients. It is also important to understand various identity theft protection services and how they work.

While investments outside of FDIC and NCUA accounts are never guaranteed, investors have important laws and regulations in place to protect them from unscrupulous financial planners or investment advisors. These safeguards include the Investor Protection Trust, state securities regulators, and the Securities Investment Protection Corporation (SIPC). In addition, various organizations also regulate their members who often pass an exam and agree to a code of ethics. Examples of these include Certified Financial Planner Board of Standards, which regulates Certified Financial Planner™ professionals (CFP Board, n.d.) and AFCPE®, which regulates Accredited Financial Counselors® (AFC).

Educate a Client About Major Acquisitions

Major acquisitions for most clients include a home and vehicles. Clients are likely to finance both of these items, often multiple times throughout their lives, therefore a financial counselor needs to be able to explain the impact of credit and interest rates to clients. For most clients, a home is their biggest investment. If a client is considering making a home purchase, it is important to educate them on various aspects of home ownership including renting versus purchasing a home, additional home costs including taxes and maintenance, and the steps to sell a home when that time comes. Financial counselors can help clients set up their budgets and run debt-to-income ratios to determine how much mortgage payment they can afford each month. Another major acquisition that deserves attention is that of a vehicle. A financial counselor should understand the basics of purchasing and leasing a vehicle, be able to educate a client on the important terms and concepts, and help them navigate those transactions.

Manage Financial Risks

Clients face numerous financial risks as they build their portfolios and live their lives, and financial counselors can educate clients on the sources of risk and how to manage those risks through the use of insurance. Financial counselors need knowledge of property and liability, health, life, disability, long-term care insurance, and liability umbrella policies, some of which are often part of employee benefit packages. Financial counselors should be able to provide education about different insurance terms such as deductibles and co-pays.

Discuss Investment Basics with a Client

As the final two sections of the chapter, investments, retirement and estate planning, are considered, it is important to re-emphasize that unless a financial counselor is properly licensed they should not be providing legal, tax, or investment advice. In all of these areas, education is appropriate, while specific recommendations and preparing documents such as a will or a tax return, are not. Financial counselors need to have a referral network of professionals in each of these areas that they know and trust. For more information about referrals, refer to Chap. 3.

For investments, this would include fundamentals such as setting goals for retirement or college funding and terms such as dollar-cost averaging, diversification, asset allocation, and how investments work. It also includes helping clients understand various investment choices, such as stocks, bonds, mutual funds, real estate, and higher risk investments, such as commodities or precious metals, and investment vehicles such as an IRA, 401(k), 403(b), and taxable investment accounts. Financial counselors may feel that their clients are not in a position to consider investing, but as a client moves towards financial health, exploring these principles with a client can help prepare them to take advantage of the higher growth potential of investments and to take advantage of free money, such as a match in an employer-sponsored retirement plan.

Educate a Client About Financial Aspects of Retirement and Estate Planning

While specific retirement planning needs to be referred to a financial planner and estate planning and document preparation needs to be referred to an estate planning attorney, financial counselors can provide important education in these areas. Retirement planning education includes education about various types of retirement accounts and how they work such as IRAs, 401(k) accounts, Roth accounts, and pension plans. They should also understand how rollovers for these types of accounts work, the penalties for early withdrawal, and contribution limits.

Estate planning is critical to a financial plan, and financial counselors can educate clients about wills, trusts, powers of attorney, and medical directives. Financial counselors can discuss the importance of these documents, what they each do, and encourage them to keep them up-to-date when life events happen, such as marriage, divorce, birth of a child, or death of a family member.

Financial counselors need to have a solid education in each of these areas and need to stay updated with changes to the industry. Financial counselors should strongly consider getting involved in organizations such as AFCPE and FPA (Financial Planning Association). FPA has local chapters that financial counselors would be welcome in, and both AFCPE and FPA hold national conferences and other educational events where financial counselors can network with others and stay updated on changes and research in the financial services field.

How Informed Practitioners Can Use Research to Enrich Their Practice and Their Clients

The last section of the chapter will briefly discuss how informed practitioners benefit from research. Because of the specialization of labor and pragmatic activities, there has been a divide between researchers and practitioners. Nevertheless, to think of research and practice as a bipolarity is obsolete. The current trend in the creation of new knowledge is to include three players: practitioner, researcher, and client. The practitioner, researcher, and client must work together to identify what works, for whom, and under what conditions. This approach ensures that financial services, when used as intended, will have the most effective outcomes as demonstrated by the research. It will also ensure that programs with proven success will be widely disseminated and will benefit a greater number of people.

The concepts of an informed-practitioner model draw on paradigms models established in the behavioral and medical sciences. Within the informed-practitioner framework, practitioners are trained to have a working understanding of research principles and methodologies. This understanding enables them to apply critical tools in an evaluation and draw on academic literature to design and implement evidence-based interventions with their clients. Evidence-based practice (EBP) is a process in which the practitioner combines well-researched interventions with clinical experience and ethics, and client preferences and culture to guide and inform the delivery of treatments and services (Anderson, 2006; Slavin, 2002; Social Work Policy Institute, n.d.).

Informed practitioners are not expected to be significant *producers* of research. Rather they are positioned as educated *consumers* of research who can utilize related research to inform their practices. There are a number of journals that financial counselors can read to be educated consumers of research, including the *Journal of Financial Counseling and Planning*, produced by AFCPE, the *Journal of Financial Planning* produced by the Financial Planning Association (FPA) and the *Journal of Financial Therapy*, produced by the Financial Therapy Association (FTA). In addition, attending conferences provides an opportunity for informed practitioners to network with researchers and discuss first-hand how the information could enrich their practices or how they might collaborate on future research. AFCPE, FPA, and FTA all host annual conferences with academic presentations.

To be able to fully utilize research, a practitioner needs to know what to look for in a research article. The AFCPE Research Task Force created a helpful resource: "How to Read Research Articles: A Guide for Practitioners" (n.d.) that walks practitioners through the eight questions to ask as research is reviewed. These questions are: (1) What's the research question? (2) What do we already know? (3) What's the conceptual (or theoretical) framework? (4) Who is in the study? (5) What method was used? (6) What's the variable of interest? (7) What are the findings and implications? (8) How can this enhance my practice? A copy of the worksheet can be found in the appendix.

Attention must be devoted to integrating research findings into the practice of financial counseling. To translate such strategic objectives into effective delivery would require the financial counseling industry to identify core competencies for both the entry-level and the established financial counselor. One way to do that is to integrate research-based training for new professionals in the counseling accreditation processes, and to require the practicing professional to stay abreast of new developments by accumulating hours of continuing education.

Conclusion

In this chapter, we have defined the terms financial knowledge, financial literacy, and financial capability, and defined that the goal of financial counseling is ultimately to help clients progress towards financial capability through knowledge, literacy, and implementation of recommended practices. Core competencies financial counselors need to understand have been outlined and we have discussed research and how financial counselors can become consumers of financial research. In an ever-changing financial world, it is recommended that financial counselors continue to enhance their knowledge of the core competencies by staying up-to-date with the literature and attending conferences. By constantly updating their knowledge, financial counselors will be equipped to serve their clients, no matter what financial challenges their clients are facing.

References

AFCPE. (n.d.-a). *AFC core competencies*. Retrieved from https://www.afcpe.org/certification-center/accredited-financial-counselor/afc-core-competencies

AFCPE. (n.d.-b). *How to read research articles: A guide for practitioners*. Retrieved from http://www.afcpe.org/uploads/programs/BROCCOLI%20BANTER%20-%20HOW%20TO%20READ%20RESEARCH%20ARTICLES.pdf

Anderson, N. B. (2006). Evidence-based practice in psychology. *American Psychologist, 61*(4), 271–285.

CFP Board. (n.d.). *Regulation of financial planners*. Retrieved from https://www.cfp.net/public-policy/public-policy-issues/regulation-of-financial-planners

Experian. (2017). *What is a credit utilization rate?* Retrieved from http://www.experian.com/blogs/ask-experian/credit-education/score-basics/credit-utilization-rate/

Federal Deposit Insurance Corporation. (2014). *How are my deposit accounts insured by the FDIC?* Retrieved from https://www.fdic.gov/deposit/covered/categories.html

Greninger, S. A., Hampton, V. L., Kitt, K. A., & Achacosa, J. A. (1996). Ratios and benchmarks for measuring the financial well-being of families and individuals. *Financial Services Review, 5*(1), 57–70. Retrieved from https://pdfs.semanticscholar.org/269d/5f90e8ce1951d74c61e2a3f8ed116c4eb021.pdf

Grist, N. (2016). Moving towards an evidence-based consensus on core counselor competencies. *The Professionalizing Field of Financial Counseling and Coaching*, 17–18. Retrieved from http://www.professionalfincounselingjournal.org/assets/cfe-fund-professionalizing-field-of-financial-counseling-and-coaching-journal2.pdf

Huston, S. J. (2010). Measuring financial literacy. *Journal of Consumer Affairs, 44*(2), 296–316. https://doi.org/10.1111/j.1745-6606.2010.01170.x/epdf

Internal Revenue Service. (2016). *Free tax return preparation for qualifying taxpayers.* Retrieved from https://www.irs.gov/individuals/free-tax-return-preparation-for-you-by-volunteers

Loftsgordon, A., & O'Neill, C. (2017). *Solve your money troubles: Strategies to get out of debt and stay that way* (16th ed.). Berkeley, CA: Nolo.

Lytton, R. H., Garman, E. T., & Porter, N. M. (1991). How to use financial ratios when advising clients. *Proceedings of the Association for Financial Counseling and Planning Education, 2,* 2–23.

MyFICO. (n.d.). *Amounts owed.* Retrieved from http://www.myfico.com/credit-education/amounts-owed/

National Consumer Law Center. (2016). *Guide to surviving debt.* Boston, MA: National Consumer Law Center.

National Credit Union Administration. (2014). *How your accounts are federally insured.* Retrieved from https://www.ncua.gov/Legal/GuidesEtc/GuidesManuals/NCUAHowYourAcctInsured.pdf

Organisation for Economic Co-operation and Development. (2014). *PISA 2012 results. Students and money. Financial literacy skills for the 21st century* (Vol. VI). Paris: OECD Publishing. https://doi.org/10.1787/9789264208094-en

Organisation for Economic Co-operation and Development. (n.d.). *Our mission.* Retrieved from http://www.oecd.org/about/

Oxford Dictionary. (n.d.). *Knowledge.* Retrieved from https://www.oxforddictionaries.com/

Paperno, B. (2017). *Forget the 30 percent credit utilization 'rule'—It's a myth.* Retrieved from http://www.creditcards.com/credit-card-news/credit-utilization-30-percent-rule-myth-1586.php

President's Advisory Council on Financial Capability. (2013). *Final report: President's advisory council on financial capability.* Retrieved from https://www.treasury.gov/resource-center/financial-education/Documents/PACFC%20final%20report%20revised%2022513%20(8)_R.pdf

Slavin, R. E. (2002). Evidence-based education policies: Transforming educational practice and research. *Educational Researcher, 31*(7), 15–21. https://doi.org/10.3102/0013189X031007015

Social Work Policy Institute. (n.d.). *Evidence-based practices.* Retrieved from http://www.socialworkpolicy.org/research/evidence-based-practice-2.html

Thaler, R. H., & Sunstein, C. R. (2008). *Nudge: Improving decisions about health, wealth and happiness.* New York, NY: Penguin Books.

The Motley Fool. (n.d.). *What is a credit utilization ratio?* Retrieved from https://www.fool.com/knowledge-center/what-is-a-credit-utilization-ratio.aspx

VantageScore. (2016). *Did you know...The optimal credit card utilization percentage is...* Retrieved from https://thescore.vantagescore.com/article/285/did-you-know-optimal-credit-card-utilization-percentage

Wiggins, G., & McTighe, J. (2012). *Understanding by design* (expanded 2nd ed.). Alexandria, VA: Association for Supervision and Curriculum Development.

Chapter 3
The Practice of Financial Counseling

Sissy R. Osteen, Megan Ford, and Jennifer Wilson

Introduction

Financial counseling is a helping profession, and financial counselors strive to help clients improve their lives both financially, and through interventions that may improve their general sense of well-being. It is important to acknowledge that the nature of the client/financial counselor relationship is a professional one that demands standards and adherence to best practices to protect the client's interests and well-being. The relationship is central to everything that occurs in counseling from developing trust to understanding and accepting the fact that the relationship will ultimately end. The relationship between a client and a financial counselor will be unique, and unlike other relationships that are developed with friends and colleagues. The power differential between client and counselor adds another layer of responsibility and respect for these perceptions, any anxiety that can result from them, and any resistance the client may feel to making needed changes. This chapter explores how the relationship is developed, maintained, and supported by explanation and definition of the scope of counseling and the focus on meeting the goals of the client.

Electronic supplementary material: The online version of this chapter (https://doi. org/10.1007/978-3-319-72586-4_3) contains supplementary material, which is available to authorized users.

S. R. Osteen (✉)
Department of Human Development and Family Science, Oklahoma State University, Stillwater, OK, USA
e-mail: sissy.osteen@okstate.edu

M. Ford
College of Family & Consumer Sciences, ASPIRE Clinic, University of Georgia, Athens, GA, USA

J. Wilson
Department of Personal Financial Planning, Texas Tech University, Lubbock, TX, USA

© Springer Nature Switzerland AG 2019
D. B. Durband et al. (eds.), *Financial Counseling*,
https://doi.org/10.1007/978-3-319-72586-4_3

Where to Begin

A strong client–counselor bond is key to client engagement and behavior change. Building a trusting and supportive relationship with the client is foundational to work as a financial counselor. The client must feel safe, supported, and believe in the abilities of the financial professional to truly consider, and implement, the ideas and recommendations that are agreed upon between the counselor and the client. Without this, clients may struggle to be open and will likely find little success in the financial counseling process. Some wonder why the relationship between counselor and client is so important and may ask "Can't the client just receive information and education and achieve the same result?" From what is known regarding outcomes in traditional mental health practice, the answer is probably not. In fact, what the client generalizes about the counselor's role might create a barrier to counseling that will only start to break down when the relationship has been firmly established. Without a supportive, honest, and caring relationship, the client will have little motivation to accept the reality of the current situation and move forward (Wall, 2002). Research from the therapy realm acknowledges the relationship with the client as fundamental to successful therapeutic work (Hatchett, 2017; Paniagua, 2014) and positive intent of the counselor is associated with positive outcomes for the client (Hill, Helms, Spiegel, & Tichenor, 2001). As the financial counseling process often draws inspiration from traditional therapeutic approaches, it seems that the fundamental importance of the client/financial counselor relationship would be no different. However, knowing where to begin and initiating this process with clients can be difficult.

One of the complexities in outlining where to begin is the representation of various starting points and ways in which the counselor can establish a good working relationship with their clients (Nichols & Schwartz, 2007). Creating and solidifying a professional helping relationship with a client will manifest differently for different practitioners. Many counselors initiate this by building rapport, establishing the relationship, or developing an alliance. Most of these phrases are used interchangeably within the therapeutic and financial counseling professions, and they all highlight the ways in which the practitioner helps the client feel more comfortable, trusting, and confident in the counseling process. Through the implementation of techniques like active listening, empathy, mirroring, and pacing (covered in more detail in Chap. 8), financial counselors can begin to build a foundation of trust and support with their clients—ultimately leading to a more effective working relationship and a solid platform for the financial counseling work. Research conducted on trustworthiness and trust reflect that counselors can build trust if they possess awareness of how they express themselves (verbally and non-verbally) and understand how they provide information. Exhibiting knowledge, being available when needed, and communicating respectfully all build trust (Eriksson & Nilsson, 2008). Trustworthy behaviors include: competency, predictability, fairness, communication, showing interest, and sharing control (Erdem & Aytemur, 2008). Ultimately, trust will be built when the counselor is forthcoming, honest, and follows through. Tools like full disclosure concerning any fees that will be charged or any conflicts of interests or relationships, providing a picture of the scope of the counseling relationship, and acting respectfully while helping the client address the reality of the current situation are foundations to a good working relationship and build trust over time. Relaying to the client what will occur during the counseling process and addressing any expectations or concerns they may have will help them feel at ease. When the counselor is consistent in modeling to the client that the primary focus of counseling is to help the client meet their goals and needs, or consistently reinforces the client's efforts towards change, the relationship becomes more solid.

Influence of Diversity

Naturally, a financial counselor will encounter clients from diverse backgrounds. It is important for a financial counselor to appropriately acknowledge differences, as well as personal biases, and develop an awareness of how the differences may impact the development of the client/counselor relationship and the implementation of the counseling practice. The first Association for Financial Counseling and Planning Education® (AFCPE®) standard of practice (SP-1; see Table 3.1) highlights the importance of nondiscrimination in work as a financial counselor: "Counselors respect diversity and must not discriminate against clients because of age, color, culture, disability, ethnic group, gender, race, religion, sexual orientation, marital status, or socioeconomic status" (AFCPE, n.d.-b, ¶ 1). Part of this respect involves cultural competence and making it a personal priority to discover how cultural elements influence a client's view of money and their work with a financial counselor. For example, some cultures, such as Asian or Asian American groups, find it difficult to seek help outside of the family (Mojaverian, Hashimoto, & Kim, 2013) and are somewhat mistrustful of the advice that comes from professionals (Paniagua, 2014). In an instance like this one, the financial counselor would be wise to explore this cultural nuance with the client and emphasize the rapport-building phase to overcome any innate uneasiness that may be present. The counselor could address any potential differences by saying something as simple as, "I understand that family plays a significant role in how decisions are made in your culture. Could you tell me a little about how this influences your decisions?" This also calls for consideration for how rapport-building efforts may need to look different for specific client populations. In another example, some American Indian/Native American populations handle direct eye contact differently and may not look someone directly in the eyes out of respect. Since nonverbal cues are integral to communication, it is crucial for financial counselors to identify these differences; otherwise, the client could be perceived mistakenly as disengaged, uninterested, or avoidant. Counselors themselves may hold certain stereotypical views of individuals from certain cultures and must use particular care to control for any bias they hold based upon those stereotypes. Financial counselors are encouraged to honor the standards of practice and to best serve diverse clients. More diversity topics are covered in Chap. 4.

Best Practices and Standards in Financial Counseling

Helping to frame the counselor/client relationship and its boundaries are the Standards of Practice set forth by the AFCPE, which outline the necessary considerations for best practices and for financial counselors (AFCPE, n.d.-b). Further, ethics are a hallmark of traditional therapy and counseling practice. Recognized as a crucial underpinning for appropriate and effective helping relationships—financial counselors have adapted (with permission) their own ethical guidelines for practice by drawing inspiration from the American Psychological Association's code (see AFCPE Code of Ethics, AFCPE, n.d.-a). These important resources should be used as primary benchmarks for practitioners. As this chapter explores the scope of financial counseling practice and elements of the client/counselor relationship, Table 3.1 identifies the practice standards specifically related to the counseling relationship and the paragraphs that follow address considerations for each standard.

Table 3.1 AFCPE standards of practice related to the counseling relationship

Standard of practice one (SP-1):	Nondiscrimination: Counselors respect diversity and must not discriminate against clients because of age, color, culture, disability, ethnic group, gender, race, religion, sexual orientation, marital status, or socioeconomic status
Standard of practice two (SP-2):	Disclosure to clients: Counselors must adequately inform clients, preferably in writing, regarding the counseling process and counseling relationship at or before the first meeting begins and throughout the relationship
Standard of practice three (SP-3):	Dual relationships: Counselors must make every effort to avoid dual relationships with clients that could impair their professional judgment or increase the risk of harm to clients. When a dual relationship cannot be avoided, counselors must take appropriate steps to ensure that judgment is not impaired and that no exploitation occurs
Standard of practice four (SP-4):	Sexual intimacies: Counselors must not engage in any type of sexual intimacies with clients and must not engage in sexual intimacies with former clients within a minimum of 2 years after terminating the counseling relationship. Counselors who engage in such relationship after 2 years following termination have the responsibility to examine and document thoroughly that such relations did not have an exploitative nature
Standard of practice five (SP-5):	Protecting clients during group work: Counselors must take steps to protect clients from physical or psychological trauma resulting from interactions during group work, financial education classes or seminars
Standard of practice six (SP-6):	Advance understanding of fees: Counselors must explain to clients, prior to their entering the counseling relationship, financial arrangements related to professional services
Standard of practice seven (SP-7):	Termination: Counselors must assist in making appropriate arrangements for the continuation of treatment of clients, when necessary, following termination of counseling relationships
Standard of practice eight (SP-8):	Inability to assist clients: Counselors must avoid entering or immediately terminate a counseling relationship if it is determined that they are unable to be of professional assistance to a client. The counselor may assist in making an appropriate referral for the client

Adapted from AFCPE (n.d.-b)

Defining the Role of the Counselor

Many financial counselors have experienced the client who believes the counselor will tell them what to do about their current financial problems or that they will be able to get a loan from the counseling organization to pay off a debt. These clients and situations highlight the need for providing a clear definition of the role of the counselor. Likewise, it is imperative that the counselor understands their own role in the relationship and how they respond to clients. This personal understanding may depend upon the theoretical underpinnings of the counselor's approach. For instance, theories can vary by focus, whether insight or action-focused. Theories like psycho-analytic, existential, and humanistic views focus on client insight to illuminate how and why the client is behaving the way they are and the issues that result from their actions. Action-focused theories like behavioral, strategic, and problem-solving approaches emphasize what actions the client can institute that will lead to the desired change (Kottler, 2008). When counselors listen, attend, and reflect back what they have heard they help clients hear themselves. The counselor can play a vital role in helping the client obtain new insights (Hill, Thompson, Cogar, & Denman, 2001). If the counselor is more intent on helping a client obtain insight into how they arrived at their current situation, the role may consist of listening, and gaining a broader historical perspective. The action-oriented counselor may help the client disclose facts that help generate solutions and lead to corrective actions. Whatever the approach, the counselor sets the tone by creating trust and rapport in an environment that allows a clear exchange of concerns and information and always focuses on the goals of the client. A larger discussion on theories and frameworks takes place in Chaps. 6 and 7.

Managing Client Expectations

Individuals and couples seek and enter financial counseling for a variety of reasons. Some initiate services for assistance planning for a life change like marriage, buying a home, or starting college. Others come in because they are experiencing issues managing money due to overuse of credit, divorce, or death or illness of a family member. Some clients come into counseling because they have been shamed or coerced by others, while some may have been referred by a trusted professional to address financial issues that are spilling over into other areas of life. Clients who seek counseling may have already exhausted all other options and experience high levels of commitment to or motivation to change. In some of these instances, one session may be adequate to move them forward (Kottler, 2008). Clients may expect to be helped or supported, may worry about what others think of them for seeking counseling, or worry they will be shamed or scolded by the counselor for the current state of their finances. The counselor can provide information and a framework for how the client and counselor will work together to address the client's goals. These steps are vital to managing expectations.

Establishing the Client/Financial Counselor Relationship

Pulvino and Pulvino (2010) identified how financial counseling progresses through four strategic stages: initiating, exploring, understanding, and acting. The stages are described in Table 3.2.

Client Intake

Counseling intake is a vital part of collecting client data to proceed with counseling and to address any reporting requirements. The intake process can be conducted prior to the first session or can occur during exploration. Some counseling agencies

Table 3.2 Four strategic stages of counseling

Initiating	First interaction with the client; it can include intake. The importance relies on counselors providing a welcoming environment and positive interaction (firm handshake, smile, eye contact, not asking questions that the client has already answered on the intake form) to begin the client/counselor relationship. This can be achieved by implementing a variety of communication strategies and active listening techniques to help clients establish trust with the financial counselor and feel motivated to move forward with the counseling process
Exploring	During this stage, the client/counselor relationship has been initiated, either as a new or continuing relationship. The next strategy involves exploring the client's needs, purposes, or goals and gathering client information. The counseling relationship may have a general focus of exploring through planning or problem solving
	Planning focuses on exploring needs and goals, which may involve obtaining additional information from or for the client. Through this stage the client may become interested in financial topics, which may result in the counselor conducting research on these topics and then presenting resources and information to the client
	Problem-solving consists of remedial counseling, which involves reviewing the client's situation and identifying: Is the presenting problem the real problem? Is there a current solution? What type of problem is it? Who owns the problem? What solutions has the client tried? What are the client's resources?
Understanding	This stage of the client/counselor relationship occurs when the counselor and client generate plans for problem-solving or achieving goals. Plans generated are dependent on the type of financial goals. Emphasis should be on strategies for generating possible alternatives for the identified problem or goal. Options include:
	Alternatives are suggested by the financial counselor
	The client is encouraged to generate alternatives
	Both the financial counselor and the client generate alternatives
Acting	In this stage, counselors or clients carry out alternatives chosen while in the understanding stage. The ongoing evaluation of how well the alternatives are working to achieve the goals that were established or to solve current problems is necessary. If the evaluation results indicate that goals are not being achieved, counselors and clients may return to the stages of exploring or understanding

may have funders or accrediting associations that require information on clients that is reported on an annual basis, thus the intake process is tied to the objectives of an agency or to the individual financial counselor. Collecting this information on an initial intake form will allow the financial counselor and client to proceed through the session without taking time to address these specifics. For the financial counseling process to be comprehensive, it is important to know all the factors associated with the financial situation for the individual or family. This can include: income sources and amounts, family structure, who in the household is employed, debts owed, due dates, interest rates, months delinquent, monthly living expenses, and periodic expenses. The forms to collect this information may be emailed, integrated into a website, or mailed to the client to complete before the first session with a list of documents that should be brought like tax returns, pay stubs, bill statements, insurance policies, student loan papers, utility bills, etc. Some financial counselors may not collect this information until after the first session has commenced but may use a standard form to collect and record the information during the session. A counseling intake packet may include a counseling consent form, a budget or spending plan sheet to list expenses, and a creditor sheet for listing debt information. Since periodic or irregular expenses that require savings are often overlooked expenses, a periodic expenses sheet can also be included. These forms will serve as a basis for discussion with the client. For some counselors, it may be important for the client to complete at least some of this information before coming to the session, when possible. Studies have found that clients feel impatient and rate the counselor as not helpful when the counselor is gathering a lot of data (Hill, Helms, et al., 2001) so it is important to temper information gathering with attending to the client no matter the stage. Gathering the data prior to the first session provides the opportunity for the counselor to confirm information that is listed and talk through options while providing a more supportive environment. On the other hand, gathering the data during the session allows the counselor to observe nonverbal cues and note any issues that may need to be explored later. Initial intake can be the first step in identifying goals for counseling or making appropriate referrals. Table 3.3 provides sample questions to ask the client when they request an appointment, which will help set the scope of counseling, identify the severity of the issues, the willingness and comfort level of the client, and whether a referral to other resources is necessary. Sample worksheets for use in the intake process are provided in the Appendices.

Table 3.3 Sample intake questions

Client intake
Having a set of questions in place before the initial counseling session can potentially identify if a referral is needed for a client prior to receiving financial counseling. Identifying the need for a referral early in the counseling process can move a client towards achieving their financial goals more efficiently.
1. What are the main issues you are having with your finances?
2. What types of challenges are you experiencing because of these issues?
3. What other services or professionals have you contacted to assist you?
4. What needs do you have that are not currently being met?

Consent or Explanation of Services

Several factors and processes need consideration during the relationship establishment and rapport-building phase, specifically related to managing the client's
expectations. Transparency and honesty during first sessions are important for
establishing engagement and trust with the client. It is also critical to outline expectations related to the services provided. This information can include but is not
limited to the following: how the counseling session will proceed, what actions and
follow through are expected of the client, what are the counselor's qualifications,
what fees are charged for service, how often meetings will be held and how long the
meetings will be, the extent of the counseling services, and confidentiality and any
exceptions (Hutchinson, 2012). Some agencies that provide financial counseling
employ a written client's bill of rights (Consumer Credit Counseling Service,
InCharge, Money Management International). This form spells out the specifics of
what the client can expect and even includes the complaint resolution process for
clients who feel their rights have been violated or their needs have been unmet. This
type of document can help assure the client that the counselor will be respectful,
nonjudgmental, trustworthy, and will focus on the needs and goals of the client. The
document will also provide the client with a voice and a sense of power in the relationship. Some clients may feel more comfortable knowing their voice will be heard
and that they are allowed to express concerns if any arise. This document may also
reduce the likelihood of misperceptions.

Dealing with Resistance or Unmet Expectations

Chapter 11 discusses managing client conversations in more detail, but since this
plays a significant role in counseling success, it will be mentioned here as well.
Clients will resist when they think they are not being treated fairly, are having their
values or beliefs devalued, feel they are being coerced by the counselor, or are being
forced into counseling (Egan, 2013). Many counselors react to these "difficult"
clients by feeling the stress that accompanies interactions with them. Counselors are
much more effective when they deal with their own personal responses and control
reactivity. Client resistance can be a normal response to change. Clients come to
counseling because they know change must occur, but they do not know what that
change entails. For the counselor, client resistance can be an opportunity to assess
whether they are practicing any of the behaviors that elicit client resistance and
control those behaviors in themselves. For instance, is the counselor moving too
quickly? Are there any topics that make the client shut down? Intentionality on the
part of the counselor may help reduce client resistance. Going back to basic listening skills can diminish client resistance, rebuild engagement, and provide opportunities for the client talk more openly about what is causing the resistance

(Nelson-Jones, 2012). In those cases, where resistance seems to be interfering with progress, the counselor can ask a direct question about what seems to be leading to the hesitation on the part of the client, such as "Is there something that is bothering you about this conversation?" or "How could we get to an agreement about the way to move forward?"

Action Plans

The action plan represents the final picture of all the assessments made during the counseling session (Hutchinson, 2012). An action plan is the written instrument that specifies the goals and direction that help the client make a commitment and summarizes the content of the counseling session. Personal ownership is the greatest level of commitment during the action phase of the relationship (Egan, 2014). This stage in the process, more than any other, should be client-led. Only the client knows what they are willing to do, how they are going to do it, and when. It is important for the client to plan the course of action rather than simply complying with actions put forth by the counselor since the counselor might later be blamed for any failure in the plan. During the stage of specifying actions, the role of the counselor would be to clarify goals, desired outcomes, skills, and preferences voiced by the client. Planning may include helping the client choose options to meet goals, encouraging specificity in implementing options, developing steps and a time frame, and measuring the client's level of commitment to obtain stated goals (Nelson-Jones, 2012). An action plan worksheet may be provided to a client to outline the intent for the future or to help the client remember what they wanted to do. Some counselors even put a short recap of a client bill of rights on the action plan so they can discuss how the session went. As a final step, the counselor can share contact information to the client if they have any questions or need support, and the date of the next appointment. A sample action plan worksheet is provided in the appendix.

Ending the Relationship

In many cases, financial counseling is brief and targeted towards particular financial issues that are identified by the client. Brief interventions are usually based upon problem-solving (Kottler, 2008). Many clients have never prepared a written budget or listed and added up their debts. For those clients, the first session provides enough insight into their current situation to help them make some decisions about future directions. Some clients will need more guidance, information, and encouragement to work through longer term changes, while others feel empowered by the information they receive to move forward on their own. For every person who starts financial counseling, eventually, the relationship will end.

Terminating the client/counselor relationship presents many meanings, both realistically and symbolically (Hutchinson, 2012) and like other phases requires attention and care from the counselor. Financial counseling relationships are forged to help the client meet identified goals. Typically, the relationship will end when the goals are met or the client feels that they have made good progress. A general time-line for counseling is usually given at the beginning session and this can set the expectation for how long the relationship will last. Checking in with the client at each session to talk about how they are feeling about the progress will assist client and counselor to each see when the ending may come.

How to End

Sometimes clients terminate counseling on their own, even when the counselor does not feel the client is ready. This type of client termination can be because the client feels they have made good progress, they have reached a personal goal, they have had a life change, or they are not ready to proceed. Nelson-Jones (2012) out-lines five formats for terminating the relationship: fixed, open termination when goals are attained, faded, termination with booster sessions, and scheduling fol-low-up contact. These formats range from fixed (specific number of sessions) to faded (gradual withdrawal) to scheduling follow-up contact by phone or email (Nelson-Jones, 2012).

Whatever the structure of the counseling termination, it is an ending. This is an ending to a relationship that was supportive and helpful. Counseling is sometimes referred to as the third leg on a three-legged stool because it provides stability to a system that is unsteady due to the stress of current issues and helps the clients feel supported. The counselor/client relationship is built over time around need and trust. Ending this relationship may be difficult for both counselor and client. The primary job of ending the client/counselor relationship is allowing the client a chance to reflect on what the counseling process and the counselor have meant to them (Hutchinson, 2012).

The most appropriate time for the relationship to end is when the client's goals have been met. The relationship does not need to extend any longer than necessary (Hutchinson, 2012). Mutual agreement makes the ending easier, but there are times when termination is not mutual. When counselors find that clients are not following through on the goals they identified in their action plans and sessions are not prov-ing beneficial, they have a responsibility to discuss future options with the client, including termination. This step can include letting the client know that even though things are not working now, you will be available if they decide later to continue, or that you will be referring them to an appropriate resource.

Client Referrals

Identifying Referrals

A key element in effective financial counseling is providing an effective referral source based on client needs. There are several situations or conditions presented in counseling that warrant referral (Singh, 2007):

- When counselors uncover issues or concerns that are out-of-scope or beyond the counselor's area of expertise on the subject matter or abilities (adequate credentials or certifications in the field of financial counseling)
- When counselors feel their personality and the client's are not compatible and this is interfering with the counseling process
- When clients are relatives or personal friends
- When clients are hesitant to share their issues with the counselor for whatever reason
- When, after several counseling sessions, the counselor feels that the relationship has not been effective, and the client has not made progress towards their financial goals

Contained within Table 3.4 is a list of topics that may warrant referring the client to a specialist.

Referrals may be identified throughout the financial counseling process based upon the information provided by the client. Referral identification may occur:

Prior to the financial counseling initiation : Probing questions included in the intake process can help a counselor identify if a referral is needed prior to starting financial counseling. Table 3.3 provides sample questions to include on a client intake form to screen for potential referral needs. For example, if the counselor learns the client is facing a home foreclosure, a referral to an attorney or legal services would be a priority to resolve before beginning the financial counseling process. Likewise, if the client expresses that they have no money for food or need a job, these needs must be addressed before the financial counseling process begins.

During the exploring stage of financial counseling : When clients are ready to pursue their financial goals, a counselor may determine a referral is needed through discovery questions or when developing a client action plan. An unexpected life event may influence the need to utilize a referral. For example, the client mentions during a session he or she is still grieving over the loss of a family member. This would be an opportunity to provide a referral if the client seems unable to handle the situation. If the client responds they are currently seeking help, then it would be appropriate to ask that the session be postponed until they feel ready to discuss financial matters.

Completing the financial counseling process : A referral may occur when the client has successfully achieved the financial goal and is ready for the next step in the

Table 3.4 Client session out-of-scope topics

Out-of-scope topics	Referral type
Filing bankruptcy, divorces, adoptions, alimony, child custody/support, credit disputes, wills/living wills, powers of attorney, foreclosure, identity theft, individual rights, citizenship, housing/renting issues, or estate planning	Legal services
Insurance/risk management, employee benefits, investment, income tax, retirement, or estate planning that may involve incorporating products into the client's financial plan	Financial planning
Depression, anxiety, interpersonal and relational conflicts, pre-marital counseling, couple or marital conflict, infidelity, abuse/violence, grief and loss, stress management, major life changes, child–parent issues, family transitions, divorce concerns, work/school issues, sexual issues, or other personal distress	Marriage, family, individual, or group therapy
Tax preparation, disputes with the internal revenue service (IRS) (collections, examination notices, appeals), audits, federal tax litigations, tax credit controversies, or identity theft	Tax/accounting services
Substance use or abuse	Addiction services
Career identification, job searching, application process, resume and cover letter building, or interviewing tactics	Career services
Financial counseling may be integrated into an organization or agency that provides multiple services where the counselor may have multiple roles for the organization. During a session, if a client mentions a specific topic that the counselor also has expertise in with the agency, and it is not an urgent matter or related to a solution, it is important for the counselor to stay focused on the task at hand. It would be in the best interest of the client and the counselor for the client to schedule another appointment and specifically meet on that topic	
For example, Volunteer Income Tax Assistance (VITA) services are integrated frequently in asset building programming/services. During a session, a client mentions to the counselor they have not filed their taxes. Since the counselor is also an IRS certified VITA tax preparer, this would be an opportunity for the counselor to inform the client about the free tax prep services and to make an appointment with a VITA tax preparer (which could also be their financial counselor). This allows for the meeting to stay on pace while also making an internal referral (more on section "Referral Sources")	

action plan or to conclude the plan. For example, the client may be referred to a qualified financial planner who can help the client to take steps to develop and protect assets.

Referral Sources

Internal Referral

An internal referral connects clients to other services that are held within the same agency. An internal referral is appropriate when a counselor needs to refer to another counselor based on a personality conflict, when the client has asked for an internal referral or the client needs additional services offered within the same agency—for example, tax preparation, small business consulting, credit counseling, or legal services. To provide internal referrals and maintain client rapport, the agency needs to: (a) Identify protocols and train agency employees on the procedures and steps for referring clients to other agency services. In addition, the agency can provide informative follow-ups with each internal service to collect feedback and continuously improve the client referral process. (b) Establish expectations between the client and financial counselor through a "Client Internal Referral Form," which explains the referral purpose; for example, seeking additional services or terminating the current client/counselor relationship. (c) Identify expectations between the financial counselor and the internal service through terms of agreement and client confidentiality forms. Additionally, the counselor may act as a liaison between the client and referral source if needed. (d) Educate the internal referral on how to guide the client back to financial counseling. A post-service process with recommendations from the internal referral source to the counselor stating the client is ready for financial counseling will facilitate this. (e) Follow up with the client regarding the referral experience.

External Referral

The counselor can make an external referral for services that are not affiliated with the agency. Collaborating with external referrals is useful in the profession of financial counseling because these resources can help clients meet their goals. Establishing and following protocols is essential for establishing an external referral process because once the referral is made the service will be conducted by another provider. Effective external referrals can be facilitated through agency trainings and providing updated information about the partnerships to continuously improve the client referral process.

The following is necessary to elicit from the partnered agency to ensure this is a suitable referral: (a) The services available and requirements to obtain services, (b) the mission, vision, and values of the referral source and how the organization aligns with the target population the agency works with, (c) research credentials, services, and programs, (d) a memorandum of understanding (MOU) defining the referral expectations, and (e) point of contact, eligibility requirements, services, intake process, and the post-service process.

Counselors need to be aware of which services require specialized skills or credentials, and to make sure the external agency has adequate qualifications before referring clients for services. Not all entities will have credentials, but websites may list that they are "trained" or "certified." Before establishing a relationship, contact the agency or the financial counselor to clarify the level of training and qualification of the service providers. Table 3.5 provides a few examples of qualifications to look for in particular services when identifying potential external referrals.

Table 3.5 Examples of service providers and related credentials

Service provider	Credential
Financial Advisor	Certified Financial Planner™ practitioner; CFP® Professional
Financial Counselor	Accredited Financial Counselor®; AFC®
Housing Counselor	HUD Certified Housing Counselor
Therapist or Counselor	Licensed Marriage and Family Therapist Licensed Professional Counselor
Social Worker	Certified Social Worker Clinical Social Worker
Accountant/Tax Preparer	Certified Public Accountant
Attorney	J.D., Attorney at Law
Substance Abuse	Certified Alcohol and Drug Counselor

Referral Effectiveness

Financial counselors need to measure the effectiveness of referrals. This can be accomplished through an additional intake form, a survey, or through direct communication with the client. Discovery statements like, "Let's discuss where you are with the situation after meeting with X" and "Tell me how you feel about the possibility of reaching a resolution after the meeting with X?" It is important to solicit this information and ensure that confidentiality between the client and the referral source is maintained. The counselor should refrain from asking clients about specific discussions with their referral, as this could jeopardize the relationship between the client and counselor. The purpose is to make sure the referral provided assistance, so the client can make progress towards their financial goals.

Community Collaboration

In addition to identifying external referrals, developing a community resource plan with a list of local programs and contacts can be a helpful tool during client sessions. Some communities have a formal resource directory that has been developed and if not, the financial counselor can utilize the United Way directory by telephoning 2-1-1 or searching for a web-based version of the directory. Counselors need to be familiar with local, state, and national resources to assist clients. It is recommended to have a resource guide readily available for clients who may need emergency assistance or an external referral. It is important for a financial counselor to understand when to connect clients with community resources and/or a referral. Based on the level of severity, providing resources can be supplemental to a financial situation whereas a referral may put the financial counseling process on hold while the client works through another situation first. Table 3.6 is an example of how to begin designing a community resource guide.

Table 3.6 Sample community resource guide

Category title[a]						
Agency's name	Services/programs provided	Cost of services	Eligibility requirements	Location	Point of contact	Website
Name:						
Name:						

[a]Category title examples: legal, childcare, food assistance, clothing, healthcare, social work, etc.

Conclusion

Financial counseling is a helping profession that assists clients through prevention and intervention services designed to help them meet their goals. The practice of financial counseling requires education and skills, core ethical characteristics like professionalism and honesty, the ability to address diversity in clientele, the capacity to build relationships with clients, and the ability to work together to establish goals and direction, while recognizing the normal resistance to change. Financial counselors need to have good observational skills so they can help clients confront issues and move forward and know when issues have been resolved or will not be resolved and the counseling relationship needs to come to an end. Financial counselors also need to know their own limitations and the limitations of the services they offer and make appropriate referrals when needed.

The counseling relationship has a beginning, a middle, and an end. Each step provides opportunities for the counselor to act with integrity and intentionality while they focus on the needs of the client. The client has the opportunity to learn in a respectful and supportive environment that encourages action towards the goals they choose. Both counselor and client have the potential for growth.

References

Association for Financial Counseling and Planning Education. (n.d.-a). *AFCPE Code of Ethics*. Retrieved from https://www.afcpe.org/resource-center/professional-standards/code-of-ethics

Association for Financial Counseling and Planning Education. (n.d.-b). *AFCPE Standards of Practice*. Retrieved from https://www.afcpe.org/resource-center/professional-standards/standards-of-practice

Egan, G. (2014). *The skilled helper: A problem-management and opportunity-development approach to helping* (10th ed.). Belmont, CA: Brooks/Cole Cengage Learning.

Erdem, F., & Aytemur, J. O. (2008). Mentoring—A relationship based on trust: Qualitative research. *Public Personnel Management, 37*(1), 55–65. https://doi.org/10.1177/009102600803700104

Eriksson, I., & Nilsson, K. (2008). Preconditions needed for establishing a trusting relationship during health counselling—An interview study. *Journal of Clinical Nursing, 17*(17), 2352–2359. https://doi.org/10.1111/j.1365-2702.2007.02265.x

Hatchett, G. T. (2017). Monitoring the counseling relationship and client progress as alternatives to prescriptive empirically supported therapies. *Journal of Mental Health Counseling, 39*(2), 104–115. https://doi.org/10.17744/mehc.39.2.02

Hill, C. E., Helms, J. E., Spiegel, S. B., & Tichenor, V. (2001). Development of a system for categorizing client reactions to therapist interventions. In C. E. Hill (Ed.), *Helping skills: The empirical foundation* (pp. 41–60). Washington, DC: American Psychological Association.

Hill, C. E., Thompson, B. J., Cogar, M. C., & Denman, D. W. (2001). Beneath the surface of long-term therapy: Therapist and client report of their own and each other's covert processes. In C. E. Hill (Ed.), *Helping skills: The empirical foundation* (pp. 147–168). Washington, DC: American Psychological Association.

Hutchinson, D. (2012). *The essential counselor: Process, skills, and techniques* (2nd ed.). Los Angeles, CA: Sage Publications.

Kottler, J. A. (2008). *A brief primer of helping skills*. Los Angeles, CA: Sage Publications.

Mojaverian, T., Hashimoto, T., & Kim, H. S. (2013). *Cultural differences in professional help seeking: A comparison of Japan and the U.S. frontiers in psychology, 3*, 1–8.

Nelson-Jones, R. (2012). *Basic counselling skills: A helper's manual* (3rd ed.). Los Angeles, CA: Sage Publications.

Nichols, M. P., & Schwartz, R. C. (2007). *The essentials of family therapy* (3rd ed.). Boston, MA: Pearson.

Paniagua, F. A. (2014). *Assessing and treating culturally diverse clients: A practical guide* (4th ed.). Thousand Oaks, CA: Sage Publications.

Pulvino, C. J., & Pulvino, C. A. (2010). *Financial counseling: A strategic approach: Communication skills for financial professionals* (3rd ed.). Sarasota, FL: Instructional Enterprises.

Singh, K. (2007). *Counselling skills for managers*. New Delhi, IN: Prentice Hall India, LTD.

Wall, R. W. (2002). *Financial counseling in practice*. Honolulu, HI: Financial Wealth Associates.

Chapter 4
A Systemic Approach to Understanding Diversity in Financial Counseling

Alycia N. DeGraff and Daniel Dillon

This chapter presents an approach to understanding individuals and the worlds in which they exist to help financial counseling service providers become more mindful of important issues that may go unrecognized. The opening section of this chapter presents an overview of systems theory—an articulation of how individuals exist and develop within their environments. Next, several dimensions of diversity are defined and discussed to provide context for how people experience, relate to, and behave in their worlds. The final section reviews a series of models and techniques to help financial counselors adopt a systems theory lens and better appreciate differences among clients.

This chapter discusses diversity consciousness as an ongoing and lifelong practice. "Cultural competency" has become a neologism in recent years, especially in workplace settings where it is applied to diversity-related trainings. While these efforts are well intentioned, inherent in the phrase "cultural competency" is the notion that a person can attend such trainings and achieve a comprehensive understanding of diversity. This chapter asserts that the process is active and ongoing.

The remaining discussion uses a systemic lens to consider the ways in which dominant group norms and values work to maintain power structures that affect all human relationships—including those of the counselor and client—and provides suggestions for increasing diversity consciousness and sensitivity in financial counseling settings.

A. N. DeGraff (✉)
University of Georgia, Athens, GA, USA
e-mail: alycia.degraff@live.com

D. Dillon
Program Evaluation Consultant, Austin, TX, USA

© Springer Nature Switzerland AG 2019
D. B. Durband et al. (eds.), *Financial Counseling*,
https://doi.org/10.1007/978-3-319-72586-4_4

A Brief Introduction to Systems Theory and Systemic Thinking

A "systemic" thinker or service provider seeks to understand individuals and the systems in which they exist. Systems theory posits that people only exist within the context of their systems, and therefore, understanding the system helps to better understand the person. The system in which an individual exists gives meaning to race, ethnicity, culture, sex, gender, sexual orientation, class, religion, ability status, and education.

General systems theory, developed by Von Bertalanffy and Sutherland (1974), is an interdisciplinary theory originating from the field of biology. General systems theory proposes that relationships between individual parts constitute a whole, and that the whole is greater than the sum of its parts. To understand the whole, one must understand and account for the relationships between individual parts and environments. Murray Bowen's application of systems theory to families (Papero, 1990) applies concepts of general systems theory to individuals and their families and contends that individuals can only be understood as they exist within these family systems. Ecological systems theory (Bronfenbrenner, 2005) is presented here as a systemic theory to understanding individuals and the systems they inhabit.

Ecological systems theory is an evolving theory of human development that looks at how an individual develops within a series of systems that both shape the individual and respond to influences from their presence (Bronfenbrenner, 2005). In this section, we borrow Bronfenbrenner's most recent reconceptualization of ecological systems theory, the process-person-context-time model (PPCT; Rosa & Tudge, 2013), to explain concepts, assumptions, and developmental phenomena. The PPCT model places proximal processes at the core of human development. Proximal processes are the roles that the individual plays in their own development through increasingly complex reciprocal interactions with other people, objects, and symbols (Bronfenbrenner & Morris, 2006). Personal characteristics can be generative and disruptive to the individual's development and can influence interpersonal processes between the micro- and meso-systems. In order to understand an individual's development, beliefs, and values, it is important to consider the context of their interactions. Bronfenbrenner describes that *context* in four levels of interactive systems: micro-, meso-, exo-, and macrosystems. A diagram of the ecological system is shown below (Fig. 4.1).

- *Microsystem.* In the traditional, individual-focused application of ecological systems models, the microsystem describes the relationship between an individual and the immediate environment. It involves a pattern of relationships, activities, and roles seen in settings such as work, family, social groups, and school. Proximal processes in the microsystem create and sustain the development of culture.
- *Mesosystem.* The mesosystem is the relations between the various microsystems, which contain the developing individual. It is a system of microsystems. For

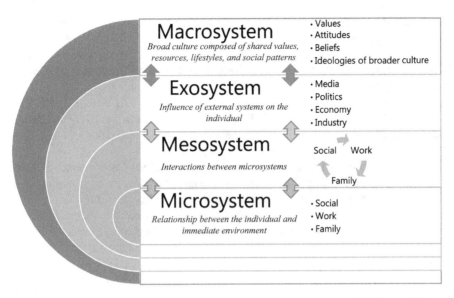

Fig. 4.1 A visual representation of the ecological system. Author depiction of PPCT model (Rosa & Tudge, 2013)

individuals, these relationships between formal and informal networks are significant, as they promote physical, psychological, social, and spiritual well-being (Mancini, Martin, & Bowen, 2003). In this model, the mesosystem is conceptualized to support the connections between the microsystems.

- *Exosystem.* The third level of interaction is the exosystem, where individuals are influenced by systems with which they are not directly engaged.
- *Macrosystem.* The last level is that of the macrosystem, which describes a broader culture composed of shared values, resources, lifestyles, and social patterns. The macrosystem subsumes all the other systems and is reciprocally influenced by, and influencing of them (Tudge, Mokrova, Hatfield, & Karnik, 2009).

> *Bronfenbrenner refers to proximal processes of complex and reciprocal interactions as the primary mechanism for development. Each of the context levels (micro-, meso-, exo-, and macrosystems) interacts bidirectionally. These processes are progressively more complex and must occur on a regular basis for development to occur.*

A deeper understanding of individuals and the systems in which they exist is central to tailoring the practice of financial counseling to the individual client. Within each system level, the dominant group's values and assumptions are often maintained in both implicit and explicit ways. These values can enter the counselor–client relationship from both sides of the exchange. For example, the financial services industry has long lacked the racial and gender diversity seen in other fields. Women and people of color have been historically underrepresented in the financial sector, leading to a predominance of perspectives and experiences common to white male professionals. Without consideration of how these perspectives might fail to adequately serve women, people of color, or those with limited means, financial counselors can unintentionally assign values and assumptions that misinform their practice of financial counseling. Taking care to consider clients' lived experiences can help counselors to develop a more conscious conceptualization of their cases, and in return, deliver better counsel.

The next section of this chapter defines various dimensions of human diversity through a systemic lens to help prepare financial counselors for engaging with clients from different backgrounds. It is important to note that definitions can be limiting and are subject to change over time. Those presented here should be considered a starting point. Equipped with a basic understanding of diversity topics, the chapter then discusses how financial counselors can practice greater awareness to gain a deeper understanding of clients and their respective experiences.

Diversity Constructs Through a Systems Perspective

This section provides definitions of several constructs that influence one's identity or sense of self; these constructs also orient an individual's personal microsystem. Constructs such as gender, race, ethnicity, or religious affiliation impact how individuals experience and perceive the world. The constructs that inform identity are associated with issues of power and carry wide-ranging implications for an individual's lived experience. Financial counselors should strive to build an awareness of these concepts into their practice to arrive at a better understanding of clients and the systems in which they exist.

Sex, Gender, and Sexuality (APA, 2007; VandenBos, 2015)

- Sex is the assignment of biological, physiological, and reproductive characteristics of a person's body into three categories: male, female, or intersex. Sex is typically assigned at birth based on appearance of genitalia.
- Gender refers to culturally constructed aspects of masculinity or femininity. Gender can be thought of as a binary continuum with masculinity and femininity at each end, where most people fall somewhere between the extremes; some people also reject the conventional gender binary and identify as non-conforming, non-binary, or genderqueer. Gender expression refers to how one expresses their gender, whereas gender identity refers to how one sees oneself. Behaviors that

match culturally constructed expectations are called gender-normative, whereas culturally incompatible behaviors are called gender non-conforming. An individual's gender expression may or may not match their gender identity or gender assignment (the gender they were assigned at birth).

- Sexuality, or sexual orientation, refers to sexual and emotional attraction. An individual may be sexually and/or emotionally attracted to men, women, both, neither, genderqueer individuals, or any other gender identity and expression. Individuals may identify as lesbian, gay, heterosexual, bisexual, queer, pansexual, asexual, or any other identification.
- Queer is an umbrella term used to describe sexual orientation, gender identity, or gender expression that does not conform to societal norms. Queer is a reclaimed, once pejorative term that is embraced by members of many sexual minority groups. The use of the word queer by non-queer people may have a negative impact on those who identify as queer due to the term's pejorative history.
- Social gender expectations form and describe the behaviors and characteristics that are deemed "appropriate" for individuals (Risman, 2004). Gender expectations can be limiting and hinder possibilities for all genders and sexes. Because gender is socially constructed (not based on biology), behaviors and characteristics that are deemed gender "appropriate" change over time and across cultures. For example, in the 1950s it was gender-normative for masculine males to be the breadwinner and manager of household finances, while feminine females were expected to take care of household chores and childrearing. Over the last half century, the USA has experienced a shift away from traditional gendernorms towards a more egalitarian approach to household earnings and childrearing.
- Extensive research on the topic of financial management and control in heterosexual partnerships outlines the disparities between genders across several dimensions. In low-income households where finances are highly controlled by the male, female partners tend to be more financially disadvantaged; as income increases, management and control are more likely to be given to the male partner while breadwinning female partners tend to minimize their capability for financial control in an attempt to maintain gender-normative financial expectations (Vogler, 1998; Vogler, Lyonette, & Wiggins, 2008; Vogler & Pahl, 1994). In recent decades, these long-running gender norms have collided with structural changes in the US economy that have worked to erode the number of jobs available to low-education, low-skilled men; at the same time, women have become increasingly likely to attend and graduate from college, suggesting that the gender pay gap will continue to narrow and upend gender-normative earnings arrangements.
- Seeking to understand gendered expectations of financial management in clients' households can help financial counselors to understand the underlying forces that inform and maintain clients' financial behaviors.

Race and Ethnicity

- Race is a categorical description of individuals based on skin color and other inherited visible differences. Race is not based on biology (AAPA, 1996; Smedley & Smedley, 2005). It is socially constructed, meaning society has placed individuals into categories in which shared assumptions can be made as a psychological short-cut. Socially constructed racial categories include Black, Asian, and White.
- Ethnicity refers to the social, cultural, and sometimes national group of a person. Ethnic descriptives can include assumptions of gender, class, race, religion, or other characteristics of a group of people. Examples of ethnicity include Hispanic, Arab, and Irish. Sometimes, ethnicity and nationality can be the same, as with German; *nationality* describes the political state to which someone belongs. A person can be categorized, based on skin color, for example, into the Black race, of Hispanic ethnicity, or of Brazilian nationality; however, this may or may not be how they self-identify.

Racial and ethnic minority groups in the United States have endured a long history of both social and state-sanctioned discrimination, fostering a degree of distrust in prevailing institutions (e.g., inequities in the criminal justice system; redlining and housing discrimination; residential segregation and under-resourced schools). Financial counselors must be conscious of the ways in which these experiences impact clients—not only historically, but today.

Class

- Class, or social class, is the classification of people based on their social or economic status. Socioeconomic status (SES), a related term often used in the social sciences, is defined as "the social standing or class of an individual or group... often measured as a combination of education, income, and occupation" (APA, 2007).

According to the American Psychological Association, low SES negatively affects physical health, psychological health, family well-being, education attainment, work stress, family-work role conflict, job security, and employment (APA OSES, 2017). In lower SES communities, it can be difficult to access public transportation, health clinics, quality groceries, safe schools, or good jobs, creating additional obstacles to financial stability and personal well-being. In the USA, race/ethnicity and SES are often intertwined (e.g., Dressler, Oths, & Gravlee, 2005); for many, racial, ethnic, and socioeconomic inequalities operate simultaneously, exacerbating barriers to educational resources, health care, and wealth accumulation. These forces can render clients from low SES and minority backgrounds more financially vulnerable than other clients.

Education

- The process of learning can be divided into formal and informal education. Formal education is typically delivered by trained teachers in a school or university setting. It is often classroom-based, though online courses are increasingly available through formal educational institutions. Informal education takes place outside of the classroom through conversations with family, friends, or coworkers. Informal education can also be self-directed, such as visiting museums, reading books, or exploring topics online. Formal learning is the most widely recognized and valued form of education in our culture. Educational inequality refers to the unequal distribution of academic resources. Many individuals live in communities where formal education resources are limited, hampering their access to equal education.

> *Financial education is often absent from public school curricula; instead, many people receive an informal financial education from their families, social groups, or online resources. For those that grow up in lower SES families, reliable financial education may be limited, making it difficult to navigate personal financial decisions.*

Mental Health

- Mental health refers to one's psychological or social well-being. It is important to differentiate mental health diagnoses from the symptoms of a mental health problem. A mental health diagnosis is given by a mental health professional and requires that a person meet certain criteria, including a set of symptoms over a period of time; a person can have symptoms (indicators of a potential diagnosis), but not meet full diagnostic criteria. For example, a person can feel sad but not meet diagnosis criteria for major depressive disorder, or a person might describe themselves as anxious but not meet diagnosis criteria for generalized anxiety disorder. Many mental health symptoms can affect financial behaviors and decisions.

Ability Status

- Able-bodied people are often valued over individuals with disabilities in our culture (e.g., Edwards & Imrie, 2003). There are many types of disabilities with varying degrees of severity, including physical, mental, intellectual, and sensory disabilities. Ability status affects the way that people experience the world, though these challenges are sometimes invisible. Ableist vocabulary includes words such as "crazy," "retarded," and "lame" that inadvertently target individuals with disabilities. When used carelessly, these words can be harmful or offensive by implying that anything other than able-bodiedness is inferior.

Religion and Spirituality

- Religion is a set of beliefs, system of faith, or practice of worship. There are several thousand religions in the world. Major religions include Judaism, Christianity, and Islam. Within most major religions, there are multiple denominations, such as Catholics, Protestants, Baptists, Lutherans, and Evangelicals, each of which belong to the larger Christian tradition. Unaffiliated, or non-religious, people are also a significant group, accounting for approximately one in six people globally (Hackett et al., 2012).
- Spirituality refers to the feeling of being connected to something larger than oneself; the term is often invoked in relation to personal growth and a search for ultimate meaning. The concept of spirituality has evolved over time, with different connotations in different eras. People can be both spiritual and religious, one or the other, or neither.

Religious and spiritual beliefs can heavily influence a person's financial behaviors. Historically, many religions have denounced the concept of usury, or lending money at high rates of interest. Today, tithes and offerings are part of some religious practices. Financial counselors should strive to understand how clients' religious beliefs may impact current financial behaviors.

Models, Tools, and Techniques for Diversity-Conscious Financial Counseling

Earlier in this chapter, we defined the mesosystem as the space in which microsystems (e.g., family, work, social systems) interact, the macrosystem as the setting for cultural values and assumptions, as well as some aspects of identity that orient individuals within these systems. Here we present a series of models, tools, and techniques to help financial counselors better understand and engage with the systemic dynamics affecting their clients.

Models for Diversity-Conscious Financial Counseling

Sensitizing Theory

Schwalbe et al. (2000) outline four processes that maintain unhelpful, systemic assumptions. In their study of inequality, the authors seek to "understand the interactive processes through which inequalities are created and reproduced in concrete settings" (p. 419). The authors identify four ways that inequality is perpetuated: othering, subordinate adaptation, boundary maintenance, and emotional management. We review each process and discuss what financial counselors can do to avoid cultivating these dynamics in their practice.

Othering is the creation of an inferior group in relation to, and by, a superior group. In the process of "othering," individuals are placed into categories that include assumptions and generalizations about who they are. Meanings and values are assigned to these categories, which work to "shape consciousness and behavior" (p. 422).

- Financial counselors that present themselves as a superior or professional with power can create unhelpful client–counselor dynamics. Viewing the client as part of an "other" group perpetuates distance and hierarchy between the client and counselor. Financial counselors can combat this process by taking a learner's stance when getting to know their clients; a learner's stance helps to create an equal and mutual relationship, acknowledges the client as an expert on their lived experience, and acknowledges the unique skills that a financial counselor brings to the relationship.
- Applying the concept of "othering" to working with couple or family clients can be helpful in exploring financial management roles. An example of "othering" discussed earlier in this chapter is that of gender-normed expectations: traditional male head-of-households are expected to perform the role of breadwinner and financial manager, while traditional females are expected to perform less-mature or "inferior" tasks, such as childcare and household maintenance (Mahoney & Knudson-Martin, 2009). Clients that buy in to these traditional roles may experience "othering" dynamics that affect behavior and perpetuate inequalities.

Subordinate adaptation refers to a coping strategy that individuals employ in response to being categorized as the inferior "other." Coping mechanisms of the inferior "other" include: acceptance and efforts to benefit from relations with the group in power (trading power for patronage); the formation of new systems of prestige (forming alternative subcultures); acceptance of their lower place in the hierarchy while trying to make it as comfortable as possible through socially unaccepted means to gains (hustling); or the withdrawal of participation from the hierarchy (dropping out).

- Financial counselors should work to recognize these coping strategies as signals of unhealthy client–counselor dynamics. A client that appears to be cozying up to their financial counselor may be coping with feelings of inferiority in relation to the counselor.
- Financial counselors can also apply this concept to client systems. For example, if one individual in a couple-client pair refuses to participate (i.e., "dropping out"), it might be important to understand whether they are feeling inferior to the individual that is participating in the sessions. Subordinate adaptation might also manifest as an overemphasis on the needs of others (i.e., feeling obligated to tend to the person in power) or feeling guilt around type of work and income (e.g., women feeling guilt related to full-time employment instead of fulfilling the traditional role of household maintenance).

Boundary management refers to the maintenance of boundaries between the superior and inferior "other" to protect cultural position, power, and capital. Boundary maintenance is often institutionalized in schools, governments, banks, and the workforce. Face-to-face interactions that perpetuate boundary management include selectively regulating access to "knowledge, skills, habits, values, and tastes that are acquired in the course of socialization, and which can be turned to one's advantage in particular social settings" (p. 430; citing Bourdieu, 1977; referred to as maintenance and transmission of cultural capital and controlling network access).

- Financial counseling is a form of boundary maintenance. Certain knowledge and resources are required to participate in financial counseling. For those with lower levels of knowledge and resources (or that came from systems with fewer educational resources), financial counseling can be perceived as uncomfortable, which may inhibit success in meeting financial counseling goals. Sensitivity to cultural differences (e.g., ways of interacting, types of knowledge, values, beliefs) can help financial counselors to respect clients' diverse capabilities and permeate restrictive boundaries.
- In applying the concept of boundary management to client systems, financial counselors can shed light on restrictive boundaries by exploring clients' perceptions and limiting narratives, such as the concept of a "glass ceiling" on women's earnings. Family-level system narratives can also perpetuate boundary maintenance; for example, narratives that minimize men's parental role include statements that husbands "help" with household chores or "babysit" children, or messages from employers that men should not take paternal leave after the birth of a child.

Emotional management is the process of maintaining a minimum level of emotional regulation to preserve interpersonal stability. To maintain emotional order, formal and informal rules about what can be said and how it can be said act as a form of social regulation (regulating discourse); individuals are taught how to make "useful" meaning of their emotions (conditioning emotional subjectivity); and events are scripted in the interest of a favorable, intended emotional experience.

- Financial counselors can work to combat emotional management tactics by practicing transparency and honesty. For instance, counselors that refrain from sugar-coating bad news or complicated financial directives can help to establish an authentic and trustworthy client–counselor relationship. If financial counselors practice transparency and honesty to avoid emotional management tactics, clients may mirror this transparency in their own behavior.
- Emotional manipulation and regulation happens in client systems as well. For example, two partners may speak differently about finances in the presence of a financial counselor, or in the presence of each other. Financial counselors can seek to gain a better understanding of this tactic by meeting with client couples both jointly and individually.

Ford Financial Empowerment Model

Stemming from the financial therapy movement, the Ford Financial Empowerment Model (FFEM; Ford, Baptist, & Archuleta, 2011) outlines an empowerment-based therapeutic approach to financial counseling. The motivating idea behind the model is that "to empower is to help individuals who feel inadequate in handling a situation to discover the capabilities that reside within them" (p. 22). The model has two aims—first, to identify the ways in which an individual's culture influences money perceptions, behaviors, and experiences (cultural conceptualization), and second, to help resolve the psychological, emotional, and relational (systemic) factors related to finances. The FFEM acknowledges a major limitation of its approach in that even the basic concepts of empowerment and individualism are masculine, Western values. However, the model advocates for a culturally conscious co-construction of empowerment goals that are culturally sensitive and client-defined. Techniques from the FFEM are outlined below, including specific tools financial counselors can use to gain better insight into client work.

- *Therapeutic collaboration* is developed through the establishment of trust and openness between client and service provider.
- *Cognitive-behavioral techniques* are used to explore thoughts that dictate money behaviors. Unhelpful thoughts are restructured to reflect more accurate, helpful thoughts that improve money behaviors. The process of restructuring thoughts includes:
  - *Agenda setting* to provide structure and feelings of accomplishment.
  - *Setting financial goals* to identify clients' desired outcomes and establish therapeutic alliances (aligning the service provider and client on the same team).
  - *Financial education* to provide foundational knowledge, tools, and skills.
  - *Assigning self-help materials* for ongoing education, practice, and consciousness outside of the session.

- *Narrative financial therapy techniques* "allow clients to construct stories about their lives that are relevant and meaningful to them" (p. 32; also see Freedman & Combs, 1996; White & Epston, 1990).

  - *Co-constructing client stories* help to establish beneficial schemas.
  - *De-constructing listening techniques* encourage more precise listening.
  - *Listening for and highlighting sparking moments* allow counselors to emphasize unique outcomes that do not match problem-saturated assumptions or negative experiences.
  - *Active, opening questioning* facilitates deeper thought and breadth of story development.
  - *Externalization* of problems, or re-framing a problem as something that is not inside or part of the client, helps to make the problem more manageable and easier to confront.

- *Experiential financial therapy techniques* aim to help clients uncover deeper experiences, unrecognized desires, and a broader acceptance of self.

  - *Exploring the self* aims to identify how certain problems are related to sense of self (e.g., how financial issues are linked to religious or moral values). Formulating a new understanding of the problem "can help clients make better sense of the problems and find better ways to manage them" (p. 33).

Money Scripts and Schemas

The Merriam-Webster definition of schema is "a mental codification of experience that includes a particular organized way of perceiving cognitively and responding to a complex situation or set of stimuli." A schema can be thought of as a way of perceiving and interpreting situations that informs a response. The concept of money scripts is a model of schemas related to money and psychology. Klontz and Klontz (2009) describe money scripts as unconscious, core beliefs about money that are developed in childhood and young adulthood and that drive financial behaviors. Money scripts are inherited through generations and cultures (Lawson, Klontz, & Britt, 2015), and include money avoidance, money worship, money status, and money vigilance (Klontz, Britt, Mentzer, & Klontz, 2011). For more detailed information about money scripts, please refer to Chap. 11.

Klontz et al.'s (2011) findings reiterate certain disparities across race, ethnicity, SES, and education. For example, the authors note that individuals belonging to minority groups (younger, non-white, unmarried, lower education, and lower SES) tend to engage in "money avoidance," "money worship," and "money status" scripts. Tools in the money scripts model can help financial counselors explore the cultural and psychological forces underpinning money behaviors.

Techniques for Diversity-Conscious Financial Counseling

Self-of-the-counselor work. In the field of family therapy, "self-of-the-therapist" work refers to self-examination of the "restraints and resources arising out of a therapist's lived experiences" (Timm & Blow, 1999, p. 332). It has also been defined as "the willingness of a therapist or supervisor to participate in a process that requires introspective work on issues in his or her own life, that has an impact on the process of therapy in both positive and negative ways" (p. 333). Put simply, self-of-the-therapist work is a form of self-improvement. It involves dealing with the personal issues that hinder professional engagement and nurturing the personal traits that enhance it. Financial counselors can engage in self-of-the-therapist work with the techniques outlined below. For additional information on increasing self-awareness, please refer to Chap. 5 in this book.

- *Take ongoing inventory of personal, implicit biases.* Everyone has biases and assumptions. Biases are attitudes and beliefs for or against something. Implicit biases and assumptions are those that are subtle and unconscious, positive and negative, and that people may be unwilling or unable to report (Project Implicit; Greenwald, Banaji, & Nosek, 2015). Project Implicit defines *attitude* as an evaluation of a concept such as a person, place, thing, or idea (e.g., having a favorable attitude towards an able-bodied person and a less favorable attitude towards a person that uses a wheelchair) and a *stereotype* as a belief that most members of a group have some characteristic (e.g., believing that Muslims are violent).
  - Project Implicit's *Implicit Association Test* (IAT) is an online assessment that measures implicit attitudes and biases on multiple dimensions. The results of this test are a good starting point for self-of-the-counselor work. To take the test, visit: https://implicit.harvard.edu/implicit/takeatest.html.
  - Implicit biases are difficult to eliminate (Greenwald et al., 2011). The goal of becoming more aware of implicit biases is to deny biases the chance to dictate behaviors, and further, to intentionally create new patterns of behavior that break the cycle of unconscious biases. The following are a list of techniques for doing so (informed by Project Implicit, 2011):
    - o The first step in combating implicit bias is to recognize it. Financial counselors can take IAT assessments, practice self-compassion, mindfulness, or meditation to help gain insight into their implicit biases. Several of these techniques are described more below. For financial counselors interested in deeper exploration, individualized counseling with a mental health professional can help advance personalized approaches to uncovering and challenging implicit biases.
    - o Once identified, one approach for resisting implicit bias is to compensate for one's inherent preferences. Financial counselors can often have a bias towards clients with higher net worth. Intentionally diversifying client caseloads can compensate for this bias.
    - o Another technique for confronting implicit bias is to identify and avoid stimuli that instill or reinforce prejudice. For example, one might examine

and reconsider sources of media consumption that portray minority groups in stereotypical ways (e.g., movies that portray women as subordinates, or news channels that pander to one-dimensional representations of racial or religious minorities).

Practicing self-compassion. Compassion is the expression of concern, empathy, kindness, and assistance in response to the suffering of *others* (Neff, 2003). Compassion *for oneself* in the process of challenging pre-existing assumptions can aid in the difficult and uncomfortable experience of doing so (Ying, 2009). Neff (2003) details six factors in self-compassion: mindfulness, common humanity, self-kindness (positive factors), and over-identification, isolation, and self-judgment (negative factors). These factors are inversely related, in that each positive factor decreases the risk of the corresponding negative factor. In other words, increased mindfulness lowers over-identification, increased sense of common humanity lowers isolation, and increased self-kindness lowers self-judgment.

Increasing one's sensitivity to diversity is intimate and arduous work. Missteps and confusion are often part of the process, making self-compassion in these moments all the more critical. Below are several ideas for cultivating self-compassion:

- *Practice self-talk that includes statements of kindness you would give to a friend who is trying something for the first time*
- *Allow space for imperfection and remind yourself that it is okay to learn from mistakes*
- *Work with a therapist that provides a safe and confidential space to work through challenges*

Self-compassion can serve as an emotional regulation technique for financial counselors when confronting implicit biases. Research suggests that professionals who practice self-compassion are better able to cope with professional challenges (Ying & Han, 2007). Studies also show that self-compassion is linked to more curiosity, exploration, initiative, and extroversion—all characteristics that result in greater functional competence (Neff, Kirkpatrick, & Rude, 2007).

Practice mindfulness. Mindfulness is a therapeutic technique for focusing one's awareness on the present moment and acknowledging and accepting one's own feelings, thoughts, and bodily sensations without judgment. Practicing mindfulness can be a worthwhile practice for those in the financial counseling field for a number of reasons. Studies show mindfulness is negatively associated with perceived stress around professional challenges (Ying & Han, 2007). Similar research has noted that being less mindful is linked to greater emotional contagion (Ying & Han, 2007) and emotional exhaustion (Ying, 2009). Mindfulness and meditation have also demonstrated a positive effect on functional competence and mental health (Shapiro, Schwartz, & Bonner, 1998). Finally, the practice of meditation has been shown to increase self-acceptance (Morgan et al., 2013) and promote professionals' effectiveness by facilitating attentiveness, empathy, and engagement with clients (Brenner & Homonoff, 2004; Germer, 2005; Shapiro et al., 1998).

Conclusion

Diversity is a broad topic. The task of deepening our understanding of other races, ethnicities, genders, social classes, religions—or any intersection thereof—is a critical and ongoing endeavor. This chapter sets out to provide financial counselors with a primer on these topics, with the idea that a systemic approach to recognizing and appreciating the different ways in which clients experience the world can help counselors to better serve their needs. Ultimately, greater sensitivity to diversity is not an end goal in itself, but rather an active lifelong practice.

References

American Association of Physical Anthropologists (AAPA). (1996). AAPA statement on biological aspects of race. *American Journal of Physical Anthropology, 101*, 569–570.
American Psychological Association (APA). (2007). Report of the APA task force on socioeconomic status. Retrieved from http://www.apa.org/pi/ses/resources/publications/taskforce-2006.pdf.
American Psychological Association Office on Socioeconomic Status (APA, OSES). (2017). *Resources and publications*. Retrieved from http://www.apa.org/pi/ses/resources/index.aspx.
Bourdieu, P. (1977). *Outline of a theory of practice* (Vol. 16). Cambridge: Cambridge University Press.
Brenner, M., & Homonoff, E. (2004). Zen and clinical social work: A spiritual approach to practice. *Families in Society: The Journal of Contemporary Social Services, 85*(2), 261–269.
Bronfenbrenner, U. (2005). *Making human beings human: Bioecological perspectives on human development*. Thousand Oaks, CA: Sage.
Bronfenbrenner, U., & Morris, P. A. (2006). The bioecological model of human development. In R. M. Lerner & W. Damon (Eds.), *Handbook of child psychology: Theoretical models of human development* (pp. 793–828). Hoboken, NJ: John Wiley & Sons Inc..
Dressler, W. W., Oths, K. S., & Gravlee, C. C. (2005). Race and ethnicity in public health research: Models to explain health disparities. *Annual Review of Anthropology, 34*, 231–252.
Edwards, C., & Imrie, R. (2003). Disability and bodies as bearers of value. *Sociology, 37*(2), 239–256.
Ford, M. R., Baptist, J. A., & Archuleta, K. L. (2011). A theoretical approach to financial therapy: The development of the Ford financial empowerment model. *Journal of Financial Therapy, 2*(2), 1.
Freedman, J., & Combs, G. (1996). Gender stories. *Journal of Systemic Therapies, 15*(1), 31–46.

Germer, C. K. (2005). Teaching mindfulness in therapy. *Mindfulness and Psychotherapy, 1*(2), 113–129.

Greenwald, A. G., Banaji, M. R., & Nosek, B. A. (2015). Statistically small effects of the Implicit Association Test can have societally large effects. *Journal of Personality and Social Psychology, 108*(4), 553–561.

Greenwald, A. G., Banaji, M. R., & Nosek, B. A. (2011). *Project Implicit*. Retrieved from https://implicit.harvard.edu/implicit/

Hackett, C., Grim, B., Stonawski, M., Skirbekk, V., Potančoková, M., & Abel, G. (2012). *The global religious landscape*. Washington, DC: Pew Research Center.

Klontz, B., Britt, S. L., Mentzer, J., & Klontz, T. (2011). Money beliefs and financial behaviors: Development of the Klontz Money Script Inventory. *Journal of Financial Therapy, 2*(1), 1.

Klontz, B., & Klontz, T. (2009). *Mind over money: Overcoming the money disorders that threaten our financial health*. New York: Crown Business.

Lawson, D., Klontz, B. T., & Britt, S. L. (2015). Money scripts. In B. T. Klontz, S. L. Britt, & K. L. Archuleta (Eds.), *Financial therapy: Theory, research and practice* (pp. 23–34). New York: Springer.

Mahoney, A. R., & Knudson-Martin, C. (2009). *Gender equality in intimate relationships. Couples, gender, and power: Creating change in intimate relationships*. New York: Springer.

Mancini, J. A., Martin, J. A., & Bowen, G. L. (2003). Community capacity. In *Encyclopedia of primary prevention and health promotion* (pp. 319–330). Springer, Boston, MA.

Morgan, W. D., Morgan, S. T., & Germer, C. K. (2013). Cultivating attention and compassion (2nd ed.). In C. K. Germer, R. D. Siegel, & P. R. Fulton (Eds.), *Mindfulness and psychotherapy* pp. 76–93. New York: Guilford Press.

Neff, K. D. (2003). The development and validation of a scale to measure self-compassion. *Self and Identity, 2*(3), 223–250.

Neff, K. D., Kirkpatrick, K. L., & Rude, S. S. (2007). Self-compassion and adaptive psychological functioning. *Journal of Research in Personality, 41*(1), 139–154.

Papero, D. V. (1990). *Bowen family systems theory*. Upper Saddle River, NJ: Prentice Hall.

Risman, B. (2004). Gender as social action: Theory wrestling with activism. *Gender and Society, 18*, 429–450.

Rosa, E. M., & Tudge, J. (2013). Urie Bronfenbrenner's theory of human development: Its evolution from ecology to bioecology. *Journal of Family Theory & Review, 5*(4), 243–258.

Schwalbe, M., Godwin, S., Holden, D., Schrock, D., Thompson, S., & Wolkomir, M. (2000). Generic processes in the reproduction of inequality: An interactionist analysis. *Social Forces, 7*, 419–452.

Shapiro, S. L., Schwartz, G. E., & Bonner, G. (1998). Effects of mindfulness-based stress reduction on medical and premedical students. *Journal of Behavioral Medicine, 21*(6), 581–599.

Smedley, A., & Smedley, B. D. (2005). Race as biology is fiction, racism as a social problem is real: Anthropological and historical perspectives on the social construction of race. *American Psychologist, 60*(1), 16–26.

Timm, T. M., & Blow, A. J. (1999). Self-of-the-therapist work: A balance between removing restraints and identifying resources. *Contemporary Family Therapy, 21*(3), 331–351.

Tudge, J. R., Mokrova, I., Hatfield, B. E., & Karnik, R. B. (2009). Uses and misuses of Bronfenbrenner's bioecological theory of human development. *Journal of Family Theory & Review, 1*(4), 198–210.

VandenBos, G. R. (2015). *APA dictionary of psychology*. Washington, DC: American Psychological Association.

Vogler, C. (1998). Money in the household: Some underlying issues of power. *The Sociological Review, 46*(4), 687–713.

Vogler, C., Lyonette, C., & Wiggins, R. D. (2008). Money, power and spending decisions in intimate relationships. *The Sociological Review, 56*(1), 117–143.

Vogler, C., & Pahl, J. (1994). Money, power and inequality within marriage. *The Sociological Review, 42*(2), 263–288.

Von Bertalanffy, L., & Sutherland, J. W. (1974). General systems theory: Foundations, developments, applications. *IEEE Transactions on Systems, Man, and Cybernetics, 4*(6), 592–592.

White, M., & Epston, D. (1990). *Narrative means to therapeutic ends*. New York: WW Norton & Company.

Ying, Y., & Han, M. (2007, June). The importance of self-compassion to social work students: Empirical evidence. In *Second North American conference on spirituality and social work*. River Forest, IL: Dominican University.

Ying, Y. W. (2009). Contribution of self-compassion to competence and mental health in social work students. *Journal of Social Work Education, 45*(2), 309–323.

Chapter 5
The Importance of Self-Awareness for Financial Counselors and Clients

Joseph W. Goetz, Dorothy B. Durband, and Angela K. Mazzolini

How does one achieve introspection? When is stress good and when is it harmful? What are one's most fundamental values and beliefs? What provides a counselor or client with the most lasting sense of contentment or sense of meaning? *Self-awareness* as defined by Merriam-Webster is "an awareness of one's own personality or individuality." As applied to a financial counseling context, self-awareness can be conceptualized as an understanding and evaluation of one's knowledge, attitudes, biases, preferences, and their potential effects on one's own behaviors and interactions with others.

In general, greater self-awareness can engender a greater understanding of reality. In other words, financial counselors and their clients are vulnerable to cognitive and emotional biases that lead to varying levels of irrationality (Goetz & Gale, 2014). Knowing oneself offsets this potential irrationality and permeates every domain of life, including idiosyncratic tendencies, psychological predilections, desires and fears, and strengths and vulnerabilities. It would be naïve to think that a counselor's past experiences, relationships, and personal history did not affect, and interact with, those of the client. These concepts known as transference and countertransference are addressed later in this chapter.

The importance of self-awareness for financial counselors cannot be overstated, as it affects all aspects of a counselor's work with clients (Kottler, 1993). Financial counselors who are intentional in their efforts to continually enhance their self-awareness are likely to be substantially more effective in helping

J. W. Goetz
Department of Financial Planning, Housing, and Consumer Economics, University of Georgia, Athens, GA, USA

D. B. Durband (✉)
School of Family Studies and Human Services, Kansas State University, Manhattan, KS, USA

A. K. Mazzolini
Financial Counseling Consultant, Lubbock, TX, USA

© Springer Nature Switzerland AG 2019   65
D. B. Durband et al. (eds.), *Financial Counseling*,
https://doi.org/10.1007/978-3-319-72586-4_5

clients. This is due, in large part, to the fact that greater self-awareness, and more specifically a counselor's understanding of how to promote self-awareness, can be transferred to a client more easily. Client self-awareness regarding their views and biases with respect to money and financial attitudes and behaviors is extremely valuable in the financial counseling process. Some even make the argument that counselor self-awareness is a primary ethical issue (see Pompeo & Levitt, 2014), as high self-awareness decreases the likelihood of counselors unintentionally harming their clients by "unconsciously working out [their] own emotional unfinished business" at a cost to the client (Hutchinson, 2007, p. 23). A necessary step for any professional should be to consider and reflect upon their own biases and how they potentially interact with various ethical and professional standards; this is particularly important in a profession such as financial counseling, that includes both technical and psychological components (Gale, Goetz, & Britt, 2012; Ross, Gale, & Goetz, 2016).

Counseling Style and Attributes of Effective Counselors

Awareness of the counseling style and preferences for both the financial counselor and client is important to the efficiency and effectiveness of the financial counseling process. Professionals with varying styles of counseling can be equally effective; however, it is valuable for the counselor to be aware of how their preferences may be incongruent with those of the client, thereby allowing for adjustments to be made or expectations recalibrated. Counseling style may involve myriad factors, such as the theoretical orientation of the counselor, level of directiveness in communication, duration and frequency of sessions, or content-based processes, such as the amount of teaching in session.

Identifying the specific characteristics or personality traits that make for the most effective financial counselors is difficult, and is likely to vary depending on the client. Research is scant on this topic. There is, however, limited research related to the effectiveness of certain traits among counselors in general. For example, researchers have found evidence that specific characteristics, such as being naturally confident or having strong interpersonal skills, make it less challenging to connect with clients (Softas-Nall, Baldo, & Williams, 2001). Certainly, the ability to be influential and persuasive is of immense value, along with flexibility to adjust the counseling process when progress is slow. Lastly, based on the authors' experience, the counselor being able to effectively communicate optimism and hope is integral to the counseling process for many clients.

There are a number of studies that provide evidence that the most effective counselors focus on developing a strong working alliance with their clients (Bedi, 2004; Bordin, 1979; Horvath & Greenberg, 1994). Regardless of their overall counseling style, counselors who develop a partnership with their client in facing the challenges of the client are more likely to see positive outcomes. It is the strength of this strategic alliance, as well as the attributes and skills that support this alliance, that are critical to effective counseling. A well-established working alliance provides the foundation for comfort, genuineness, and truthfulness in the counselor–client relationship, which leads to more positive outcomes. Effective financial counselors create and support a strong working alliance in two primary ways:

1. Ensuring client–counselor agreement on goals and tasks involved in the process of financial counseling (i.e., managing expectations and clearly communicating steps of the process)
2. Developing an emotional bond and high level of trust between the client and financial counselor

Attributes of counselors that have a positive effect on the working alliance include: empathic effort, acceptance, genuineness, open-mindedness, sensitivity, and use of effective communication techniques and skills. Increased self-awareness among financial counselors provides an important foundation for the critical counseling characteristics of empathy and the other attributes listed above (Duan, Rose, & Kraatz, 2002). In other words, learning about oneself and how a financial counselor's past affects his or her current beliefs and behaviors helps the counselor develop a stronger sense of empathy. The concept of unconditional positive regard introduced by Rogers (1980) speaks to the value of being fully accepting of a client and assuming the client is working toward self-actualization. Being genuine with a client encourages trust and collaboration. Continuous effort is required to optimize open-mindedness, as it is natural for preconceived notions, stereotypes, and one's personal history to cloud communication with a client. Sensitivity in communication also supports a strong working alliance. As Grable and Goetz (2017) point out, financial counselors and planners often use insensitive language without being self-aware that they are doing so:

> This is due in large part to the fact that these issues [i.e., sexism, racism, and heterosexism] unfortunately permeate our culture and thus unconsciously make their way into the coding of language. Part of the challenge is that financial planners [and counselors] and other professionals are often insensitive without realizing they are being insensitive. Remember, long-standing dominant cultural practice likely leaves a powerful, sometimes unconscious, influence over the most conscientious financial planner [and counselor]. Thus, even the most experienced financial [counselors] have opportunities for improvement when the issue of sensitivity in client communication comes up. For most [professionals], the concern will not be about obviously inappropriate characterizations or treatment of people based on gender, race, age, and other characteristics. Rather, it is the more subtle variations in language, body language, and communication among financial professionals that can be perceived as insensitive by a client that may be problematic. There are countless examples of the subtleties of expressions that, with no malicious intent, can have a remarkably adverse effect on a client. (p. 163)

Financial counselors who have a high openness to feedback, and continuously seek out opportunities for improvement in their client communication, inevitably develop greater self-awareness. The desire to continue to learn and improve is one of the most important attributes a counselor can have, as it supports increasing overall effectiveness in the financial counseling process.

Effective counselors are aware of their clients' contextual factors and characteristics. Characteristics and contextual factors of the client may refer to family dynamics, socioeconomic status, sexual orientation, ethnicity, health status, job security, or social, human, and financial capital. Awareness also involves understanding clients' personal experiences with group identity, discrimination, and privilege, as recognizing one's own privilege aids in facilitating empathy for understanding how discrimination limits opportunities and for understanding others who may lack privilege (Birkenmaier & Sherraden, 2016). The most effective financial counselors is likely one who has high self-awareness of his or her own psychological processes and biases regarding money, best practices and research evidence related to each client, skill deficits and strengths, whether a client feels understood, and the perceived strength of the working alliance.

This awareness is crucial, along with an ability to provide an explanation for, and plan to help, the client reduce distress or change behaviors. Being influential and possessing a sophisticated set of interpersonal skills and a resolute desire for feedback, continuing education, and greater self-awareness are central to effective financial counseling. As the chapter heading suggests, self-awareness is at the foundation of positive attributes of any financial counselor. The next section examines various components of self-awareness.

Components of Self-Awareness

Conscious and unconscious factors from both the counselor and client affect the financial counseling process. The role of unconscious influence may affect one's work as a financial counselor. As explained by Hutchinson (2007):

> Many of Freud's original ideas have been challenged by other theories both in and out of psychoanalytic school of thought: however, the idea of the unconscious is broadly accepted by most major approaches to counseling and psychotherapy. Theorists may disagree about the specific nature and origins of material held in the unconscious, but they generally believe that we all function with elements of our past stored in our memories just beyond the grasp of our daily awareness. A function of most counseling is to help people access more of this material, to draw it into the realm of conscious awareness. (p. 26)

Financial counselors' self-awareness of their unconscious and conscious beliefs, attitudes, and tendencies will vary based on other components of self-awareness, including: (a) training factors, (b) personality factors, (c) situational factors, and (d) financial socialization factors. With more training, financial counselors are likely to develop greater self-awareness, particularly when components of the training are focused on self-discovery and self-evaluation. A well-established financial counseling education or training program will also cover established domains of competency including mastery of various subject areas. Through this process of education and training, counselors develop greater self-awareness of what they do, and do not, know.

It is important for a financial counselor to be aware of their own personality characteristics and how those may affect the financial counseling process. For example, if a financial counselor is by nature an impatient person, she or he will need to develop compensatory skills as not to allow this factor to adversely affect the counseling process. Other personality traits such as being naturally inquisitive or driven can be beneficial but are not necessarily effective and may also need to be monitored, depending on compatibility with the client's personality characteristics. Working style, personality preferences, or personality assessments (i.e., psychometrically validated scales that provide a sense of where one falls within a broader population) may be helpful in providing insights for financial counselors. Examples include the Myers–Briggs Type Indicator®, Clifton StrengthsFinder®, Kolbe A™ Index, Thomas–Kilmann Conflict Mode Instrument, and DiSC®, but there are many others.

A financial counselor should be aware of how their current financial status, as well as their past financial socialization, might affect their perspectives and emotions when working with clients. Socialization processes acquired in childhood allow the development of skills and knowledge (Fox, Bartholomae, & Gutter, 2000). Financial socialization is a process that is influenced by numerous means such as families, peers, media, and teachers influencing individuals as they develop financial values, attitudes, skills, and behaviors (Gudmunson, Ray, & Xiao, 2016). As suggested by Gudmunson and Danes (2011), though everyone is financially socialized, some forms of socialization may lead to detrimental attitudes, beliefs, and behaviors. This awareness is important as to not overly project financial counselors' experience onto their clients. Transference and countertransference are two natural tendencies that can hinder the financial counseling process. Transference refers to how a client's financial socialization (i.e., past financial-related experiences) and related emotions were not fully resolved and may, in turn, affect the financial counseling process. Countertransference is similar, but on the part of the financial counselor, as explained by Grable and Goetz (2017):

> All financial planners [and counselors] have conscious and unconscious feelings from their past that may be triggered by a client's words or behaviors. These feelings may hinder or help client-financial [counselor] communication, but in either case, it is important to recognize when transference and countertransference are occurring within the communication process. In transference, the client transfers their feelings associated with a past event or person to that of their financial planner [or counselor], potentially disrupting and hindering the communication process. For example, a planner [or counselor] may say something to the client that sounds similar to what a disloyal past significant other or adviser once said. Subsequently, the client may experience feelings of distrust rush back in, even though on an intellectual level the client knows her current [counselor] is a different person. Consider a situation when a financial planner [or counselor] makes a neutral statement, but because of transference, the client interprets the statement as criticism because he or she associates the statement (and now the financial counselor) with another authority figure, such as an overly critical father…In reaction to a client statement or behavior, a financial planner [or counselor] may also have emotional baggage that unconsciously clouds his judgment or affects his client communication. This is countertransference. (p. 65)

A common form of countertransference among financial counselors revolves around the concept of debt. Based on a person's financial socialization, it is common to have varying degrees of personal comfort with leveraging or taking on debt. This varying level of emotional comfort on behalf of a financial counselor can be incorrectly projected onto a client's situation (i.e., countertransference). For example, due to a financial counselor's experience as a child viewing their parents incessantly argue about debt, the counselor may incorrectly recommend aggressively paying down all debts, rather than examining a client's liabilities more holistically and within the context of maximizing the client's probability of success in meeting all long-term goals. This sometimes means making minimum payments on some debts or even increasing the amount of more strategic debt. When viewing debt within the context of a client's overall financial plan, debt is most appropriately viewed on a continuum of problematic to strategic. For example, recommending a client accelerate the payoff of low-interest, tax-deductible debt and consequently not having enough cash flow to fund a retirement account and receive an employer-match on contributions will, in almost all instances, reduce the probability of success in meeting long-term goals. In other words, a personal, negative bias toward debt may lead a counselor to recommend sending extra money toward mortgage or student loan debt, while the optimal financial recommendation would be to benefit from the current year tax savings and higher expected rate of investment return.

Though countertransference may often happen outside of the facilitator's [financial counselor's] awareness (Klontz, Kahler, & Klontz, 2008), unproductive communication can be reduced when financial counselors are more aware of their client's transference and their own countertransference. The self-aware financial counselor reflects on their own reaction to the client (i.e., countertransference) to examine the appropriateness and reasonableness in their response before responding. In other words, they consider whether their reactions are helpful and appropriate given the client's contextual factors or if the reaction is resulting from the financial counselor's own issues. One of the most effective ways for counselors to enhance self-awareness of countertransference is through completing a counseling log immediately following a client session or journaling to record issues or reactions of concern until resolved. Alternatively, to enhance increasing awareness of a client's transference is by asking a client about their past experiences with family and money, as well as conducting assessments about values, attitudes, and beliefs values around money. A money history questionnaire is provided at the end of this chapter.

The same assessments and exercises can be used by financial counselors to identify the impacts of their own financial socialization on biases they may have developed. More specifically, uncovering family of origin issues related to money and the money scripts that financial counselors may have can help avoid instances of negative countertransference and make counselors more aware of their own biases around money. Money scripts are typically unconscious core beliefs about money developed in childhood that span generations and drive adult financial behaviors (Klontz et al., 2008). As Shapiro (2007) noted: "the meaning and power of money in childhood has a powerful impact on how money is viewed as an adult" (p. 280). A genogram is a tool used by therapists and healthcare professionals focused on money (see Mumford & Weeks, 2003) that can help the financial counselor work with clients to visually illustrate their generational family relationships through financial attitudes and behaviors. Genograms may help couples talk about money in a way that is non-threatening and view patterns and issues between their families of origin (Britt, 2016).

As expressed by Goetz and Gale (2014):

> Behavioral finance researchers clearly show that individuals are subject to cognitive and emotional biases that may lead to suboptimal financial decisions...The field of neuroeconomics further explains these biases affecting financial behaviors from a physiological perspective and presents clear implications for financial planners [and counselors]...Despite many empirical data corroborating the fact that cognitive biases and emotions have an integral role in financial decisions and behaviors, few professionals in the financial field address their own biases or those of their clients. (p. 227)

Common cognitive and emotional biases result from magnifying the meaning of past financial experiences, exposure to financial misinformation, and emotional tendencies, but others result simply from how the human mind is wired (Goetz & James, 2008). For example, clients tend to search for patterns, which is adaptive across most domains of life, but often leads to suboptimal decisions with respect to financial decisions, such as buying and selling at the wrong times when investing in the stock market or prioritizing repayment of the wrong debts. Common biases that affect counselors and client include mental accounting, confirmation bias, familiarity bias, and various other heuristics (i.e., mental shortcuts in decision-making) (Chatterjee & Goetz, 2015). These biases can be overcome or at least muted through engaging in regular exercises to increase self-awareness.

Assessment Exercises to Increase Self-Awareness

Self-awareness can be developed in myriad ways, the most obvious being life experience and the inevitable missteps and successes along the way. As summarized by Hutchinson (2007):

> Life experience helps to shape the person of the counselor. The wider and more divergent the life experience, the greater the capacity of the counselor to do this work. Counseling is both science, represented by your professional course work and preparation, and art, represented by your personal evolution. In addition to the developing of your counseling skills, you need to develop your knowledge of contemporary thought about the forces that have shaped your clients' lives and the signs of normal and abnormal development. You need to have a working knowledge of basic diagnostic and assessment strategies. (p. 28)

Other ways to potentially accelerate the development of counselor and client self-awareness include strategies that can be immediately implemented, such as seeking feedback and constructive criticism. This may be accomplished through formal and informal work performance evaluations (i.e., eliciting feedback from supervisors, supervisees, and colleagues) and regular feedback from peers. Regularly checking in with clients and asking for their feedback on what has been the most and least helpful components of their financial counseling process is also an important mechanism for increasing self-awareness; it may be a simple concept, but many financial counselors fail to be intentional in seeking client feedback.

Another strategy to enhance self-awareness is through self-observation work or reviewing one's own sessions with clients. Audio or visual recording of client or communication work (with client consent) and then observing to complete self-evaluations is perhaps the most powerful exercise a financial counselor can perform to increase their self-awareness of communication patterns and tendencies (e.g., verbal expression, word usage, pacing, eye contact, use of silence, body language, communication techniques). Recording role-plays and client simulations can also be informative. Along with self-observation and self-evaluation, regular reviews from peers, supervisors, and clients are accepted techniques to increase self-awareness and identify opportunities for improvement. Introspective exercises, such as journaling and reflection, may also be helpful, particularly in terms of recording experiences or feelings (Green & Howe, 2012) and evaluating change over time. One technique within journaling involves tracking counselor recommendations over time to determine effectiveness and making notes of both successes *and* failures (i.e., ineffective or suboptimal recommendations or techniques). This is one of the best ways to counteract the natural inclination that counselors have to seek out, and remember, positive information and information that confirms an already-held belief (i.e., overconfidence and confirmation bias).

Completing all client-required tasks or exercises and engaging in financial counseling activities alongside a client can yield multiple benefits to the financial counselor. It provides an opportunity to reflect on the experience of sitting on the other side of the desk or table. Kahler (2008) noted both personal and professional benefits can result from becoming a consumer of one's own profession, like mental health professionals who receive personal therapy; becoming the financial counseling client, provides an ability to address one's financial blind spots and provides accountability, while enhancing one's own relationship with money. The process may help financial counselors better understand how clients see them, what they see and do not see, and become more aware of what the counselor wants them to see.

Self-Care

Self-care may not be the first thing that comes to mind when thinking of self-awareness, yet it is an important piece for financial counselors to consider. To better manage stress, avoid burnout, and maintain balance in all areas of their lives, financial counselors, as well as other helping professionals, need to implement self-care. Corey (2013) has advice for new psychotherapy counselors, though it can be translated to all helping professionals: "You cannot control stressful events, but you do have a great deal of control over how you interpret and react to these events. It is important to realize that you cannot continue to give and give while getting little in return" (p. 33). Based on a study conducted by Richards, Campenni, and Muse-Burke (2010), self-care is critical to the life of a counselor. "The results indicate that the frequency with which mental health professionals participate in self-care activities and the importance they place on them is associated with overall well-being, which suggests that self-care is important to the functioning of mental health professionals" (p. 261).

Finding a balance between work and personal life, having a support network of both friends and coworkers, and having a positive outlook—in other words, practicing self-care—can help a person better adapt to stressful situations (National Institute for Occupational Safety and Health, 1999). Self-care can fall into several categories, such as physical, psychological, spiritual, and support seeking (Richards et al., 2010). According to the Centers for Disease Control and Prevention (CDC), a healthy adult should get both aerobic and muscle-strengthening activity each week (CDC, 2014). Physical self-care incorporates physical activity that utilizes energy (Richards et al., 2010). Whether through going to the gym, practicing yoga, taking brisk walks, or even completing household chores, moving one's body is an important part of self-care because exercise can decrease symptoms of depression and anxiety. Participating in mental health counseling provides benefits such as alleviating symptoms and distress, personal development, and an increase in self-awareness. Spiritual self-care is broadly described by Richards et al. (2010) as "…a sense of the purpose and meaning of life and the connection one makes with this understanding" (p. 249). This definition covers religion as well as behaviors such as meditation. Spirituality can influence physical well-being, mental health, and self-awareness. Working in a supportive environment with supervisors who can recognize signs and symptoms of burnout, as well as with coworkers who can provide advice through difficult situations, are both important pieces of self-care. Keeping professional and personal support systems separate may also prove beneficial for maintaining a work–life balance and preventing burnout (Richards et al., 2010).

The National Institute for Occupational Safety and Health (NIOSH) defines job stress as "… the harmful physical and emotional responses that occur when the requirements of the job do not match the capabilities, resources, or needs of the worker" (NIOSH, 1999, p. 6). Consequences of stress can be both physical and mental, and can lead to many undesirable outcomes such as cardiovascular disease, musculoskeletal disease, psychological disorders, suicide, cancer, ulcers, and impaired immune function. Stress can also lead to job burnout. Job burnout for financial professionals can occur when three factors are in play: emotional exhaustion, depersonalization, and reduced personal accomplishment (Koetsten, 2005). Emotional exhaustion is a "…feeling of being 'used up' and unable to face another day. That feeling prompts individuals to emotionally and cognitively distance themselves from their work as a way to cope" (Koetsten, 2005, p. 67). Depersonalization refers to how a professional views a client. The client becomes another problem to be handled and is held at a distance. Feeling as though one's work is making little to no difference in the world is reduced personal accomplishment (Koetsten, 2005).

Practicing mindfulness-based stress reduction as a part of self-care may also provide benefits. A study performed by Schure, Christopher, and Christopher (2008) with counseling graduate students at Montana State University found that when students practiced yoga, meditation, and qigong over a semester long course, the students had positive physical and emotional outcomes. Students reported increased physical attributes, such as flexibility and strength, as well as less frequent illnesses. Students had increased clarity of thought, reflection, and self-awareness. Many students also reported feeling more grounded and having an increased sense of purpose.

Students saw changes in their ability to show empathy and compassion, which were attributed to the increased mental clarity and ability to stay focused during times of silence.

Conclusion

Across most theoretical orientations of counseling and therapy, self-awareness is a primary goal for the counselor. Increasing the self-awareness of the client can have substantial benefits in terms of communication around finances, financial behaviors, and overall progress in financial and overall well-being. A financial counselor who has successfully increased their financial and overall self-awareness is likely to be much more effective in assisting clients in increasing their self-awareness. Facing the confirmation bias head-on by actively seeking out conflicting information to one's assumptions or pre-existing beliefs, and continuously seeking feedback can inform one's understanding of potential biases. How one is perceived by others is important, so the most effective counselor will constantly seek a better understanding of the congruence between the intent and impact of their messaging.

A common component of the scientific method used to investigate and explain natural phenomena is *testing* and *retesting*. Adapted to the practice of financial counseling, we might observe that people make assumptions about themselves that may, or may not, be correct. Only through a process of testing and retesting, however, can a client or counselor really find out if their assumptions are accurate. A person may think they do not like skydiving, avocados, or people who play Dungeons and Dragons, but when tested, the results may lead to pleasant surprises. Similarly, counselors will need to experiment with various techniques to determine which ones are the most effective for them and their clients.

In sum, greater self-awareness provides a foundation for effective financial counseling. The most effective counselors are aware of their opportunities for improvement and continually seek to make these improvements. They create opportunities for receiving feedback and develop a model in which they can test whether improvements have a positive effect on outcomes. A self-aware financial counselor is more likely to be an effective financial counselor and achieve, or even exceed, expected goals.

Money History Questionnaire

1. What are your earliest memories about money? Are these memories generally positive or negative?
2. How was money discussed in your family of origin? Only when absolutely necessary? Openly without emotions? Secretly? As power?
3. How did you obtain money as a child? What did you do with the money when you got it?

4. How was money used in your family system? To control? For being good? Withheld as punishment? To motivate?
5. As a child, what was your impression of your family's wealth or class status? Looking back, how accurate do you think that impression was?
6. Who spent most of the money in your family when you were a child?
7. Do you recall ever wanting something very much and could/could not get it because there was not enough money? How did you react to this situation?
8. What was the family's attitude toward borrowing money from others in the family?
9. Who made decisions about how much money to save? For what was money saved?
10. What were some of the fears or anxieties about money in your parents' or grandparents' generation?
11. What messages about money did each generation pass on to the next generation?
12. How would you describe each generation's philosophy about wealth? What is your philosophy about wealth?
13. What were some of the most well-known habits about money in each generation? What are some of your habits when it comes to money?
14. If applicable, what was your first job outside of the family? How did the job influence you?
15. What are the basic "rules" that you tend to live by when it comes to money? You can list money sayings or money proverbs that capture your beliefs and behaviors about money.

As you look back over what you've written, briefly describe any themes or lessons that come through in your responses. Can you see more clearly how you got here or what you may need to do for healthier financial management?

Adapted with permission from questions developed by Glen Jennings, Ed.D. and James Grubman, Ph.D.

References

Bedi, R. P. (2004). The therapeutic alliance and the interface of career counseling and personal counseling. *Journal of Employment Counseling, 41*, 126–135.
Birkenmaier, J., & Sherraden, M. (2016). Cultural competence in financial counseling and coaching. *The Professionalizing Field of Financial Counseling and Coaching*, 11–12 Retrieved from http://www.professionalfincounselingjournal.org/assets/cfe-fund-professionalizing-field-of-financial-counseling-and-coaching-journal2.pdf
Bordin, E. S. (1979). The generalizability of the psychoanalytic concept of the working alliance. *Psychotherapy: Theory, Research & Practice, 16*(3), 252–260.
Britt, S. L. (2016, Fall). The intergenerational transference of money attitudes and behaviors. *Journal of Consumer Affairs, 50*(3), 549. https://doi.org/10.1111/joca/12113
Center for Disease Control and Prevention. (2014). How much physical activity do adults need? Retrieved from https://www.cdc.gov/physicalactivity/basics/adults/index.htm

Chatterjee, S., & Goetz, J. (2015). Applications of behavioral economics in personal financial planning. In C. Chaffin (Ed.), *Financial planning competency handbook* (2nd ed., pp. 751–762). Hoboken, NJ: John Wiley & Sons, Inc.

Corey, G. (2013). *Theory and practice of counseling and psychotherapy* (9th ed.). Belmont, CA: Brooks/Cole.

Duan, C., Rose, T., & Kraatz, R. (2002). Empathy. In G. Tryon (Ed.), *Counseling based on process research: Applying what we know* (pp. 197–231). Boston: Allyn & Bacon.

Fox, J. J., Bartholomae, S., & Gutter, M. (2000). What do we know about financial socialization? *Consumer Interests Annual, 46,* 217.

Gale, J., Goetz, J., & Britt, S. (2012). Ten considerations in the development of the financial therapy profession. *Journal of Financial Therapy, 3*(2), 1–13. https://doi.org/10.4148/jft.v3i2.1651

Goetz, J., & Gale, J. (2014). Financial therapy: De-biasing and client behaviors. In H. K. Baker & V. Ricciardi (Eds.), *Investment behavior: The psychology of financial planning and investing* (pp. 227–244). New York: John Wiley & Sons.

Goetz, J., & James, R. (2008). Human choice and the emerging field of neuroeconomics: A review of brain science for the financial planner. *Journal of Personal Finance, 6*(2), 13–36.

Grable, J., & Goetz, J. (2017). *Communication essentials for financial planners: Strategies and techniques.* Hoboken, NJ: John Wiley & Sons, Inc..

Green, C. H., & Howe, A. P. (2012). *The trusted advisor fieldbook: A comprehensive toolkit for leading with trust.* Hoboken, NJ: John Wiley & Sons, Inc..

Gudmunson, C. G., & Danes, S. M. (2011). Family financial socialization: Theory and critical review. *Journal of Family Economic Issues, 32*(4), 644–677.

Gudmunson, C. G., Ray, S. K., & Xiao, J. J. (2016). Financial socialization. In J. J. Xiao (Ed.), *Handbook of consumer finance research* (2nd ed.). New York: Springer.

Horvath, A. O., & Greenberg, L. S. (Eds.). (1994). *The working alliance: Theory, research, and practice.* New York: John Wiley & Sons, Inc..

Hutchinson, D. (2007). *The essential counselor: Process, skills, and techniques.* Boston: Houghton Mifflin Company.

Kahler, R. S. (2008). Becoming consumers of the profession we practice. *Journal of Financial Planning, 21*(11), 56–64.

Klontz, B., Kahler, R., & Klontz, T. (2008). *Facilitating financial health: Tools for financial planners, coaches, and therapists.* Cincinnati: National Underwriter.

Koetsten, J. (2005, October). Reducing stress and burnout for financial planners. *Journal of Financial Planning, 18*(10), 64–74.

Kottler, J. (1993). *On being a therapist.* San Francisco: Jossey-Bass.

Mumford, D., & Weeks, G. (2003). The money genogram. *Journal of Family Psychotherapy, 14*(3), 33–44.

National Institute for Occupational Safety and Health. (1999). *Stress...at work.* DHHS (NIOSH) Publication No. 99-101. Retrieved from: https://www.cdc.gov/niosh/docs/99-101/default.html

Pompeo, A. M., & Levitt, D. H. (2014). A path of counselor self-awareness. *Counseling and Values, 59,* 80–94.

Richards, K. C., Campenni, C. E., & Muse-Burke, J. L. (2010, July). Self-care and wellbeing in mental health professionals: The mediating effects of self-awareness and mindfulness. *Journal of Mental Health Counseling, 32*(3), 247–264.

Rogers, C. (1980). *A way of being.* Boston: Houghton Mifflin.

Ross, D. B., Gale, J., & Goetz, J. (2016). Ethical issues and decision making in collaborative financial therapy. *Journal of Financial Therapy, 7*(1), 17–37.

Schure, M. B., Christopher, J., & Christopher, S. (2008, Winter). Mind-body medicine and the art of self-care: Teaching mindfulness to counseling students through yoga, meditation and qigong. *Journal of Counseling and Development, 86*(1), 47–56.

Shapiro, M. (2007). Money: A therapeutic tool for couples therapy. *Family Process, 46,* 279–291.

Softas-Nall, B., Baldo, T., & Williams, S. (2001). Family of origin, personality characteristics, and counselor trainees' effectiveness. *Psychological Reports, 88*(2), 199–201.

Chapter 6
Classic Theories for Use in Financial Counseling

Angela K. Mazzolini and Sissy R. Osteen

Introduction

Financial counseling is a field that has roots in several disciplines including medicine, home economics, and mental health counseling. Theoretical approaches to financial counseling are therefore derived from a multitude of professions. It is important for the reader to understand the theories and frameworks behind the techniques that guide the work of financial counselors because a theoretical worldview will have a direct impact upon how: (1) a counselor hears and assesses client issues, (2) decides on an approach to help the client understand and accept their responsibility and possible need for change, and (3) the counselor plans and conducts an actual session. Each theory lays out basic beliefs about human thought, behavior, and developmental paths as well as an expected outcome for the counseling intervention. It can pinpoint a particular approach to issues that clients may present in counseling. A theory is, after all, "a plausible or scientifically acceptable general principle or body of principles offered to explain phenomena" (Merriam Webster, 2018, para. 1). The closer that a theory aligns with the beliefs and observations of the counselor, the easier it is for the counselor to understand the issues and relationships that are observed in counseling.

According to Brew and Kottler (2017) Theory in counseling and therapy emerged in four movements from Freud's model that focused on unconscious motives and urges, to Adler and his humanism (which also inspired Roger's person-centered work), onto the focus on current thinking and its influence on behavior. The fourth movement is

A. K. Mazzolini (✉)
Financial Counseling Consultant, Lubbock, TX, USA

S. R. Osteen
Department of Human Development and Family Science, Oklahoma State University, Stillwater, OK, USA
e-mail: sissy.osteen@okstate.edu

© Springer Nature Switzerland AG 2019
D. B. Durband et al. (eds.), *Financial Counseling*,
https://doi.org/10.1007/978-3-319-72586-4_6

more current and contextual and will receive broader coverage in the chapter on contemporary theories.

It should also be noted that there is no one right technique or theory, but in fact, most counselors will take an approach to financial counseling that integrates more than one theory. Counselors use techniques that fit their own style and worldview. A counselor's theoretical base for counseling is developed and evolves over time. It begins with self-awareness about personal life philosophy, further develops through experiences and insights, and eventually leads to an intentionality in the application of counseling practice (Halbur & Halbur, 2006). Each theoretical orientation can influence the counselor's approach. According to Corey (2001), "Valuable dimensions of human behavior can be overlooked if the counselor is restricted to a single theory." (p. 26). Corey (2017) also cautions that counselors should avoid using any particular theory to justify a personal bias. Because every client is different, it is imperative that financial counselors have different tools to use with diverse personalities among clients, and among diverse populations.

In order to help understand why and how each theory is different, the authors have created a timeline that includes the year or period the theory was introduced and those credited with developing the theory. This is not an all-inclusive list, but focuses on the theories and frameworks highlighted in this chapter and the next. These theories were chosen based on the authors' familiarity and usability in financial counseling. They are each presented as an *overview* and are *not* all encompassing of each theory. The authors hope to give financial counselors a glimpse into the theories that are being utilized in other professions, but that have great application opportunities for financial counseling. Readers are encouraged to seek out more in-depth training on theories and techniques that are of interest to them.

To assist with the application of the various theories, a case study will also be introduced in each of the two chapters and the different theories and frameworks will be utilized to better explain the application to financial counseling.

Timeline

1895: Sigmund Freud began developing psychoanalysis
1911: Alfred Adler broke away from psychoanalysis and developed his own theory
1940s: Gestalt Theory developed by Fritz and Laura Perls
1942: Person-centered Approach developed by Carl Rogers
1955: Rational Emotive Therapy (later renamed Rational Emotive Behavioral Therapy) developed by Albert Ellis
1968: General Systems Theory proposed by Ludwig Von Bertalanffy
1980s: Solution-Focused Brief Therapy (SFBT) developed by Steve deShazer and Insoo Kim Berg and Appreciative Inquiry developed by David Cooperrider and Suresh Srivastva
1983: Transtheoretical Model of Change (TTM) developed by James Prochaska and Carlo DiClemente

1990s: Motivational interviewing (MI) developed by William Miller and Steve
   Rollnick
1992: Additions made to TTM by James Prochaska, Carlo DiClemente, and John
   Norcross
1998: Positive psychology introduced by Martin Seligman

Case Study

The following case study will be exemplified through the application of the theories
that are discussed in this chapter: Ranbir and Pranay Patel are a married couple in
their late thirties. They are a second-generation Indian-American couple. Ranbir's
family is more traditional than Pranay's. The couple met in college where each
completed an MBA. Ranbir is employed as a Chief Operations Officer for an international computer technology company where he has been employed for the last 5
years. His annual income is $150,000. Pranay indicates that she is not currently
employed but she would really like to be. Ranbir's family feels that she should stay
at home and raise children. They have been married for almost 5 years but have no
children despite constant pressure from Ranbir's family to continue the family
name. The couple comes in for counseling with credit card debt as the stated concern. Ranbir explains that Pranay is the primary user of the card and has a habit of
online shopping that is "out of control."

Psychoanalysis

No conversation about psychotherapy theories is complete without a discussion of
the Psychoanalytic Theory developed by Sigmund Freud (Freud, 1973). Freud's
greatest contributions to theory were related to the development and structure of
personality. Freud proposed that the personality consists of three systems, the id, the
ego, and the superego (Corey, 2017). Freud also proposed that consciousness was a
very small part of the way the mind functions. He believed the unconscious, including such things as dreams, slips of the tongue, and even forgetting, offered more of
an explanation for behavior than conscious thought. According to Freud, unconscious content was usually related to wishes or desires and if the wishes or desires
were not socially acceptable, the subject was in conflict. The theory's focus on the
unconscious also proposes that individuals may not be aware of what guides their
actions (Kottler, 2008). In his early career, Freud focused on hypnosis as a way to
uncover the unconscious mind and thus the motivations for actions. He later moved
to free association. Free association is a technique used to allow the client to talk
freely (say whatever comes to mind) about themselves. This helps them avoid the
influence of defense mechanisms. The theory proposes that during this free flow of
words or thoughts, the client may trip themselves up and reveal deeper motivations
(McLeod, 2009).

Other assumptions of psychoanalytic thought include anxiety (tension that leads an individual to action); and ego defense mechanisms (e.g., repression, denial, projection, compensation, and sublimation) (Corey, 2001). It is this list of defense mechanisms that illustrate how Freud's concepts have carried over to contemporary theories.

Application

Counselors working from a psychodynamic perspective hold certain assumptions about client issues: (1) difficulties are connected to childhood experiences, (2) clients may not be aware of the true motives for their actions, and (3) counseling is a transference relationship where the counselor stays neutral and the client projects their hidden motivation onto the counselor (McLeod, 2009).

Mental health professionals spend years learning about psychoanalysis before working with clients, so it is unlikely that financial counselors will use a technique like dream analysis to reveal a client's unconscious thoughts, but financial counselors might find use for other techniques from psychoanalysis. Free association could help when a client cannot understand why he or she is stuck in a pattern of behavior. A client may perceive that a deep seeded belief may be irrational, yet does not know where the belief came from or how to overcome it. It is more important to understand that Freud believed that individuals were motivated by these unconscious beliefs and unresolved issues. In the case of the Patels, the counselor would take a longer-term approach by letting the couple discuss any unresolved issues in the past, even those that involve past generations. A free association exercise might illuminate the stereotypical beliefs about gender roles and the resistance to change. Theoretically, this type of insight could result in a correction of distortions and reduction in reactivity.

Adlerian Therapy

Alfred Adler was originally a colleague of Freud's and follower of psychoanalytic thought. The relationship between the two was ended in dramatic fashion when Freud and other members of the Psychoanalytic Society voted Adler out when they decided that his ideas strayed too far from the psychoanalytic movement (Maniacci, 2012). Adler's assumption of holism differed significantly from Freud's three systems of personality. In fact, Adlerians propose that, "the person is an indivisible unit, that the person needs to be understood in his or her totality. From this vantage point, dividing the person into id, ego, and superego, or parent, child, and adult states is not beneficial." (Mosak & Maniacci, 1999).

Adler's future work focused on individual psychology and moved away the influence of inner forces toward how the individual responds to life-changing problems as they strive to attain mastery and success within the context of social interest

(Moore, 2012). According to Adlerian theory, individuals are motivated to strive toward superiority in a socially useful way. This "superiority" is actually a situation that the individual has assessed, through observation and interpretation, to be a better condition than the current "inferior" position. The progression toward superiority occurs in a relational context, can proceed in a way that is either socially useful or socially useless, and the way that one strives toward superiority indicates mental health (Watts, 2012). Striving for superiority, without social interest or considering needs or desires of others in the group or community, reflects a self-centered focus. Adlerian psychology addresses the idea of superiority/inferiority in relationships and how the individual that senses they are in the position of inferiority can deny cooperation to the other person (Walton & Kern, 2016). The position of inferiority will not be sustained forever, as the person in this position will continue to strive toward a better situation.

Lifestyle or style of life is in important concept in Adlerian theory as it is in most individual psychological theory. Adler believed that style of life was an individual's unique way of developing by overcoming problems and striving toward goals. Lifestyle also consists of the way the individual views himself/herself and the world (Lombardi, Melchior, Murphy, & Brinkerhoff, 2006). Adler believed that a person's perception of their world influences their personality and once subjective perceptions of the world are established individuals find ways to confirm what they have come to believe through a selective attention process (Oberst & Stewart, 2003).

There are eight basic assumptions of Adlerian theory: (1) holism, (2) teleology, (3) the creative self, (4) striving for superiority, (5) soft determinism, (6) phenomenology, (7) social field theory, and (8) idiographic orientation (Mosak & Maniacci, 1999). Key concepts and principles of these assumptions underlie Adlerian theory that could have a direct influence on how counseling could proceed. These concepts, as presented by Dinkmeyer and Sherman (1989), include the following:

1. Individuals must be considered as a whole, as an entire person and personality (holism). Focusing exclusively on parts or aspects of the individual will obscure the whole (Mosak & Maniacci, 1999). Adler considered the individual a unified whole where conscious and unconscious complemented each other rather than existed in conflict (Lundin, 1989).
2. Behavior is purposeful and directed toward a certain goal. Helping family members see the purpose of the other's behavior can help clarify the reasons for the behavior and eventually align their goals (teleology).
3. The creative self, also referred to as the creative power, is a very important assumption of Adlerian theory that proposes that people are active in decision-making who are shaped by their experiences and behaviors (Peluso, 2012). Adler also believed that all behavior was directed toward a goal.
4. The way that a person behaves is associated with their need to overcome feelings of inferiority and move toward superiority (striving for superiority). Striving toward a better situation is a major motivation for individuals (Mosak & Maniacci, 1999).

5. Soft determinism is seen as the middle ground between nondeterminism and determinism. Determinism focuses on causality but nondeterminism sees no connection between cause and effect. Soft determinism is distinguished by terms like influences and possibilities (Mosak & Maniacci, 1999).
6. Behavior results from personal subjective observations and perceptions (phenomenology). Adler was convinced that behavior resulted from the meaning that individuals derive from their observations and interpretations (Mosak & Maniacci, 1999).
7. Behavior has social meaning and can be understood and changed when it is viewed within a social context (social field theory).
8. The idiographic orientation focuses on the particular characteristics of any given individual.

Application

Considering the tenets of Adlerian psychology, Slavik (2006) proposed that there are four options or outcomes for counseling. The counselor can help the client change their thinking, change their behavior, change their perceptions, or manipulate their outcomes. Adlerian theory offers guidance for addressing the issues identified by the Patels. As a constructivist theory that proposes that behavior has meaning and is goal-directed, the counselor could focus on understanding a fuller context of how each person developed socially. Since a major tenet of the theory is that individuals are firmly lodged within the social context of the past and present (Freeman & Urschel, 2003), there is a seemingly clear opportunity with the Patels, to gather information about how "firmly lodged" they are in the social and cultural norms and contexts they experienced. Adler believed that the individual's perception of a situation was what mattered more than the actual situation because it is the perception and reaction that helps the individual build a lifestyle (Oberst & Stewart, 2003). Discussing feelings of inferiority or superiority may help the Patels understand the underlying goal behind Pranay overspending or the reason there is resistance to her working when she has expressed the desire to be employed.

Gestalt Therapy

Fritz and Laura Perls developed Gestalt therapy in direct opposition to psychoanalysis. Perls was influenced by Freud's concepts, but his ideas differed in several significant ways. Gestalt therapy stressed the holistic approach to personality rather than the more mechanistic view of psychoanalytic theory, it valued examination of the present situation instead of repressed early childhood experiences, and the approach focused on process more than on content (Corey, 2001). Several basic principles underlie Gestalt Therapy Theory including holism, field theory, the figure formation process, and organismic self-regulation (Corey, 2001). According to Perls (1992), "'Gestalt' is a holistic concept. A gestalt is a structured entity that is more than, or different from, its parts" (p. 52). Gestalt theory proposed that the individual was to be considered as a whole, and an emphasis was placed on how the individual fit within the environment (the field). Field theory focuses on the context that everything is related and moves and changes in tandem. The concept of figure formation describes how an individual organizes the context or environment and determines which aspects are the most significant at any time (the figure) and which aspects remain in the background. Another premise of Gestalt is that humans operate in homeostasis or self-regulation. When an organism or system operates in conditions that are out of balance for too long, it becomes sick. "For the individual to satisfy his needs, to close the gestalt, to move on to other business, he must be able to sense what he needs and he must know how to manipulate himself and his environment, for even the purely physiological needs can only be satisfied through the interaction of the organism and the environment." (Perls, 1973, p. 18).

The last two tenets of Gestalt illustrate that while man is a whole organism (instead of being parts of a whole), man does not operate independently. According to Gestalt, man is a unified organism and the body and mind work together instead of as separate entities, as suggested by psychoanalysis. When a person experiences themselves on three levels of fantasizing, play-acting, and doing, then they will have a greater understanding of themselves. Based on this assumption, psychotherapy, then, is not about repressed memories or the unconscious, but about integrating thoughts, feelings, and actions, even those from the past, to create a wholeness in a person. Contact boundary is the final basic premise. "No individual is self-sufficient; the individual can exist only in an environmental field. The individual is inevitably, at every moment, a part of some field. Individual behavior is a function of the total field, which includes both the person and the environment. The nature of the relationship between him and his environment determines the human being's behavior." The contact boundary is where a person and his or her environment meet and the psychological events happen. "Our thoughts, our actions, our behavior, and our emotions are our way of experiencing and meeting these boundary events" (Perls, 1976, p. 56). Perls uses the biological response to being thirsty to help explain contact boundary. If someone is thirsty, that person feels a lack of fluid and so the need is felt as a negative. A glass of water is a positive experience and when the person has had enough water to feel satisfied, the outcome is a zero sum. The gestalt is closed.

When humans try to operate on their own, outside of contact with others, or are unable to close the gestalt, neurosis can occur (Perls, 1973). In a gestalt, a thirsty man drinks. In a person experiencing neurosis, there may be a barrier to prevent a thirsty man from seeking water, but may seek out other ways to fulfill his desire. Gestalt therapy then helps to bring the person back to the main premises to close the gestalt: Life happens in a system, not in a vacuum; organisms tend toward self-regulation; body and mind work together to achieve the self-regulation; the environment around a person will determine their behavior.

Application

Financial counselors can relate the ideas of Gestalt therapy to their own clients. Clients do not exist separate from their environments, especially when dealing with money. Some techniques that are associated with Gestalt therapy that financial counselors may find helpful are the empty chair technique, and the reversal exercise. Sometimes clients have a conflict or unresolved feelings toward another person or toward themselves. The empty chair technique involves placing an empty chair across from the client and having them speak to the person who could be sitting there. The absence of an actual person in the chair reduces the anxiety of a confrontation and allows the client to say things they would never actually say to another person. They may verbalize feelings they did not even realize they had. A client may also assume the role of the person in the empty chair to be able to imagine the situation from the other person's point of view. "The goal of this exercise is to promote a higher level of integration between the polarities and conflicts that exist in everyone. The aim is not to rid oneself of certain traits but to learn to accept and live with the polarities" (Corey, 2017, p. 215).

A reversal exercise allows a person to face the thing that brings them anxiety and make contact with the parts of themselves that are in denial or hidden (Corey, 2017). The counselor asks the client to exhibit the opposite of their normal behavior, so if working with a couple and one partner is always quiet and soft-spoken, he or she would be asked to be loud and gregarious. Or, in the case of the Patels, each could discuss the pleasures and frustrations of being employed and staying at home shopping. This would allow each partner to express their thoughts and feelings in ways they typically would not be able to and help the other partner hear a different perspective. This may lead to better understanding and resolution of the conflict.

Person-Centered Approach

Much like Gestalt, the person-centered approach, developed by Carl Rogers, is built on the concept that humans have the capacity to change and grow. The central hypothesis is as follows:

It is that the individual has within him or herself vast resources for self-understanding, for altering the self-concept, basic attitudes, and his or her self-directed behavior and that these resources can be tapped if only a definable climate of facilitative psychological attitudes can be provided (Rogers, 1979, p. 98).

The three conditions that allow for growth are transparency or congruency, unconditional positive regard for the client, and empathetic understanding. According to Rogers, if the counselor creates these conditions, the client will be more accepting of himself or herself, be able to listen to their inner dialogue more accurately, and will develop a more genuine attitude toward themselves.

"These tendencies, the reciprocal of the therapist attitudes, mean that the person is a more effective growth enhancer for him or herself" (Rogers, 1979, p. 99).

There are no techniques specific to person-centered approach. Rogers' theory proposed that when the three conditions were met, and the client was able to translate the counselor's conditions to their own self-awareness, then the client's behavior would be more creative in finding ways to meet his or her goals. He believed in the actualizing tendency "which is the inherent tendency of the organism to develop all its capacities in ways which serve to maintain or enhance the organism" (Rogers, 1959, p. 196). Since this theory relies heavily on the counselor/client relationship, it is important for the counselor to have self-awareness in order to provide the conditions that will bring about behavior change in the client.

Application

Pure, traditional person-centered practice requires the counselor control their own attitudes and responses and let the client lead. More contemporary forms of person-centered practices are more directive, but still adhere to the underlying principles (Sommers-Flanagan & Sommers-Flanagan, 2004). The person-centered approach can be translated into many counseling settings. Making sure that a client feels heard and understood and that the counselor is being honest and open with the client is imperative to building rapport. (More information about the importance of building rapport can be found in Chap. 3.) During times when a client faces conflict or does not complete agreed upon tasks, it is important for the counselor to remain positive about the ability for the client to change, but the counselor may need to share their disappointment or provide feedback in order to be genuine with the client. If the counselor can provide the unconditional positive regard, genuineness, and empathy toward the client that serves as the basis for the person-centered approach, the client will be able to make positive changes in their financial life. In the case of the Patels' situation, the counselor can focus on hearing each of them out, respecting the perspectives that they provide, and providing a positive, caring environment where they can attain greater self-awareness and feel understood.

Rational Emotive Behavioral Therapy

As with many psychotherapy theories, Rational Emotive Behavioral Therapy (REBT) was developed as a counterpoint to psychoanalysis. Albert Ellis, the developer of REBT, was not satisfied with the effectiveness and efficiency of psychoanalysis. He began reading the works of Greek and Roman philosophers who "emphasized the primacy of philosophic causation of psychological disturbances – a viewpoint that was not popular in America in the 1950's – and deemphasized the part played by psychoanalytic psychodynamic factors" (Ellis & Dryden, 2007, p. 1). The foundation of REBT was built around the principle that "…people are disturbed not by things but their view of things…" (p. 15). The purpose of REBT is to move clients from irrational thoughts to rational ones to help clients reach their own goals (Ellis & Dryden, 2007).

Ellis' theory is probably best known for using the ABC approach to counseling. A is the activating event, B is the belief about the activating event, and C is the consequences of the activating event and of the beliefs about the event. Using the equation of A + B = C, REBT therapists will help clients change their irrational beliefs to produce different consequences (Ellis & Dryden, 2007).

Disputing Irrational Beliefs (DIBS) is one technique used in REBT. The counselor asks the client to write down their unhealthy or irrational belief and then begins to dispute it either through detecting, debating, or discriminating. Detecting looks for words such as "ought," "never," "should," or "must." Debating involves using questions "…such as 'Where is the evidence…?' 'In what way is this Belief accurate or inaccurate?' and 'What makes it so?'" (Ellis & Dryden, 2007). Discriminating involves distinguishing between wants and needs. DIBS is often given as homework between sessions.

Emotive techniques are an important part of REBT. As in Rogers' approach, REBT therapists have unconditional acceptance of clients. They may employ very limited self-disclosure if it helps a client dispute an irrational belief. Another emotive technique counselors may use is role reversal, "where [clients] forcefully and dramatically adopt the role of their rational 'self,' whose goal is to successfully dispute self-defeating beliefs as articulated by their irrational 'self'" (Ellis & Dryden, 2007, p. 63). Risk-taking is another technique, where clients are asked to push themselves out of their comfort zone and face their fears. To illustrate, Ellis gave an example of when he went out in public and forced himself to speak to 100 women to overcome his fear of approaching women (Ellis & Dryden, 2007). When he was 19, he forced himself to go to the Bronx Botanical Gardens and approach women who were sitting alone on a park bench. He gave himself 1 min to converse and to ask each woman out on a date. While none accepted, he believed this practice helped him overcome his fear of talking to women (Corey, 2012). Clients may also be encouraged to repeat rational statements passionately and forcefully in partnership with the other exercises.

A behavioral technique that is most associated with REBT is desensitization, where clients are put in uncomfortable situations or asked to imagine anxiety provoking situations that arouse their fears. The client is also taught techniques for relaxing in order to overcome their fears (Corey, 2017). Ellis was not a proponent of gradual desensitization, but rather of flooding, or being exposed to the object of one's fear at the height of anxiety. Other behavioral techniques include relaxation techniques and modeling behaviors. A therapist might also work with a client on building life skills, such as cooking, cleaning, personal hygiene, and nutrition, where they are absent.

Application

Because REBT is more technique-heavy than previous theories covered in this chapter, it may be easier to see how a financial counselor could use this theory in practice. It is common for counselors to work with clients who have irrational beliefs about money and so disputing those beliefs and helping clients create rational beliefs becomes an important part of financial counseling. The Patels could be challenged to look at the situations they describe in a new way and determine whether the beliefs that guide their decisions are reasonable or rational. Ranbir could be asked to consider his anxiety related to Pranay working while Pranay could focus on anxiety surrounding the families' reaction to her getting a job outside the home.

General Systems Theory

General systems theory, the precursor to modern family systems theories (Whitchurch & Constantine, 1993) was developed as an approach to understanding how complex systems work, how components are interrelated, and how this relationship meets objectives (von Bertalanffy, 1968). Founders of the Mental Research Institute (MRI), including Bateson, Mead, Hayley, and Jackson, conducted seminal systems theory work connecting systems theory and family processes (White, Klein, & Martin, 2015). Inarguably, families could be described as complex systems and understanding the roles and rules of the system and how the parts interact can illuminate how the system operates and how likely it is that change can occur.

Assumptions of the systems framework include: (1) Parts of the system are connected and influence each other, (2) The whole system must be seen in order to develop an understanding, (3) A system and its environment interact in ways that influence both system's behavior and the environment, (4) All systems have a method of feedback, and (5) Systems are not real or tangible things. Systems theory is a way to viewing interactions, how meanings have developed over time, and how these affect family functioning (White et al., 2015).

Some of the concepts of systems theory can help the counselor understand family interactions, how the family interacts with the environment, what rules maintain the system, how much impetus or resistance there is to change, and what the change will mean to the system. A *system* is a set of interrelated parts that can be understood by viewing it as a whole and in connection with the environment in which they interact. *Boundaries* exist between a system and the environment through which energy and information flow. Boundaries can be very rigid or highly permeable. *Rules of transformation* are internal rules of the system that determine how information is transformed into behavior. *Feedback* is a circular loop for returning systems outputs into the system as inputs. Positive feedback (deviation amplifying) can interfere with the system ability to reach a goal while negative feedback (deviation dampening) may more likely lead to the change. *Variety* refers to the system's ability to adapt to change. *Equilibrium* is a balance of inputs and outputs. Systems can be seen as homeostatic as they exhibit a tendency to focus on maintaining equilibrium by using feedback and control. *Subsystems* are the various levels or components of the system. These components and their impact on the functioning of the family need to be considered separately for a full understanding of what is occurring and what effect will any change have (White et al., 2015).

Application

Understanding how systems concepts can help define what is occurring in the family can provide the counselor with direction for gathering information, determining goals, and aligning efforts toward meeting those goals. Parts of the system interact with each other and the environment or other subsystems. In the case of Ranbir and Pranay, the counselor would want information about the couple subsystem, the in-laws, and the parent/son, parent/daughter subsystems to understand how the system is structured and how relationships interact to influence behavior. The counselor could also focus on boundaries and how permeable or rigid they are. The influence of external inputs, like the opinions of the in-laws, can have a dramatic impact depending upon how firm or permeable the boundaries are. What type of feedback is presented that may prevent the couple from meeting their goals? Would any of their goals be seen as unbalancing the equilibrium in the larger system and is there enough variety for the system to adapt to change?

Systems theory as a worldview offers a good perspective on what might be going on with the Patels. Counselors must be cautious though about making assumptions and conclusions that are based upon theory. The focus on counseling is to help clients develop new understandings and learn new skills that will help them meet their goals. According to Kottler (2008), the counselor can apply the theory to a session by exploring patterns of interaction, how the system is organized, alliances between the members, and how power is distributed among the members.

Conclusion

It is possible that financial counselors are using many of the theories and techniques discussed in this chapter without realizing the source. Mental health counselors spend years in training to perfect and apply the techniques presented in this chapter and the next. These chapters provide an overview for financial counselors to explore in more depth which theory and techniques can work best. It is important for financial counselors to know the background of these theories so that they can choose one (or more) that fits with their personality and works best for clients. The theory that works best may be the one the financial counselor naturally gravitates toward, but it may also come from the practice of operating from different theories and using different techniques.

Just as financial counselors are not all the same, clients all come with different needs and personality types. When a financial counselor becomes comfortable with using a specific theory, he or she may have a client that does not respond well to that theory or techniques. It is possible that financial counselors will choose multiple theories from this chapter and from the next to build an integrative approach from which to operate, which will allow the financial counselor to meet the needs of the clients in a more suitable fashion. It is important to approach this in an intentional way rather than piecing together different techniques.

Finally, financial counselors are encouraged to seek out additional training in whichever theory or theories from which they choose to operate. Many of the theories presented as overviews here are quite in-depth and the financial counselor will most assuredly benefit from other training. There are books and online resources for each theory mentioned above. The more understanding a financial counselor has of multiple theories and techniques guided by those theories, the better will be the outcomes in assisting their clients.

References

Brew, L., & Kottler, J. A. (2017). *Applied helping skills: Transforming lives*. Thousand Oaks, CA: Sage.

Corey, G. (2001). *Theory and practice of counseling and psychotherapy* (6th ed.). Belmont, CA: Wadsworth/Thompson Learning.

Corey, G. (2012). *Theory and practice of group counseling* (8th ed.). Belmont, CA: Brooks/Cole.

Corey, G. (2017). *Theory and practice of counseling and psychotherapy* (10th ed.). Boston, MA: Cengage Learning.

Dinkmeyer, D., & Sherman, R. (1989). Brief Adlerian family therapy. *Individual Psychology, 45*(1 & 2), 148–158.

Ellis, A., & Dryden, W. (2007). *The practice of rational emotive behavior therapy* (2nd ed.). New York, NY: Springer.

Freeman, A., & Urschel, J. (2003). Adlerian psychology and cognitive-behavioral therapy: A cognitive therapy perspective. In R. Watts (Ed.), *Adlerian, cognitive, and constructivist therapies* (pp. 71–88). New York, NY: Springer Publishing.

Freud, S. (1973). The complete introductory lectures on psychoanalysis. In A. Richards (Ed.) and J. Strachey (Trans.), *The Pelican Freud Library*. Middlesex, England: Penguin Books.

Halbur, D. A., & Halbur, K. V. (2006). *Developing your theoretical orientation in counseling and psychotherapy*. Boston, MA: Pearson Education.

Kottler, J. A. (2008). *A brief primer of helping skills*. Thousand Oaks, CA: Sage.

Lombardi, D. N., Melchior, E. J., Murphy, J. G., & Brinkerhoff, A. L. (2006). The ubiquity of life-style. In S. Slavik & J. Carlson (Eds.), *Readings in the theory of individual psychology* (pp. 207–216). New York, NY: Routledge.

Lundin, R. W. (1989). *Alfred Adler's basic concepts and implications*. Muncie, IN: Accelerated Development Publishers.

Maniacci, M. P. (2012). An introduction to Alfred Adler. In J. Carlson & M. P. Maniacci (Eds.), *Alfred Adler revisited* (pp. 1–10). New York, NY: Routledge.

McLeod, J. (2009). *An introduction to counseling* (4th ed.). New York, NY: McGraw-Hill.

Merriam Webster (2018). Definition of theory. Retrieved from https://www.merriam-webster.com/dictionary/theory

Milliren, A., & Clemmer, F. (2006). Introduction to Adlerian psychology: Basic principles and methodology. In S. Slavik & J. Carlson (Eds.), *Readings in the theory of individual psychology* (pp. 3–14). New York, NY: Routledge.

Moore, B. A. (2012). The progress of mankind. In J. Carlson & M. P. Maniacci (Eds.), *Alfred Adler revisited* (pp. 35–40). New York, NY: Routledge.

Mosak, H. H., & Maniacci, M. P. (1999). *A primer of Adlerian psychology: The analytic-behavioral-cognitive psychology of Alfred Adler*. Philadelphia, PA: Brunner/Mazel.

Oberst, U. E., & Stewart, A. E. (2003). *Adlerian psychotherapy: An advanced approach to individual psychology*. New York, NY: Brunner-Routledge.

Peluso, P. R. (2012). Personality as a self-consistent unity: A contemporary view. In J. Carlson & M. P. Maniacci (Eds.), *Alfred Adler revisited* (pp. 57–70). New York, NY: Routledge.

Perls, F. (1973). *The gestalt therapy approach & eye witness to therapy*. Palo Alto, CA: Science and Behavior Books.

Perls, F. (1976). *The gestalt approach & eye witness to therapy*. New York, NY: Bantam Books.

Perls, L. (1992). Concepts and misconceptions of gestalt therapy. *Journal of Humanistic Psychology, 32*(3), 50–56.

Rogers, C. R. (1959). A theory of therapy, personality, and interpersonal relationships, as developed in the client-centered framework. In S. Koch (Ed.), *Psychology: A study of a science* (Vol. 3, pp. 184–256). New York, NY: McGraw-Hill.

Rogers, C. R. (1979). The foundations of the person-centered approach. *Education, 100*(2), 98–107.

Slavik, S. (2006). Models, theories and research in individual psychology. In S. Slavik & J. Carlson (Eds.), *Readings in the theory of individual psychology* (pp. 3–14). New York, NY: Routledge.

Sommers-Flanagan, J., & Sommers-Flanagan, R. (2004). *Counseling and psychotherapy theories in context and practice: Skills, strategies, and techniques*. Hoboken, NJ: Wiley.

von Bertalanffy, L. (1968). *General systems theory: Foundations, development, applications*. New York, NY: George Braziller.

Walton, F. X., & Kern, R. M. (2016). Address to the international conference of European Scientist's Union: Some contributions of Adlerian psychology to society. *Journal of Individual Psychology, 72*(2), 148–158.

Walton, F. X. (2012). The fundamental views of individual psychology. In J. Carlson & M. P. Maniacci (Eds.), *Alfred Adler revisited* (pp. 11–18). New York, NY: Routledge.

Watts, R. E. (2012). On the origin of the striving for superiority and of social interest. In J. Carlson & M. P. Maniacci (Eds.), *Alfred Adler revisited* (pp. 41–56). New York, NY: Routledge.

Whitchurch, G. C., & Constantine, L. L. (1993). Systems theory. In P. G. Boss, W. J. Doherty, R. LaRossa, W. R. Schumm, & S. K. Steinmetz (Eds.), *Sourcebook of family theories and methods: A contextual approach* (pp. 325–352). New York, NY: Plenum Press.

White, J. M., Klein, D. M., & Martin, T. F. (2015). *Family theories: An introduction*. Thousand Oaks, CA: Sage.

Chapter 7
Contemporary Theories and Frameworks for Use in Financial Counseling

Kristy L. Archuleta, Sarah D. Asebedo, and Lance Palmer

Introduction

Meet Jackie, a single mother who just turned 35 years old. She has two children, James (12 years old) and Taylon (10 years old). She has come to you for financial counseling because she is feeling financially overwhelmed. Two weeks ago, she found THE HOME she wanted to purchase. It had been on the market for 1 week when her friend, Elizabeth, told her about it. Jackie was so excited when Elizabeth told her about the three bedroom home near the school where she teaches. She has always wanted to own a home to provide a stable living environment for her and her children, and a house near the school where she works and her children attend seemed perfect.

She immediately contacted a realtor friend, Todd, who was happy to show her the home. Indeed, it was perfect! Todd discussed with her the process of purchasing a home and recommended that she discuss financing options with her local bank. When visiting with the loan officer at the bank and running a credit report, she discovered that her credit was too poor for the bank to finance her home. Jackie teared up. She felt like a failure. She felt like she had failed at achieving the goal of owning a home. She felt like she let down her children by not being able to provide a stable living environment. She felt hopeless. Most of all, she felt stupid for not understanding what she needed to do and what she could do to get on the right track.

K. L. Archuleta (✉)
Department of Financial Planning, Housing and Consumer Economics, University of Georgia, Athens, GA, USA

Institute of Personal Financial Planning, Kansas State University, Manhattan, KS, USA
e-mail: karchuleta@uga.edu

S. D. Asebedo
Department of Personal Financial Planning, Texas Tech University, Lubbock, TX, USA

L. Palmer
Department of Financial Planning, Housing and Consumer Economics, University of Georgia, Athens, GA, USA

© Springer Nature Switzerland AG 2019
D. B. Durband et al. (eds.), *Financial Counseling*,
https://doi.org/10.1007/978-3-319-72586-4_7

After Jackie cried and told Elizabeth about her situation, Elizabeth recalled a course she took on the topic of financial counseling in college. She recommended a financial counselor that uses a postmodern theoretical approach to financial counseling. Jackie agreed that it was time to seek help and asked Elizabeth about what she meant by postmodern theoretical approaches. Elizabeth explained that theory provides a lens to view a particular phenomenon. Theory describes, explains, or predicts phenomena. Postmodern or contemporary theories differ from traditional theories in that they view that there are multiple paths to an end solution. Theoretical approaches provide a framework to explain clients change and give interventions based on theoretical roots. Postmodern theoretical approaches suggest that one size does not fit everyone.

This chapter will introduce financial counselors to four postmodern theoretical approaches that have been borrowed from mental health professions and that can be or have been used in a financial setting, including solution-focused brief therapy, motivational interviewing, appreciative inquiry, and positive psychology. The authors begin the discussion of these approaches by introducing you to the Transtheoretical Model of Change (TTM), then use TTM to connect the case scenario and Jackie's readiness to change to the approaches.

Transtheoretical Model of Change

The Transtheoretical Model of Change (TTM) posits that change is a multi-stage and fluid process. With an understanding of the stages of change, financial counselors can help individuals effectively modify their financial behavior. According to Prochaska, DiClemente, and Norcross (1992), the five stages of change within the TTM are: (1) pre-contemplation, (2) contemplation, (3) preparation, (4) action, and (5) maintenance. The key to helping clients progress through the stages of change is to understand and apply the ten cognitive, affective, and behavioral processes of change that clients are already using or will use to support behavior change. Key to the TTM's assumptions of how lasting change occurs is that the benefits of making a change must outweigh the downside of the change before any lasting change can occur.

Pre-contemplation marks the beginning stage. Individuals have no intention to change, often resist acknowledging a problem exists, or may be unaware of the problem entirely. During this phase family and friends may recognize a change is needed but are unsuccessful in their persuasion efforts. Change might be observed due to pressure from others; however, any progress is often lost once the pressure subsides. Overall, an individual in pre-contemplation will not acknowledge change is needed and is more than 6 months away from behavior change.

Key processes that move individuals out of pre-contemplation include raising awareness of the consequences of the behavior, helping the individual recognize positive or negative emotions associated with the behavior, and helping the person recognize the effect their behavior has on other people. These processes begin to increase the benefits of behavior change in the person's mind, and help them move into later stages.

Following pre-contemplation is the contemplation stage of change. Individuals in the contemplation stage are willing to acknowledge a problem exists, but lack any commitment or intention to take action towards addressing the problem. Individuals in this stage are often within 6 months of changing their behavior. However, without a commitment to move forward, there is a tendency to become stuck in the contemplation stage as individuals can struggle with evaluating the pros and cons of taking action.

The same cognitive and affective processes that motivate individuals out of pre-contemplation continue to be very important to someone seeking to move from the contemplation stage. Awareness of behaviors and effects on others increases, and the emotional responses to the behavior may also deepen. Additional processes that are beneficial are self-reevaluation, the ability for the person to redefine his or her self-image in a more desirable state, recognition that the desired change is supported by society, and opportunities to practice the desired change.

The preparation stage typically occurs when an individual is less than a month away from exhibiting a major and consistent change in their behavior. Incremental change is observed in this stage. For example, if an individual needs to save more, they might start spending less on certain expenditures or delaying purchases. Overall, intention to change is high in the preparation stage and early signs of behavior change can be observed.

The processes of change at this stage are shifting from cognitive and affective processes to behavior modification processes. Key processes exhibited in this transition include the individual making a commitment to change, seeking help from others to support behavior change, and identifying different ways of doing things.

The action stage is characterized by observable and significant progress towards behavior modification. Successfully altering behavior within the action stage can take anywhere from 1 day to 6 months. During this time, individuals spend a considerable amount of energy on key change processes including modifying their environment and experiences to achieve their goal; external recognition is received as others notice the progress made, or the individual rewards himself. It is important to note that the action stage does not signify behavior change as more work is necessary to complete and maintain this change. However, at this point many of the early cognitive and affective processes of change have diminished in importance and the individual is focused primarily on behavioral processes of change.

The hallmark of the maintenance stage is ongoing management of the changed behavior. In this stage behavior change is stabilized and consistent results are observed. Maintenance efforts can last anywhere from 6 months to a lifetime and often involve the continued practice of behavioral processes of change including supporting relationships, managing one's environment to reduce temptations, and recognizing the positive aspects of change. Individuals can relapse to an early stage at any point in the process and will need to spend time working through the earlier stages of change.

Case Study Application

The TTM provides a framework to understand where clients are in the process of change (Kerkmann, 1998). Through this understanding, solutions can be generated that align with the client's state of mind. For example, an action-oriented solution would be inappropriate and ineffective for a client in the pre-contemplation stage; that is, how can someone take action when they do not yet acknowledge or know a problem exists?

Jackie is just now becoming aware of the limitations of her financial situation due to her recent mortgage loan rejection. Prior to this event she felt as though she was functioning well financially, yet was not aware that her financial situation would prohibit her from purchasing the home. Jackie has moved into the contemplation stage of change with the realization that she cannot achieve one of her important financial goals. While she lacks knowledge about her financial situation and is unsure how to move into the preparation and action stages, she is in the process of transitioning into preparation because she reached out to a friend and financial counselor for help—an observable action that suggests movement towards preparation and action. A financial counselor can have a significant impact on clients in the contemplation stage and emerging preparation stage as people often get stuck when facing complex decisions, especially when a lack of knowledge is present.

This chapter will demonstrate how a financial counselor can help move Jackie from the contemplation stage to the preparation stage using four contemporary theories and frameworks for financial counseling: Motivational Interviewing, Solution-Focused Brief Therapy, Positive Psychology, and Appreciative Inquiry.

Motivational Interviewing

Motivational Interviewing (MI) is similar to Solution-Focused Brief Therapy (SFBT) in many ways, including a strengths-based, client-centered, collaborative approach that meets clients where they are in the change process (Stermensky & Brown, 2014). For example, MI uses scaling-like questions to identify readiness for change. MI also emphasizes the need for a strong alliance between counselor and client, helping clients determine their own motivations for change. Although there are several similarities between Solution-Focused Brief Therapy (SFBT; discussed later in the chapter) and MI, MI focuses on clients' ambivalence and pushes to increase intrinsic motivation (Stermensky & Brown, 2014). Ambivalence, in the MI approach, is the state of being uncertain or having mixed emotions about a something or someone, which keeps a client from moving forward. However, like SFBT, evidence exists for MI's effectiveness in a variety of multidisciplinary settings including medical and mental health (Lundahl, Kunz, Brownell, Tollefson, & Burke, 2010).

Miller and Rollnick (2013) defined motivational interviewing in three ways. The most simplistic definition is: "Motivational interviewing is a collaborative conversation style for strengthening a person's own motivation and commitment to change" (p. 12). The most useful practitioner definition exerts: "motivational interviewing is a person-centered counseling style for addressing the common problem of ambivalence about change" (p. 29). In other words, motivational interviewing is the process by which clients are motivated to change.

Principles and Assumptions

Levensky, Forcehimes, O'Donohue, and Beitz (2007) summarized the four principles of motivational interviewing as: (a) express empathy, (b) develop a discrepancy, (c) roll with resistance, and (d) support self-efficacy. Expressing empathy is different than expressing sympathy (e.g., feeling sorry for the client). Empathy is expressed through communicating that the counselor understands what the client is experiencing—the counselor can put themselves in the client's shoes, per se. To develop discrepancies, a counselor helps clients identify the differences between behaviors and intended outcomes. It is important for clients to recognize these inconsistencies themselves rather than the counselor outright telling them (Levensky et al., 2007). When clients appear to be resistant, the counselor "rolls" with it rather than engaging in the resistance. Resistance may mean that the counselor has moved on too quickly in the process and in response the client may argue, disengage, or may change the subject. The counselor can support self-efficacy by creating hope that change can occur, encouraging the client to identify their own solutions, and helping the client recognize that they are responsible for the carrying out of the changes (U.S. SAMHSA, 1999).

The four processes of motivational interviewing are described as both "sequential and recursive" (Miller & Rollnick, 2013, p. 26). These processes include: engaging, focusing, evoking, and planning. As noted previously, a strong working alliance must exist between counselor and client when using this approach. Engagement is the process of building and maintaining the alliance. Focusing is concentrating on what the client came in to talk about. The counselor may also have an agenda of what they want to address with the client and that may be included. The idea behind focusing is to clarify the direction of counseling. Evoking refers to helping the client figure out why and how they will change. In other words, therapists help clients create an argument for themselves about changing or creating motivation to change. Planning is committing to change and developing a specific plan to change. In this process, clients move from talking about whether they should change, and why, to when and how to change.

Key Interventions

Miller and Rollnick (2013) described MI as more than a set of techniques, rather it is a way of being with clients. The way of being with clients not only reflects the principles and assumptions identified above, but also four main skills are needed to implement MI appropriately and to move the clients through the four processes.

Skills to achieve MI goals include asking open-ended questions, affirming, reflective listening, and summarizing. Asking open-ended questions versus closed-ended (i.e., yes/no) questions is essential to exploring clients' goals and values. Asking open-ended questions helps clients to articulate their experiences and is an opportunity for the counselor to learn about the client's hopes and desires. Affirming refers to acknowledging and validating the client in their successes, such as the counselor thanking the client for meeting with him or her. Reflective listening is listening to understand what the client is saying. When utilizing reflective listening, the counselor summarizes what he/she heard the client say to confirm that the counselor understood what the client said. The client can then confirm or reject the counselor's interpretation of what was said. Reflective listening is essential in motivational interviewing, helping to build rapport between counselor and client and move the client towards readiness to change. Reflective listening can also be used to reduce a client's resistance by reflecting the meaning of what the client said rather than countering what the client said (see Levensky et al., 2007 for an example). Summarizing is a long reflection of what was said during the session (Miller & Rollnick, 2013). Summarizing demonstrates that the counselor has been listening during the session and creates a "what else?" opportunity for clients where they can fill in the missing gaps that the counselor missed. In the planning process, summaries draw together the person's "motivations, intentions, and specific plans for change" (p. 34).

Case Study Application

A financial counselor using a MI approach with Jackie will want to help Jackie explore her goals and values to help motivate her to move from contemplation to preparation and then to action. The financial counselor may ask open-ended questions that will not only elicit information about Jackie's goals and values, but also will help Jackie recognize her motivation to change and build rapport between the financial counselor and Jackie. The financial counselor may ask questions such as, "Tell me what matters most in your life" and "what do you hope your life looks like a few years from now?" Similar to the SFBT scenario, Jackie may describe that her children and family are what matters most and providing for her children is important. She may explain that in a few years she hopes to be a homeowner and can manage her money successfully. The financial counselor can use reflective listening to check to make sure Jackie was understood correctly. A reflective statement could be, "it sounds like your family and children are what matters most to you and your primary reason to own a home and be financially stable." The financial counselor may go on to affirm Jackie by stating, "it's great that you came in today to work on meeting your goals."

These skills in this phase essentially "prime the pump" by emphasizing why Jackie is seeking help. To help continue to move Jackie from contemplation, a financial counselor will continue to ask open-ended questions, like "what would be helpful to you so that you can achieve the goal of owning your own home?" Jackie can then explain that her credit score is too low for a mortgage and that she needs to understand why. The financial counselor can then reflect to Jackie and either teach her to read the report or help her access her credit report, identifying outstanding debt and credit behaviors that are lowering her score.

After reviewing the credit report, the financial counselor can ask another open-ended question such as, "What do you think would make the biggest difference in paying down debt?" The financial counselor knows that Jackie needs to get a handle on her income and expenses but the financial counselor needs Jackie to come up with the idea. Jackie may then say, "After reviewing my credit report, I obviously have trouble paying bills on time and I am only paying the minimum amount on my credit cards. I didn't know that this would impact my credit score so much. I need to make a calendar and write bill due dates on it and create a budget so that I can figure out how much extra I can afford to pay on them. I have not been good with creating and keeping a budget." This is an opportunity for the financial counselor to help Jackie recognize her ambivalence and respond, "Life is really busy, but you are here and that shows that your financial situation and providing for your children are important to you."

The financial counselor can ask Jackie a scaling question to help move her from the preparation to action phase, such as "On a scale from 1 to 10, how prepared are you to start increasing your credit score?" and "On a scale from 1 to 10, what is your commitment to improve your readiness score?" These scaling questions can also be used in follow-up sessions to continue to assess her readiness for change. The financial counselor can conclude the session with a long reflective statement. The reflective statement not only helps the client know that the financial counselor heard the client correctly, but also can be used to help the client process emotions and thoughts by hearing them through someone else's words.

Solution-Focused Brief Therapy

Solution-Focused Brief Therapy (SFBT) is a brief form of psychotherapy where the therapist and the client co-construct new meaning via solution talk by focusing on clients' strengths and desired outcomes from the past and for the future (Bavelas et al., 2013). The approach was developed by Steve de Shazer and Insoo Kim Berg and colleagues in the early 1980s after observing what seemed to work well with their clients in the Milwaukee-based Brief Family Therapy Center (BFTC). While the approach was pragmatically developed, the developers of SFBT have been clear that SFBT is not a theory itself, rather it is model of intervention that is theoretically rooted. The approach is grounded in the work of Milton H. Erickson and the Mental

Research Institute (MRI) in Palo Alto, as well as in Wittgensteinian philosophy, Buddhist thought (de Shazer & Dolan, 2007), family systems theory and social constructionism (Nichols, 2008).

SFBT focuses on the present where problems are maintained and the future where desired outcomes occur, rather than looking at the past where problems developed. de Shazer recognized that understanding what caused the problem was necessary, rather focusing on what a client can do about the problem is more helpful (de Shazer & Dolan, 2007). This was a different approach than the typical therapeutic approaches that focused on how and why the problem occurred. A number of studies exist, suggesting promising outcomes for SFBT intervention (Bavelas et al., 2013; Franklin, Zhang, Froerer, & Johnson, 2017; Kim, Smock, Trepper, McCollum, & Franklin, 2010). The application of the SFBT model has also displayed positive outcomes in a financial setting, sometimes referred to as financial therapy or solution-focused financial therapy (Archuleta et al., 2015; Archuleta, Mielitz, Jayne, & Le, 2017; Palmer, Pichot, & Kunovskaya, 2016). Archuleta, Grable, and Burr (2015) provide a more in-depth description about the application of SFBT in a financial setting. They described incorporating financial homework and financial education into the SFBT process.

Principles and Assumptions

SFBT assumes clients are ready to change and can change, but sometimes need help recognizing how to do so. de Shazer (1994) believed that how a client talks about a problem is different than the way they talk about solutions. The conversational language and the social interactions between therapist and client can help clients change by recognizing what is important to the client (Bavelas et al., 2013). If therapists and clients can change the way they talk about a problem, they can change their perception of the problem and what to do about it; this is the key assumption about how change occurs—a shift in language through co-construction. Clients then shift the way they think about problems and solutions which allows for space for change outside of the room and in interactions in the world.

Solution-focused brief therapists employ a curious and not-knowing stance. The therapist makes no judgement, allowing for client to determine what is a problem and what is not (O'Hanlon & Weiner-Davis, 1989). This type of assessment helps clients come up with their own (or co-constructed) solutions, which they are more likely act upon. SFBT also assumes that problems do not occur all of the time, there are exceptions and clients have to look for those exceptions to see what is happening when the problem is not occurring or when it is being managed well. Since clients are considered to be experts on their own lives, therapists help clients tap into the strengths they possess which they are more likely to act upon (O'Hanlon & Weiner-Davis, 1989).

de Shazer and Dolan (2007, pp. 1-3) described eight major tenets of SFBT: (a) "if it's not broke, don't fix it"; (b) "if it works, do more of it"; (c) "if it's not working, do something different"; (d) "small steps can lead to big changes"; (e) "the solution is not necessarily directly related to the problem"; (f) "the language for the solution development is different from that needed to describe a problem"; (g) "no problems happen all of the time, there are always exceptions that can be utilized"; and (h) "the future is both created and negotiable." Financial counselors who adopt an SFBT model need to buy into these tenets in order to implement the interventions into practice successfully.

Key Interventions

SFBT uses several key interventions to facilitate client change. It differs from some of the other approaches in this chapter such as appreciative inquiry and MI because its key interventions are very intentional. Some of the hallmark interventions of the approach are setting goals, the miracle question, scaling questions, formula first session task, highlighting exceptions, coping questions, and compliments (de Shazer & Dolan, 2007; Nichols, 2008). Although this chapter is not long enough to overview all the interventions associated with SFBT, three key interventions are reviewed.

One key intervention to SFBT is the miracle question. The miracle question helps clients to think about what their life would look like if a miracle occurred, specifically paying attention to what the client would be doing differently. The miracle question asks clients to visualize how their life would be different if the problem did not exist. The client is then asked to identify specific ways of knowing that change occurred. Ultimately, the miracle question sets the stage for clients to identify their desired goals (Thomas & Nelson, 2007; Stith et al., 2012). Other interventions, such as small steps, are used to help identify ways in which the client can reach those desired outcomes. The process of the miracle question helps the counselor and client co-construct the client's visualization of the future, which can be translated into goals. The financial counselor can use the miracle question process to clearly summarize and articulate goals.

Then, the financial counselor can move to using scaling questions. Scaling questions are used to help clients find where they see themselves on any given topic. One way to use scaling questions is to ask clients where they are in reaching their goals. de Shazer and Dolan (2007) suggested using a miracle scaling question by asking clients to scale from 0 (where they were when they decided to seek help) to 10 (being the day after the miracle occurs). Scaling questions can be used to assess a variety of issues including motivation to complete a goal, confidence in ability to achieve a goal, and commitment to accomplishing a goal (de Shazer & Dolan, 2007).

To implement SFBT into the financial counseling process effectively, the alliance between the counselor and the client must be strong. One way in which counselors build this alliance is by taking genuine curiosity in the client and listening to understand. Focusing on what the client wants in life helps a client feel understood and respected and is important to building a strong alliance (Turnell & Lipchik, 1999). de Shazer and Dolan (2007) noted that SFBT therapists spend most of their time "listening attentively for signs of previous solutions, exceptions, and goals."

Case Study Application

As has already been established, Jackie is in the *contemplation* stage and a financial counselor will be looking to help move her to the *preparation* and *action* stages. A financial counselor using a SFBT approach can help with this process by asking the miracle question once goals are established (note Jackie's goals). Bavelas et al. (2013) pointed out that the miracle question can have multiple versions, but that it goes something like this:

> "I am going to ask you a rather strange question [pause]. The strange question is this: [pause] After we talk, you will go back to your work (home, school) and you will do whatever you need to do the rest of today, such as taking care of the children, cooking dinner, watching TV, giving the children a bath, and so on. It will become time to go to bed. Everybody in your household is quiet, and you are sleeping in peace. In the middle of the night, a miracle happens and the problem that prompted you to talk to me today is solved! But because this happens while you are sleeping, you have no way of knowing that there was an overnight miracle that solved the problem. [pause] So, when you wake up tomorrow morning, what might be the small change, or the first thing that you notice is different, that will make you say to yourself, 'Wow, something must have happened—the problem is gone!'" (Berg & Dolan, 2001, p. 7).

The financial counselor can then follow up with questions to help clients become more specific about the miracle that occurred and move from content to process types of answers (Archuleta, Grable, & Burr, 2015). Follow-up questions could be (Archuleta, Grable, & Burr, 2015; Bavelas et al., 2013; Nichols, 2008):

> What would tell you that a change has occurred?
> What is the first thing you might notice?
> How would your family notice that a change had happened?
> What would tell significant people in your life that a change had occurred?
> How would they know that the problem was gone?

Jackie may describe her miracle is that she would live in a safe neighborhood where she feels safe and close to friends and her children's friends. She may further explain that she would feel relieved and free from worry about her debt and her credit. She may know the problem is gone when she feels confident she can pay the mortgage and all her bills. The financial counselor can then use scaling questions to ask Jackie, "On a scale from 0 to 10 with 0 being where you were experiencing the highest level of stress from your circumstance and 10 being the day after the miracle, where do you see your financial stress today?" (de Shazer & Dolan, 2007, p. 61).

Jackie may describe being at a 3. As a mechanism to identify current strengths, the financial counselor may then respond with, "how did you manage to get to a 3?" Jackie may describe being a three because she made the phone call to seek help so she is taking steps in the right direction. In addition, she has sought out a real estate agent and mortgage banker and knows there are things that need to change. She just doesn't know what to do next. Asking how she got there gives Jackie the opportunity to reflect upon the things she has already done and is currently doing that made her a 3 rather than a 0 or 1. Additionally, asking about the differences between a 3, 2, 1, and 0 help to provide nuanced details and validation of what she has already done well.

Moving Jackie from preparation to action stages of TTM, the financial counselor can ask Jackie, "what is the smallest thing you can do to move up on the scale?" Jackie may respond by stating that she needs to understand why her credit is too low to qualify for a loan. The financial counselor can teach Jackie how to check her credit report and then review it with her. Throughout the process, the financial counselor has been attentively listening to Jackie and recognizes that Jackie's goals are to build stability for her children and herself, to be worry free, and build her confidence around money management. These are additional emotional areas that the financial counselor cannot ignore and should address with Jackie. The financial counselor will ask what each of these areas look like. What does stability look like? What does worry free look like? What will you be doing when you are worry free? What does confidence with money management look like? How will you know you are confident managing your money? Miracle scaling questions could be asked around these specific topics as well.

Positive Psychology

Positive psychology is a field of scientific study within psychology that focuses on the development of human strengths and virtues (Peterson & Park, 2003). Positive psychology emerged as a field in 1998 under the leadership of Martin Seligman to promote the expansion of psychology research and practice beyond the treatment of mental illness. Today, positive psychology has gained prominence within a variety of professions where one's psychological functioning affects outcomes (e.g., education, health).

When it comes to money, psychology has been shown to significantly affect financial decision-making and financial outcomes. Given the prevalence of behavioral finance and psychology within financial counseling and planning, Asebedo and Seay (2015) introduced positive psychology to the peer-reviewed financial literature and demonstrated how positive psychological theory, tools, and exercises can be applied to financial goals and behavior. Positive psychology's signature "well-being theory" (Seligman, 2012) provides a useful framework that informs how financial counselors can help clients achieve a flourishing life by aligning their financial goals and resources with the psychological elements that contribute to well-being.

Principles and Assumptions

Well-being theory posits that five psychological elements contribute to a flourishing life (Seligman, 2012): positive emotions, engagement, relationships, meaning, and accomplishment (PERMA). Positive emotions are momentary in nature and can be forward-looking (e.g., optimism), present focused (e.g., happiness), and reflective (e.g., life satisfaction). Well-being theory states that the frequent experience of positive emotions contributes to a flourishing life. While positive emotions are important, it is only one of five components of well-being. The second component is engagement. The concept of engagement originates from Csikszentmihalyi's (1997) "flow" concept, which represents a psychological state of mind where an individual is fully immersed and absorbed in a particular task or activity. Third, positive, healthy, and supportive relationships are a critical component to attaining well-being across the life course according to well-being theory and multiple studies (e.g., see Holt-Lunstad, Smith, & Layton, 2010). Meaning is the fourth component of well-being and encompasses a sense of belonging to something greater and having purpose and meaning in one's life. Accomplishment is the fifth and final component of well-being and refers to the feeling of success, mastery, and achievement because of one's efforts. Well-being theory suggests that the combination of these PERMA elements contributes to a full and flourishing life.

Key Interventions

While many positive psychological interventions exist that are useful within the financial context (see Asebedo & Seay, 2015), this chapter focuses on applying well-being theory as an intervention for financial behavior. The first step to incorporating well-being theory into practice is measuring and assessing clients' existing well-being levels. Fortunately, positive psychology research has developed a robust set of scales that can be used to assess well-being through the PERMA elements. The University of Pennsylvania has developed a resource devoted to positive psychological measurement; their Authentic Happiness website (see www.authentichappiness.sas.upenn.edu/testcenter) provides user-friendly scales that financial counselors can administer to clients to evaluate their well-being levels. These scales serve as the starting point for conversations with clients about their well-being. It is important to note that well-being theory focuses on the psychological outcome of PERMA as opposed to specific tasks or activities that lead to PERMA, as the latter can vary greatly from person to person. Consequently, it is important for financial counselors to structure their inquiry appropriately. For example, instead of asking a client "What is your favorite hobby?" consider reframing the question to "Tell me about the last time you experienced a sense of deep engagement where you lost track of time? What were you doing? How long ago has it been since you've experienced this?" By focusing on the psychological outcome of PERMA, the financial counselor will obtain a deeper and more informative response. Understanding the client's existing well-being status gives insight to the financial counselor about how to most effectively apply a financial or counseling intervention.

The CFPB Financial Well-Being Scale (see Chap. 13) is a related and complementary scale to PERMA; it is focused specifically on financial well-being, defined as "a state wherein a person can fully meet current and ongoing financial obligations, can feel secure in their financial future, and is able to make choices that allow them to enjoy life" (Consumer Financial Protection Bureau, 2017). Those who score higher on the CFPB Financial Well-Being Scale may have more flexibility to allocate their financial resources to the activities, products, and experiences that support the PERMA elements. However, those who have less financial flexibility (i.e., a lower score on the CFPB Financial Well-Being Scale) can still greatly benefit from a PERMA intervention, as research suggests that those with greater well-being (i.e., most often using happiness and life satisfaction measures) interact with their money in a financially prudent and positive manner (e.g., see Guven, 2012; Lyubomirsky, King, & Diener, 2005). More specifically, Guven (2012) found evidence supporting a causal link between increased happiness and saving. While more research needs to be conducted in this area, existing research suggests that a PERMA intervention might serve as a catalyst that helps an individual make financially wise decisions and work towards greater financial well-being. When financial resources are significantly limited, however, the financial counselor will have to be more creative with the PERMA intervention. For example, Asebedo and Seay (2015) point out that the PERMA elements can also be achieved by activities that require time with little to no financial input: positive relationships can be supported by spending more time with family and friends, or meaning could be achieved through volunteering. Time and money are our two largest fixed resources; all clients across the financial well-being spectrum can benefit by exploring how they are spending both their time and money in ways that support the PERMA elements.

An example of a financial counseling intervention using well-being theory (PERMA) entails helping the client discover how they are currently spending their financial resources to align with the PERMA elements. This intervention helps clients realize how they are spending money in ways that facilitate well-being maximization such that adjustments can be made. This exercise is facilitated by helping the client organize their discretionary expenses into PERMA categories, assuming fixed expenses meet basic needs. With this framework in place, the financial counselor can work with the client to determine how the client's financial resources are being allocated to support well-being. Moreover, the financial counselor can work with clients to determine how they are spending their time to facilitate well-being, as the PERMA elements do not need to require financial input. Table 7.1 provides a basic framework a financial counselor can use to help their client explore how they are using their time and money to support well-being—not only today, but also how they envision supporting these elements in the future.

Case Study Application

Well-being theory provides a useful framework within which to view Jackie's situation. Before Jackie can move into the preparation—and ultimately action—stage, she needs to gain a better understanding of her income and expenses. Through the lens of well-being theory, Jackie can begin to view her expenses (including savings needed for the home purchase and future home-related expenses such as maintenance) by how those expenses contribute to her well-being. Moreover, well-being theory significantly

Table 7.1 Well-being time and money envisioning exercise

	Today (time and money)	Future (time and money)
Positive emotion		
Engagement		
Relationships		
Meaning		
Accomplishment		

shifts the conversation away from cutting expenses (which can be demotivating or paralyzing) to spending money where it matters (which is more motivational). The cash flow exercise facilitates Jackie's own personal discovery of expenses that may need to decrease such that she can more effectively allocate her money to other areas of her life that matter the most. Additionally, Jackie may find that she needs to spend more money or time pursuing one of the PERMA elements, such as relationships or accomplishment. This may mean spending more time with family and friends or pursuing a new hobby or sport. Overall, the well-being theory intervention can help Jackie realize how to experience a flourishing life, whether or not she becomes a homeowner. She may even find that she can strengthen her financial position such that she is able to accomplish her home purchase goal in the near future. It is also possible that Jackie discovers the home purchase is not necessary, or that it can wait for a few years. The well-being approach through positive psychology is a future-oriented intervention that helps clients focus on what really matters in life, while also delivering the financial education necessary to move from the contemplation stage to the preparation stage.

Appreciative Inquiry

Appreciative inquiry originated at Case Western Reserve University through the work of David Cooperrider and Suresh Srivastva as an organizational change management approach in the mid-1980s. The conceptualization and theory of appreciative inquiry continued to be developed by Cooperrider and colleagues at Case Western Reserve University and through the associated Global Excellence in Management Initiative. Originally developed as an organizational change theory, appreciative inquiry has been adapted for use in a variety of organizational, interorganizational, community, small group, and individual coaching settings (Whitney & Trosten-Bloom, 2010).

Whitney and Trosten-Bloom (2010) describe Appreciative Inquiry (AI) as "The study of what gives life to human systems when they function at their best....This approach to personal change and organization change is based on the assumption that questions and dialogue about strengths, successes, values, hopes, and dreams are themselves transformational" (p. 1). AI is the deliberate process of recognizing and affirming past and present strengths and success coupled with an openness to discovering future possibilities.

Several practitioners and researchers have proposed how AI can be an effective financial planning and counseling intervention model (Delgadillo, Palmer, & Goetz, 2016; Jacobson, 2009; Pullen, 2001). Jacobson advocates that AI is an ideal model to engage clients during the discovery phase of the relationship because it helps clients recognize and focus on their strengths, motivations, and aspirations. Similar to other counseling interventions discussed, questions (and how they are asked) is a core characteristic of AI. Positively framed questions result in generative discussions, or continued discussion and exploration of strengths and aspirations. Generative discussions also cultivate the client's intrinsic motivation for change.

Principles and Assumptions

AI is built upon a foundation of eight principles which are operationalized using the Five-D cycle. The eight foundational principles are the: constructionist; simultaneity; poetic; anticipatory; positive; wholeness; enactment; and free-choice (Whitney & Trosten-Bloom, 2010). The constructionist principle is that language is a tool that creates our perception and vision of what is possible and thereby influences our actions and behaviors.

Language influences perception of reality and therefore can substantially alter how people behave in reality. The simultaneity principle follows that, as people are asked questions such as, "What is working well?" the process of answering the question immediately begins to shift perceptions of the situation to parallel the way the question was asked. In other words, a person will respond with more positivity when asked, "What is working well?" as opposed to more negatively and problem-focused when asked, "What is the problem?" Closely related is the anticipatory and enactment principles which assert that when current strengths are identified and the image of the goal is clearly imagined and explained, then the identified strengths and clarity of the future vision begin to influence current behavior. In other words, having someone articulate their vision of their preferred future-self influences their current behavior. The poetic and wholeness principles are similar in that every situation has multiple interpretations and perceptions and each perspective is valid.

The final principles are the positive and free-choice principles. Underlying these principles is the critical aspect of language and how it is used. The positive principle asserts that as the counselor asks positive questions, chooses to focus on positive elements, and construes events positively, then the client has greater opportunity for positive change. The client's free-choice regarding what they can and will choose to pursue is what will ultimately determine the outcomes. For financial counselors, AI reinforces that the client, not the counselor, holds the key to success. AI is simply an approach and process that the financial counselor can use to help the client discover and design their desired future. When a financial counselor strays from, or runs against these principles, the benefits of AI for the client are diminished.

Key Interventions

These principles are operationalized using the Five-D cycle of define, discover, dream, design, and destiny. Clearly defining what the client wants to work on is the first step. Lack of clarity can lead to frustration for all involved. Asking people to tell a story about when the client's financial management was working best, asking about what is most important to that person, or asking about a time the client felt energized about their finances are generative questions that help discover clients' strengths and abilities that they can use to reach their dream.

Dreaming is the process of envisioning what could be. This is where goal-setting takes place and for AI; this step is only possible if the define and discover steps have been followed. Designing is developing a strengths-based roadmap to achieve the imagined goal. Clients can compare what they are currently doing with what the design process outlines and make small changes which center their efforts on their strengths. Destiny is the iterative process of the Five-D cycle applied on an ongoing basis by the client (Tschannen-Moran, 2010).

The counselor should always be mindful of his or her own language. It is essential that the language from the counselor be positive, forward-looking, and strengths-based. Clients will often talk of roadblocks, failures, and problems. The counselor should always validate the client's concerns and challenges, but the counselor should also have the capacity to construct his or her own language in a way that brings the client back to engaging in the Five-D cycle. The foundational principles of AI help guide the financial counselor's language. For example, after a client shares some current financial challenges the financial counselor can validate those concerns and then ask a question such as, "I am impressed that you are dealing with these challenges as well as you are and that you are taking the initiative to address them in a positive way. Will you tell me about a time when your finances were helping you achieve success in your life, when your money supported your goal achievement? How were you generating income at that time and how were you using your money so that your goals were being accomplished?" By choosing to focus on the client's strengths, such as his or her ability to manage and seek help with the current situation, as well as positive exceptions to the current situation, the financial counselor has already begun to create a world wherein the client is proactive, has strengths, and takes initiative to achieve their goals. By framing the response in this way, the client is simultaneously beginning to think and respond within this new framework.

Case Study Application

AI could be an effective approach to help Jackie transition more fully into *preparation* and from there into *action*. Clearly defining Jackie's purpose in meeting with the financial counselor provides the focus and scope of the initial effort and is the first step in the Five-D cycle. A simple question that could further refine the define stage could be, "What would need to be different about your current situation to allow you to feel like you can move forward towards your goal of providing a safe place for your children?" Or, "What is it that we could work on together that will allow you to feel that our efforts were successful?" The financial counselor can determine that Jackie's purpose in visiting is to understand how to improve her credit score so that she can qualify for a loan. Additional issues will inevitably follow, but the initial motivation for working with a financial counselor should be identified and addressed and serve as the focal point of the engagement.

The discovery phase allows the financial counselor to explore some of Jackie's strengths. Questions such as, "Jackie, as a single working mother of two children you have had to overcome many challenges. Please tell me about how you successfully overcame difficult challenges in the past." Or another question that seeks to help Jackie articulate her strengths could be, "Tell me about a time when you felt like your family's financial situation was better than normal. What were you and your family doing then that made it so good?" These questions are designed to remind Jackie of her strengths and help her realize that she is not a financial failure. Many of the feelings that are motivating Jackie to seek help are negative (e.g., feeling stupid, financial failure, inability to provide for children), and the financial counselor should seek to counter these negative feelings with real examples of success so that Jackie does not get stuck feeling hopeless. As the financial counselor listens, Jackie will identify certain strengths and other skills that solutions can be built around. This also provides a positive perspective (overcoming past challenges, realizing that she has been successful at managing money) from which to view the current situation.

In the dream stage, Jackie should be encouraged to share her desire and dream to provide a safe and stable housing situation for her children. It is important that this dream be Jackie's and that she is emotionally connected to the dream. Prompting her to provide greater detail regarding "what it will be like to…" or "how she will feel when…" is important because it provides specific goals, both large and small, that can be worked towards in the design stage. In the design stage, actionable steps are identified to help reach the goals. A simple and readily achievable goal would be for Jackie to obtain a copy of her credit report so that she can be fully informed of why her credit score is low. Other actions will be identified in the design stage that will help Jackie move fully into preparation and eventually into appropriate action. It is likely that the design stage of the process will not be fully realized until Jackie has met with the financial counselor a few times.

Conclusion

This chapter aimed to provide a brief overview of four innovative approaches for financial counseling, while also providing insight as to how these approaches can be used in practice to help individuals improve their financial behavior and outcomes—such that they can ultimately improve their lives. Positive psychology, MI, and SFBT were developed through practice and research with individuals, while AI—in contrast—was first developed as an organizational change theory. As with any new skill, time and practice are required to learn and successfully implement a new approach to working with clients. These approaches cannot be implemented by simply reading this chapter, as this chapter only briefly introduces these postmodern models of intervention. To effectively implement any of these approaches, additional study should be devoted to understanding and practicing the approach before using it with clients. Each of these approaches may require a shift in mindset for the financial counselor to incorporate the approach into their client interactions. Some of the approaches presented above may require the financial counselor to adopt an entirely new way of talking about challenges the client is facing. Positively framed questions that lead to a discussion of client strengths and aspirations are not natural for some individuals and will take practice. Thus, further reading, training, and practice are essential in developing the skills required of each approach.

References

Archuleta, K. L., Burr, E. A., Bell Carlson, M., Ingram, J., Irwin Kruger, L., Grable, J., & Ford, M. (2015). Solution focused financial therapy: A brief report of a pilot study. *Journal of Financial Therapy, 6*(1), 2.

Archuleta, K. L., Grable, J. E., & Burr, E. (2015). Solution-focused financial therapy. In B. T. Klontz, S. L. Britt, & K. L. Archuleta (Eds.). *Financial therapy: Theory, research & practice* (pp. 121–141). New York: Springer.

Archuleta, K. L., Mielitz, K. S., Jayne, D., & Le, V. (2017). *Financial goal setting, financial anxiety, and solution-focused financial therapy (SFFT): A quasi-experimental outcome study.* Research Paper presented at CFP Board Academic Research Colloquium.

Asebedo, S., & Seay, M. (2015). From functioning to flourishing: Applying positive psychology to financial planning. *Journal of Financial Planning, 28*(11), 50–58.

Bavelas, J., De Jong, P., Franklin, C., Froerer, A., Gingerick, W., & Kim, J. (2013). *Solution focused therapy treatment manual for working with individuals* (2nd version). Solution Focused Brief Therapy Association. Retrieved from http://www.sfbta.org/PDFs/researchDownloads/file-Downloader.asp?fname=SFBT_Revised_Treatment_Manual_2013.pdf

Berg, I. K., & Dolan, Y. (2001). *Tales of solutions: A collection of hope-inspiring stories.* New York, NY: WW Norton & Co.

Consumer Financial Protection Bureau. (2017). *Quick guide to the CFPB financial well-being scale.* Retrieved July 21, 2017 from https://www.consumerfinance.gov/data-research/research-reports/financial-well-being-scale/

Csikszentmihalyi, M. (1997). *Finding flow: The psychology of engagement with everyday life.* New York, NY: Basic Books.

de Shazer, S. (1994). *Words were originally magic.* New York: Norton.

de Shazer, S., & Dolan, Y. (2007). *More than miracles: The state of the art of solution-focused brief therapy.* New York, NY: Routledge.

Delgadillo, L. M., Palmer, L., & Goetz, J. (2016). A case study demonstrating the use of appreciative inquiry in a financial coaching program. *Family and Consumer Sciences Research Journal, 45*(2), 166–178.

Franklin, C., Zhang, A., Froerer, A., & Johnson, S. (2017). Solution focused brief therapy: A systematic review and meta-summary of process research. *Journal of Marital and Family Therapy, 43*(1), 16–30.

Guven, C. (2012). Reversing the question: Does happiness affect consumption and savings behavior? *Journal of Economic Psychology, 33*(4), 701–717.

Holt-Lunstad, J., Smith, T. B., & Layton, J. B. (2010). Social relationships and mortality risk: A meta-analytic review. *PLoS Medicine, 7*(7), e1000316.

Jacobson, E. A. (2009, November). Appreciative financial planning: Harnessing the power of appreciative inquiry for your advisory practice. *Investment Management Consultants Association*, 37–45.

Kerkmann, B. C. (1998). Motivation and stages of change in financial counseling: An application of a transtheoretical model from counseling psychology. *Journal of Financial Counseling and Planning, 9*(1), 13.

Kim, J., Smock, S., Trepper, T., McCollum, E., & Franklin, C. (2010). Is solution-focused brief therapy evidence-based? *Families in Society: The Journal of Contemporary Social Services, 91*(3), 300–306.

Levensky, E. R., Forcehimes, A., O'Donohue, W. T., & Beitz, K. (2007). Motivational interviewing: An evidence-based approach to counseling helps patients follow treatment recommendations. *AJN The American Journal of Nursing, 107*(10), 50–58.

Lundahl, B. W., Kunz, C., Brownell, C., Tollefson, D., & Burke, B. L. (2010). A meta-analysis of motivational interviewing: Twenty-five years of empirical studies. *Research on Social Work Practice, 20*(2), 137–160.

Lyubomirsky, S., King, L., & Diener, E. (2005). The benefits of frequent positive affect: Does happiness lead to success? *Psychological Bulletin, 131*(6), 803–855.

Miller, W. R., & Rollnick, S. (2013). *Motivational interviewing: Helping people change*. New York, NY: The Guilford Press.

Nichols, M. P. (2008). *Family therapy: Concepts and methods* (8th ed.). Pearson Education: Boston.

O'Hanlon, W. H., & Weiner-Davis, M. (1989). *In search of solutions: A new direction in psychotherapy*. New York: W.W. Norton & Company.

Palmer, L., Pichot, T., & Kunovskaya, I. (2016). Promoting savings at tax time through a video-based solution-focused brief coaching intervention. *Journal of Financial Therapy, 7*(1), 2.

Peterson, C., & Park, N. (2003). Positive psychology as the evenhanded positive psychologist views it. *Psychological Inquiry 14*(2), 143–147.

Prochaska, J. O., DiClemente, C. C., & Norcross, J. C. (1992). In search of how people change: Applications to addictive behaviors. *American Psychologist, 47*(9), 1102–1114.

Pullen, C. (2001). Financial planning and appreciative inquiry. *Journal of Financial Planning, 14*(10), 52–54.

Seligman, M. E. (2012.) *Flourish: A visionary new understanding of happiness and well-being*. New York, NY: Simon and Schuster.

Stermensky, G., & Brown, K. S. (2014). The perfect marriage: Solution-focused therapy and motivational interviewing in medical family therapy. *Journal of Family Medicine and Primary Care, 3*(4), 383–387. https://doi.org/10.4103/2249-4863.148117

Stith, S., Miller, M. S., Boyle, J., Swinton, J., Ratcliffe, G., & McCollum, E. (2012). Making a difference in making miracles: Common roadblocks to miracle question effectiveness. *Journal of Marital and Family Therapy, 38*(2), 380–393.

Thomas, F. N., & Nelson, T. S. (2007). Assumptions and practices within the solution-focused brief therapy tradition. In T. S. Nelson & F. N. Thomas (Eds.), *Handbook of solution-focused brief therapy: Clinical applications*. New York: Haworth Press.

Tschannen-Moran, B. (2010). Appreciative inquiry in coaching. In M. Moore & B. Tschannen-Moran (Eds.), *Coaching psychology manual* (pp. 52–62). Philadelphia, PA: Lippincott Williams & Wilkins.

Turnell, A., & Lipchik, E. (1999). The role of empathy in brief therapy: The overlooked but vital context. *Australian and New Zealand Journal of Family Therapy, 20*(4), 177–182.

U.S. Substance Abuse and Mental Health Services Administration, Center for Substance Abuse Treatment. (1999). Chapter 3—Motivational interviewing as a counseling style. In *Enhancing motivation for change in substance abuse treatment*. (Treatment improvement protocol (TIP) series, no. 35.). Retrieved from https://www.ncbi.nlm.nih.gov/books/NBK64964/

Whitney, D., & Trosten-Bloom, A. (2010). *The power of appreciative inquiry* (2nd ed.). San Francisco, CA: Berrett-Koehler Publishers, Inc.

Chapter 8
Key Communication and Physical Environment Concepts for Financial Counselors

Ryan H. Law, Camila A. Haselwood, and Joseph W. Goetz

Trust is at the heart of financial counseling relationships. Successful financial counseling requires honest contributions from both the client and the counselor. Clients need to trust that their privacy will not be violated, that they will not be judged by their counselor, and that the financial counselor has the expertise and skills to help them. Positive outcomes and implementation of recommendations increase in probability when a strong client–counselor relationship is present (Lambert & Barley, 2001). The way that a financial counselor communicates supports the development of a strong working alliance. In order to build that strong working alliance and trust with clients, financial counselors need to learn to communicate effectively. The importance of having good listening and communication skills in working with clients has been a topic of a small number of research studies and articles in the financial planning and counseling literature (Grable & Archuleta, 2015; Grist, n.d.; Kirchenbauer, 2014; Sharpe, Anderson, White, Galvan, & Siesta, 2007). This chapter will focus on key techniques that will help financial counselors develop their communication skills, including empathy, non-judgmental awareness, body language, asking effective questions, active listening, affirmation, and strategically arranging one's office space.

Developing these skills takes time and practice. However, financial counselors should strive to continuously enhance their communication skills as improvement in any of these interpersonal areas will be time well spent. The sections that follow provide ways of building one's skill set and should be looked at individually and as a group.

R. H. Law (✉)
Money Management Resource Center, Personal Financial Planning program, Utah Valley
University, Orem, UT, USA
e-mail: ryan.law@uvu.edu

C. A. Haselwood
Institute of Personal Financial Planning, Kansas State University, Manhattan, KS, USA

J. W. Goetz
Department of Financial Planning, Housing, and Consumer Economics, University of
Georgia, Athens, GA, USA

© Springer Nature Switzerland AG 2019
D. B. Durband et al. (eds.), *Financial Counseling*,
https://doi.org/10.1007/978-3-319-72586-4_8

Empathy

Empathy is a building block to a long-standing relationship with a client. Empathy is the ability to put oneself into a client's context and being able to perceive and understand what the client is experiencing. According to Miller and Rollnick (2013) empathy is, "seeking to accurately understand the client's internal frame of reference as a separate individual" (p. 64). When empathy is expressed or shown, a person is entering another's world, seeing through their eyes (Chung & Bemak, 2002; Miller & Rollnick, 2013). For counselors, "this means placing oneself inside the client's frame of reference and then having the ability to effectively communicate one's understanding of that world" (Chung & Bemak, p. 155).

Clients benefit from "being fully seen and fully understood" and empathy is used to attain this experience (Yalom, 2002, p. 18). When clients meet with financial counselors they are sharing their shortcomings, their fears, their goals, and the importance of understanding their thoughts and feelings should not be taken lightly. Empathizing with the client grows trust and perception that the feelings and emotions being shared are understood, it gives a starting place to grow and for changes to be made. Empathy will create trust between the counselor and the client, allowing for goals to be achieved. When a client feels that they are being understood, it opens them up to be more receptive to recommendations.

The empathy process is expressed in three ways: (1) empathic understanding, (2) empathic expression, and (3) empathic communication. Empathic understanding is an individual's ability to "infer the thoughts and feelings," empathic expression is the ability to match these thoughts and feelings (i.e., mirroring or mimicking) (Reber, Allen, & Reber, 2009), and empathic communication is the ability to communicate thoughts and feelings (Barrett-Lennard, 1981; Elliott et al. 1982; Goldstein & Michaels, 1985). Often the first expression is the only one displayed, however being able to encompass all will lead to more positive outcomes with clients.

Non-judgmental Awareness

As mentioned in the introduction, if a client feels judged for their choices they are less likely to trust a financial counselor. Both Kirchenbauer (2014) and Grist (n.d.) identify taking a non-judgmental approach as one of the key skills of financial professionals. With some clients it may be helpful to tell them that people make mistakes with money and that they are not being judged for what they have done in the past, and that by working together a solution may be found to help them move forward. The way to learn clients' money stories is to talk to them in an open, honest, and caring way. If clients feel safe, they may be more likely to open up.

In building trust and avoiding judgment, financial counselors should also be aware of client diversity (e.g., racial, gender, socioeconomic, education-level differences) that can affect the communication process. Chapter 4 of this book provides a discussion on client diversity.

Body Language

Mehrabian (1981) concluded that when a person is talking about their feelings or attitudes, their body language, or nonverbal behavior, accounts for up to 55% of their communication. Pease and Pease (2006) analyzed thousands of hours of recorded sales interviews and negotiations and they determined that body language accounts for 60–80% of the impact in a conversation. Regardless of the exact percentage, body language is important, and financial counselors need to pay attention to their own body language, as well as to the client's body language. Indicators of clients' disengagement include leaning back in their chair, potentially showing boredom, or crossing of arms to indicate they are cold or uncomfortable with the topic of conversation, or perhaps the client rarely makes eye contact or uses excessive hand gestures which may indicate anxiety or fear (Garrison, Myhre, Garman, & Hutchins, 1979).

Eye contact can communicate to a client that they have a counselor's undivided attention (Miller & Rollnick, 2013). Eye contact can also convey acceptance, warmth, and interest (Sharpe et al., 2007). Grable and Goetz (2017) recommend that one should not maintain eye contact with a client more than 70% of the time; any longer than that can cause the client to feel uncomfortable. Miller and Rollnick (2013) recommend that the speaker and listener (or counselor and client) do not directly face each other because it can be uncomfortable for the client to be directly facing the counselor and maintain eye contact for too long. If the chairs are positioned at an angle, eye contact can be made and broken more easily. See the section below on the physical environment for more on this subject.

Asking Questions and Silence

Effective questions are used to obtain information and deepen the relationship (Grable & Goetz, 2017). There are two basic types of questions: open-ended and closed-ended. A closed question can be answered with a "yes" or "no" or a very short answer, while an open question requires the person answering to go into more detail (Myhre, Harrison, Harris, & Garman, 1977; Pulvino & Pulvino, 2010). An example of a closed question is, "Do you plan to start budgeting this month?" An example of an open question is, "How did your budgeting go last month?" Open-ended questions can often be rephrased as statements, such as "Tell me about your experiences with budgeting last month." The use of the phrase, "Tell me more about..." can be a great way to invite a client to speak. It is best to use open questions in the initial interview and when one has clients that need to be encouraged to talk (Myhre et al., 1977). If one has a reluctant client who is withholding information or giving false or incomplete information one can use probes. "The kinds of probes that a financial counselor uses are questions and statements that explore the client's problem in an attempt to penetrate right to the heart of the matter" (Myhre et al., 1977, p. 9). Closed-ended questions are used to gather information and open-ended questions are to encourage the client to elaborate and gather the most accurate information (Pulvino & Pulvino, 2010; Grable & Goetz, 2017).

Questions are a crucial part of financial counseling, right down to the way that the question is worded. It is important for financial counselors to know when to use certain question forms and when not to because it can mean the difference between a client opening up or shutting down. Soliciting exceptions, scaling question, miracle questions, and hypothetical questions are all examples of question forms that may assist in guiding clients back to their goals. Soliciting exceptions is a key component for counselors as problems do not occur at all times, and it is important to look for solutions and focus on the future (Pulvino & Pulvino, 2010). An example of this interaction would be asking the client to reflect on a time when the problem did not occur, "That is interesting. Can you think of any time when this isn't true?" (Pulvino & Pulvino, 2010, p. 131). Incorporating the use of scaling questions could provide a more initiative answer, examples include, "on a scale of 0-10, 0 being not important at all, and 10 most important what number would you pick for yourself as to where you are with importance on this change?" and "why are you at a ___, and not a zero?" (Miller & Rollnick, 2013, p. 174). Miracle questions help to remove hurdles for clients and to look beyond the obstacles that are in front of them. See Chap. 7 for more information about miracle questions. Another solution could be to use a hypothetical question, such as, "what if you were out of debt? How would your life be different?" (Pulvino & Pulvino, 2010, p. 140).

In addition to asking effective questions, allowing for silence is also a significant counseling skill. Allowing silence to fill the room allows the client to reflect, gather their thoughts, and not lose their train of thought. "While there are silences that feel awkward, indifferent, or even hostile, there are also silences that feel comforting, affirming, and safe. They resonate with the ease of ... exchanging feelings and thoughts that do not quite make it into language" (Back, Bauer-Wu, Rushton, & Halifax, 2009, p. 1113). When a question has been asked that requires the client to think, the financial counselor needs to learn to be comfortable with silence. Myhre et al. (1977) encourage financial counselors to learn to get comfortable with pauses as long as 30 s or more, while Grable and Goetz (2017) indicate that financial planners start feeling stress after about 5 s of silence, therefore 10–15 s of silence is sufficient.

Active Listening

Covey (2004) identified listening as the most important skill one can develop and stressed the importance of seeking first to fully understand a person's message. Grable and Goetz (2017) echoed that listening is the single most important skill a financial professional can develop. Active listening includes attending behavior and encouragers, conversation pacing, clarification, and summarizing.

Attending Behavior and Encouragers

Attending is an important component of active listening; attending occurs when a financial counselor orients themselves physically to the client in such a way that the client knows that he or she has the financial counselor's full attention. Attending portrays a feeling of caring for the client. An acronym for counselors to remember attending skills is SOLER (Egan, 2010). S: Face the client squarely or sit squarely in relationship to the client. O: Maintain an open body position, without one's legs or arms being crossed. L: Lean forward or lean slightly toward the client to demonstrate interest. E: Make appropriate eye contact. R: Maintain a relaxed body position in these behaviors.

The counselors' use of attending encouragers to prompt clients to continue talking is another attending behavior. A nod of the head is a nonverbal encourager, while verbal examples include brief responses such as "mmm-hmmm," "uh huh," "Oh?", "I see" or "Tell me...:" or "Then what?"

Pacing and Leading

Pacing is patterning verbal and nonverbal behavior to match the client, which helps establish and build rapport (Meier & Davis, 2011). Financial counselors can pace a client's tone, rate of speech, volume, and body language. Financial counselors should not mirror every detail of the client's verbal and nonverbal behavior, but instead should pace general patterns. Following pacing, leading can then be utilized to change the tempo of the session. For example, if a client is rushing or speaking loudly, the financial counselor can match this behavior and then begin to slow down the tempo, which, if done appropriately, the client will match. Similarly if the client is leaning back in their chair the financial counselor can pace the client by subtly leaning back, then lead the client by leaning forward. There are times when a financial counselor may intentionally increase or decrease the pace, such as when they perceive that a client is not making sufficient progress or is stuck on a superfluous point.

Clarifying

Clarification is utilized when a statement or comment is made that needs further explanation or to gain clarity with the client (Myhre et al., 1977). A key rule counselors should follow is avoiding making an assumption about what a client means (Myhre et al., 1977, p. 21). When clients discuss their thoughts or experiences, they are voicing their personal experiences or perceptions (Myhre et al., 1977). It is important to take the time to fully explore and understand what a client is discussing. "Every assumption that a counselor makes has the potential to become a misunderstanding or a problem in the client/counselor relationship" this can be avoided with using clarification (Myhre et al., 1977, p. 22). There are multiple techniques that can be used to achieve clarification, including to repeat key words or phrases, rephrase what the client stated, admit confusion, and lastly ask open-ended questions (Myhre et al., 1977).

Clarification can sometimes be used in conjunction with restating, paraphrasing, and reflection, which are techniques that are used to gain clarity and to further the discussion (Cully & Teten, 2008). Every person explains experiences and feelings in a different way, no one person is the same, which is why clarification is such an important tool for counselors. Combining techniques allows for confirmation and clarification but it also allows the counselor to reflect the feelings and emotions that are being expressed (Cully & Teten, 2008). Words can hold multiple meanings, specifically, abstract words. Pulvino and Pulvino (2010) bring attention to the following words that could have multiple meanings—you, it/it's, to keep track, or money. For example, if four people were asked what money means one might say that money is evil, another that it is a tool, another that it represents freedom and finally one that says having money is bondage.

Examples of clarifying questions include, "when you say ___, what do you mean?" or "sounds to me like you're saying ___?" (Nelson-Jones, 2014, p. 151). Each clarifying question should have a purpose and the timing that they are asked should be considered as well. It is important for counselors to be clear on what is important to the client goals, in these cases the following clarification questions could be used—"you've mentioned three areas [specify]. Which one would you like to focus on first?" or "Is there anything you would like to add before we move on to…?" (Nelson-Jones, 2014, p. 157). The utilization of these questions may ensure that the client and counselor are thinking in a similar way when it comes to understanding what is truly important for the client.

Summarizing

Summarizing is paraphrasing and emphasizing the critical points of a conversation as a way of checking accuracy and assisting the client in organizing their thought process. A summary can link what was discussed in a previous conversation with the current appointment or conversation or to wrap up a conversation (Miller & Rollnick, 2013). Additionally, it allows time for the client to reflect, elaborate, or expand further on subjects (Miller & Rollnick, 2002; Miller & Rollnick, 2013; Velasquez, Maurer, Crouch, & DiClemente, 2001; Alexander, Morris, Tracy, & Frye, 2010). Clients often do not know exactly why they may be seeking a financial counselor and taking the time to summarize what has been communicated can lead to the root of the financial issue(s). Summarization ensures that all financial problems are focused on, determines the kind of financial counseling that is needed, and ensures that nothing is overlooked (Myhre et al., 1977).

In a study done by Kim, Gale, Goetz, and Bermudez (2011), summarizing was utilized to "highlight and celebrate clients progress" (p. 24). Whether summarizing is used to assist with transition, check-in, highlight events, or provide closure, the skill is of the utmost importance in order for a financial counselor to be successful with clients. Summarization can be utilized when needing to transition, close a session, or to ensure understanding of what the client has voiced.

Affirmation

Affirming statements validate, support, and encourage the client's behaviors or feelings, and are often used to point out strengths in a client that they may not fully recognize. According to Miller and Rollnick (2013), a counselor's role is to recognize and comment "on the client's particular strengths, abilities, good intentions, and efforts" (p. 33). Affirmation can aid in client retention and encourage change, as "people are more likely to spend time with, trust, listen to, and to be open with people who recognize and affirm their strengths" (Miller & Rollnick, 2013, p. 64). Pugh (1999) expresses affirmation as a way to communicate to the individual that is speaking that the listener (financial counselor) is present, which creates a ripple effect of encouraging further discussion. Affirmation is used to assist individuals in seeing the reality of their choices and to take responsibility for them (Larrabee, 1982). This realization is not made prevalent by the counselor but by the client in use of affirmation. Miller and Rollnick (2013) bring attention to an often forgotten thought, "making people feel terrible doesn't help them to change" (p. 33).

Affirmation is especially useful for financial counselors as seeking help regarding finances can be difficult for most individuals. When counselors affirm the client's feelings, it allows for change. When affirmation is being used with a client you are saying to the client that "I hear; I understand and validating the clients experiences and feelings" (Miller & Rollnick, 1991, p. 20). Affirming statements should use the word "you" instead of "I" and should focus on specifics. For example affirmation statements can be kept simple—for example, "thanks for coming in today." acknowledges a small success (Levensky, Forcehimes, O'Donohue, & Beitz, 2007, p. 55).

What follows is a sample dialogue between a financial counselor and client. This sample dialogue will help financial counselor's see how many of these communication skills can be used in a counseling session:

Counselor: Good morning, please come into my office and have a seat on the couch. I am glad we could schedule some time for you to come in and discuss your present and future financial goals.

Client: We are eager to discuss and outline a plan!

Counselor: I want to begin by stating that this meeting is confidential. Before we dive in, do you have any questions or concerns that you would like to share? (Face the client while maintaining an open body position (no crossed arms or legs).

Client: No

Counselor: Could you tell me about yourself? (Open question) (Remember to make eye contact)

Client: My husband and I have been married for 8 years, we have two kids, and love to spend time as a family by sharing experiences such as family vacations. My husband and I am very career driven but our family always comes first. (Encourage the conversation by nodding your head)

Counselor: What kind of vacations do you and your family enjoy?

Client: Now that my husband and I have kids, we enjoy traveling to locations that the whole family can enjoy. One of our goals this year is to plan the vacation in advance and budget for it as well. (Active listening: lean in when the client is talking)

Counselor: What roadblocks do you foresee that could prevent you in budgeting for the vacation? (Open question)

Client: One current roadblock is that we do not currently have a vacation fund; most of our vacations are booked because we get to the point during the year where we need a break. This is leaving us feeling stressed once the vacation is over because we felt we spent money that we should not have.

Counselor: Have you looked at setting aside money each month to a vacation fund?

Client: We have explored this but have never implemented a way to do that.

Counselor: I am glad that you shared this with me. I will make a note that this is one of your family goals. So that we can discuss a good plan to accomplish your goal, can you tell me more about your goals and what your expectations are for our sessions? (Open question)

Client: The goals that we have in mind right now are to create a larger safety net for our family, work on planning for retirement, and set up a college fund for our children.

Counselor: These are excellent goals that can definitely be achieved! When you say safety net for your family, can you give me more details on what you mean? (Affirming; Clarifying question)

Client: Right now we do not have much in savings, which worries us. If we had an emergency right now we would have to use a credit card to cover the cost. (Allow for silence after this to ensure the client has had enough time to share their thoughts)

Counselor: It sounds like this is a fear that you and your family have. (Reflection)

Client: Yes, this is a source of fear for us. We have two children and they depend on us so having no safety net keeps us up at night sometimes.

Counselor: What you expressed is a perfectly normal fear and as a team we will accomplish creating a safety net for your family. My husband and I have three children and they are our life as well. (Empathy and Affirming—allow for silence) Do you currently put a set amount into savings now?

Client: No

Counselor: Do you have a specific number that you would like to reach? (Active listening: asking questions)

Client: We would like to have at least 3–6 months of salary in a savings account.

Counselor: Great! When would you like to achieve this goal?

Client: Within the next year or two.

Counselor: These are great goals to have! Other than your goal of a safety net you mentioned working on your retirement, and setting up a college fund. (Affirming; Restating) Do you have specific goals surrounding those?

Client: Yes, we would like to be able to retire together and keep the same lifestyle that we have now. Currently our daughters are two and four. We would like to start a college fund that allows us to pay for their tuition to a 4 year college.

Counselor: Ok, we have made some great strides during our first session and I believe we have come to a good stopping point. Now that we have discussed your goals, my team and I will look at ways that we can assist you in your savings goals, retirement goals, vacation goals, and college fund goals. (Paraphrasing) Do you have any questions or concerns? (Open-ended question)

Client: No, we look forward to working with you.

Counselor: I am looking forward to working with you as well, please e-mail or call me if anything comes up before our next session.

Communication is a large part of the financial counselor–client relationship but it is not the only aspect that should be taken into consideration. The environment in which a financial counselor meets with a client is just as important and can set the tone for the relationship. The following provides helpful advice on considerations for a physical environment that is conducive to meeting with clients.

The Physical Environment

Creating a financial counseling environment that is welcoming to clients and also comfortable for financial counselors is of the utmost importance. Yet, the extent to which financial counselors give thought to their office environment is not well documented. There are a number of reasons for this potential lack of attention. First, some financial counselors may have little control over their physical environment. The layout of the office, the furnishings, and the colors may have been chosen by their employer, a property management company, or an interior decorating firm. Second, there is a lack of empirical research examining the effects of the physical environment on the financial counseling process. Furthermore, there are a number of studies that address the potential impact of the physical environment within the broader fields of counseling and therapy, as well as from the field of financial planning, that may be appropriately applied to the financial counseling field.

Financial counselors should spend more time thinking about and designing their offices because having a suboptimal setup causes clients additional stress (Britt & Grable, 2012; Grable, Heo, & Rabbani, 2014) and according to Grable and Goetz (2017):

> …client stress matters. The more stress experienced, the less likely the client will enthusiastically engage in the financial planning process. On the other hand, the more ways a

financial planner can reduce client stress within the environment, the more likely he or she is going to be viewed as competent, trustworthy, and caring by the clients (p. 50).

In a review of published research on the physical environment in counseling settings, Pressly and Heesacker (2001) identified eight elements that constitute the physical environment: accessories, color, furniture and room design, lighting, smell, sound, texture, and thermal conditions. Attention to these eight elements of the physical environment will likely be associated with decreased stress and improved client outcomes.

Accessories

Devlin et al. (2009) researched two specific accessories: credentials and family photos. Clients tended to judge therapists that had diplomas and credentials hung in their office more positively than those who did not have them displayed. Thus, it may be helpful to the counseling process for financial counselors to allocate the time and cost toward framing and presenting diplomas, awards, and various certificates (such as their AFC® or CFP® certificates) in convenient view to clients. Clients may see those diplomas and certificates on the wall as a signal that a particular counselor's expertise can be trusted. Family photos appeared to have no effect on the client's perception of the therapist (Devlin et al. (2009)). As such, if financial counselors enjoy having family photos in the office, they should feel free to include them but it is not necessary for them to be in the client's view.

Pressly and Heesacker (2001) reported that clients tend to prefer artwork that reflects natural settings, such as animals, water, and landscape, as compared to pictures of urban scenes, people, or abstract art. One creative option is to lease artwork or to exhibit varying local artists' work on a periodic basis, as this may add value to the client's experience when visiting the office. Indoor plants provide benefits such as stress reduction (Bringslimark, Hartig, & Patil, 2009) and tend to represent growth, renewal, and life (Carpman & Grant, 1993). Growing plants and changing artwork symbolize an environment that welcomes and supports change.

While displaying diplomas, licenses, awards, artwork, and plants, it is important to remember that there needs to be a balance, as waiting rooms and client rooms should be free from clutter. Avoid over-furnishing and over-decorating to prevent an environment that may be over-stimulating and chaotic leading to client distress.

An experimental study done by Grable and Britt (2012) recommended that one's office lobby should not have financial news programs running as they increase stress. Positive financial news created the highest levels of stress as a client may feel regret for not taking action, and stress levels from financial programs tended to be higher for men than women. While further research in this area needs to be done, it is most likely a good idea to turn off financial news programs and even eliminate any money related magazines from the lobby.

Financial counselors should also maintain a supply of tissues, pens and pencils, paper, a calculator, and a calendar for scheduling future appointments. Having these supplies on hand ensures that the financial counselor will be prepared for their appointments.

Color

The most important thing to remember about using wall color is that it should be pleasing to the financial counselor and staff since they will be the ones spending the most time in the space. According to Pressly and Heesacker (2001), blue is a good color for an office (such as an accent wall). The colors blue and violet decrease blood pressure, pulse, and respiration. When other colors are used in artwork and plants, neutral wall colors work well.

From a financial counselor's perspective, color does not appear to influence work productivity (Kwallek, Woodson, Lewis, & Sales, 1997) with the exception of sterile white being not particularly conducive to work productivity (Kwallek & Lewis, 1990). Therefore, as with other strategies from this chapter, it is better to place client interest first and opt for a blue accent wall or neutral colors for the office.

Furniture Arrangement

The top source of environmental stress for clients is the office seating arrangement (Britt & Grable, 2012; Grable & Goetz, 2017). A physical barrier of any kind, including a desk, is a stressor for the client, and that some other type of seating arrangement, such as a couch, may be beneficial. Meeting with a client in a room that has a couch and armchair can create a less stressful environment for clients as compared to a traditional office arrangement with chairs placed around a table or on opposite sides of a desk (Britt & Grable, 2012). Having a couch reduces physical barriers between a financial counselor and client, thus enhancing the development of a trusted relationship and encouraging the exchange of information (Britt & Grable, 2012).

The traditional office layout involves the financial professional sitting behind an impressively large desk in high-back leather chair, while the client sits on the other side, often in chairs of a lower height thereby forcing the client to look up to the financial counselor (Grable & Goetz, 2017). Although this setup may feel comfortable to the counselor, it is a suboptimal structural arrangement in terms of building a strong working alliance with the client, and may even increase the stress of the client.

Lighting

If a counseling session can be conducted in a room with a window, the natural light may help facilitate self-disclosure on the part of clients. A combination of natural light, soft lighting, and full-spectrum lighting may benefit both counselors and clients (Pressly & Heesacker, 2001). To minimize distraction, Grable and Goetz (2017) recommended that seating be arranged so windows are behind the client.

Smell

Smell should be a consideration in a financial counseling office environment. Care should be taken with using air fresheners or scented plug-in devices as some clients might be sensitive to these. Some clients may not like the smell of, or may even be allergic to, perfumes and cologne. Care should always be taken that the financial counselor and staff are free of fragrances and have fresh breath. Keeping the office clean and the garbage taken out will help keep the smell of the office pleasant.

Sound

As noted previously, privacy is critical to financial counseling. If clients feel that others can overhear them, it can result in decreased self-disclosure. Devices such as white noise machines will mask sounds heard from the hallway or waiting room and prevent people outside from hearing voices within.

Music within the workplace can influence cooperative behavior among employees (Kniffin, Yan, Wansink, & Schulze, 2017) although the influence on financial counseling client behavior is unknown. Sillings, a music director who creates playlists for companies, recommends that if a task requires focus, elevator music or classical music would be suitable which could certainly transfer to a financial counseling environment (Vozza, 2016).

Texture

Texture refers to features of a room that make it seem soft and comfortable or hard and cold (Pressly & Heesacker, 2001). Recommendations include using soft, textured surfaces and using flat or satin sheen paint to soften the room.

Thermal Conditions

Thermal conditions refer to the temperature and humidity of a space. According to Woodward (2013), the temperature of an office impacts movement, mood, and pace. Warmth is conducive to making people friendlier and creates a desire to connect. While the exact temperature of the office is a matter of personal preference, the Occupational Health and Safety Administration (n.d.) recommends that workplace temperatures are in the range of 68–76 °F (20–24 °C), and that humidity is kept in the range of 20–60%.

Considerations for Virtual Appointments

The environment for a virtual session is as important as a physical office. With video conferencing tools at our fingertips the virtual era is giving financial counselors a whole new tool to use for client meetings. The same amount of time and care should be put into how a virtual environment will look to a client. The image that is displayed will set the tone for the meeting. It will be important to ensure that the client understands how to start a video conference, if a client cannot enter the meeting as easily as opening a door you will begin the meeting with frustration. During the call, no distracting noises should occur, it should be treated as though the person is truly in front of the financial counselor. Since the virtual era is new, further research is needed to determine client's perceptions regarding meetings in a virtual space. All other recommendations included in this chapter about communication skills are just as important in a virtual session as they are in person.

Conclusion

The financial counseling profession is built around building relationships, and the first step in building a successful relationship is communication. Communication is the backbone within relationships which carries tremendous weight, as it can make or break a client–counselor relationship.

Financial counselors should strive to improve their communication skills with a focus on empathy, non-judgmental awareness, body language, asking effective questions, active listening, affirmation, and strategically arranging one's office space. A financial counselor's office should be warm and inviting, utilizing accessories such as awards and diplomas as well as plants and paint colors that decrease stress. Meeting spaces should be arranged in a way that will decrease client stress. Attention should be given to lighting, smell, sound, texture, and thermal conditions within the office.

Everything from a counselor's ability to ask the right questions to how an office is laid out holds significant value and plays a role in the client's stress level. No one skill is enough; rather, the value of incorporating many skills together will allow for further discovery with one's clients and long-lasting trust. Learning these skills and utilizing them together will allow financial counselors to be more effective across a variety of counseling sessions.

References

Alexander, P. C., Morris, E., Tracy, A., & Frye, A. (2010). Stages of change and the group treatment of batterers: A randomized clinical trial. *Violence and Victims, 25*(5), 571–587. https://doi.org/10.1891/0886-6708.25.5.571

Back, A. L., Bauer-Wu, S. M., Rushton, C. H., & Halifax, J. (2009). Compassionate science in the patient-clinician encounter: A contemplative approach. *Journal of Palliative Medicine, 12*(12), 1113–1117. https://doi.org/10.1089/jpm.2009.0175

Barrett-Lennard, G. T. (1981). The empathy cycle: Refinement of a nuclear concept. *Journal of counseling psychology, 28*(2), 91.

Bringslimark, T., Hartig, T., & Patil, G. G. (2009). The psychological benefits of indoor plants: A critical review of the experimental literature. *Journal of Experimental Psychology, 29*, 422–433.

Britt, S., & Grable, J. (2012). Your office may be a stressor: Understand how the physical environment of your office affects financial counseling clients. *The Standard, 30*(2), 5 and 13.

Carpman, J. R., & Grant, M. A. (1993). *Design that cares: Planning health facilities for patients and visitors* (2nd ed.). Chicago: American Hospital Publishing.

Chung, R. C. Y., & Bemak, F. (2002). The relationship of culture and empathy in cross-cultural counseling. *Journal of Counseling & Development, 80*(2), 154–159.

Covey, S. R. (2004). *The 7 habits of highly effective people: Powerful lessons in personal change.* New York, NY: Free Press.

Cully, J. A., & Teten, A. L. (2008). *A therapist's guide to brief cognitive behavioral therapy.* Retrieved from https://depts.washington.edu/dbpeds/therapists_guide_to_brief_cbtmanual.pdf

Devlin, A. S., Donovan, S., Nicolov, A., Nold, O., Packard, A., & Zandan, G. (2009). Impressive? Credentials, family photographs, and the perception of therapist qualities. *Journal of Environmental Psychology, 29*(4), 503–512.

Egan, G. (2010). *The skilled helper: A problem management and opportunity development approach to helping* (9th ed.). Belmont, CA: Brooks Cole.

Elliott, R., Filipovich, H., Harrigan, L., Gaynor, J., Reimschuessel, C., & Zapadka, J. K. (1982). Measuring response empathy: The development of a multicomponent rating scale. *Journal of Counseling Psychology, 29*(4), 379.

Garrison, J. E., Myhre, D. C., Garman, E. T., & Hutchins, D. E. (1979). *Building basic financial counseling skills: A leader's guide for group training of financial counselors.* Blacksburg, VA: Virginia Polytechnic Institute and State University Extension Division.

Goldstein, A. P., & Michaels, G. Y. (1985). *Empathy: Development, training, and consequences.* Lawrence Erlbaum.

Grable, J. E., & Archuleta, K. L. (2015). Principles of communication and counseling. In C. R. Chaffin (Ed.), *CFP board financial planning competency handbook* (2nd ed., pp. 115–125). Hoboken, NJ: Wiley.

Grable, J. E., & Britt, S. L. (2012). Financial news and client stress: Understanding the association from a financial planning perspective. *Financial Planning Review, 5*(3), 23–36.

Grable, J. E., & Goetz, J. W. (2017). *Communication essentials for financial planners: Strategies and techniques.* Hoboken, NJ: Wiley.

Grable, J. E., Heo, W., & Rabbani, A. (2014). Financial anxiety, physiological arousal, and planning intention. *Journal of Financial Therapy, 5*(2), 1–18.

Grist, N. (n.d.). Moving towards an evidence-based consensus on core counselor competencies. *Professionalizing Field of Financial Counseling and Coaching Journal,* 17–18. Retrieved from http://www.professionalfincounselingjournal.org/index.html

Kim, J. H., Gale, J., Goetz, J., & Bermúdez, J. M. (2011). Relational financial therapy: An innovative and collaborative treatment approach. *Contemporary Family Therapy, 33*(3), 229–241.

Kirchenbauer, L. A. K. (2014, September). The 5 essential skills of an exceptional financial planner. *Journal of Financial Planning,* 21–24.

Kniffin, K. M., Yan, J., Wansink, B., & Schulze, W. D. (2017). The sound of cooperation: Musical influences on cooperative behavior. *Journal of Organizational Behavior, 38*(3), 372–390.

Kwallek, N., & Lewis, C. M. (1990). Effects of environmental design on males and females: A red or white or green office. *Applied Ergonomics, 21*(4), 275–278.

Kwallek, N., Woodson, H., Lewis, C. M., & Sales, C. (1997). Impact of three interior color schemes on worker mood and performance relative to individual environmental sensitivity. *Color Research and Application, 22*(2), 121–132.

Lambert, M. J., & Barley, D. E. (2001). Research summary on the therapeutic relationship and psychotherapy outcome. *Psychotherapy Theory Research Practice and Training, 38*(4), 357–361.

Larrabee, M. J. (1982). Working with reluctant clients through affirmation techniques. *Journal of Counseling and Development, 61*(2), 105–109. https://doi.org/10.1002/j.2164-4918.1982.tb00739.x

Levensky, E. R., Forcehimes, A., O'Donohue, W. T., & Beitz, K. (2007). Motivational interviewing. *The American Journal of Nursing, 107*(10), 50–59 Retrieved from http://www.jstor.org/stable/29746504

Mehrabian, A. (1981). *Silent messages: Implicit communication of emotions and attitudes.* Belmont, CA: Wadsworth.

Meier, S. T., & Davis, S. R. (2011). *The elements of counseling* (7th ed.). Belmont, CA: Brooks/Cole Cengage Learning.

Miller, W. R., & Rollnick, S. (1991). *Motivational interviewing; preparing people to change addictive behavior.* New York, NY: The Guilford Press Retrieved from https://www.ncbi.nlm.nih.gov/books/NBK64964/

Miller, W. R., & Rollnick, S. (2002). *Motivational Interviewing: preparing people for change* (2nd ed.), New York, NY: Guilford Press.

Miller, W. R., & Rollnick, S. (2013). *Motivational interviewing: Helping people change* (3rd ed.). New York, NY: The Guilford Press.

Moy, J. (n.d.). Developing a comprehensive counseling curriculum. *The Professionalizing Field of Financial Counseling and Coaching Journal,* 23–24. Retrieved from http://www.professionalfincounselingjournal.org/index.html

Myhre, D. C., Harrison, B. H., Harris, R. D., & Garman, E. T. (1977, September). *Asking questions and clarifying client statements: Basic interviewing skills for financial counselors.* Blacksburg, VA: Virginia Polytechnic Institute and State University Extension Division.

Nelson-Jones, R. (2014). Clarify problem skills. *Practical counseling and helping skills* (pp. 149–174). Retrieved from http://greenmedicine.ie/school/images/Modules/Therapeutics-Relationshipes-and-Skills/149-174.pdf

Occupational Safety & Health Administration [OSHA]. (n.d.). *OSHA Technical Manual.* Retrieved from https://www.osha.gov/dts/osta/otm/index.html

Pease, A., & Pease, B. (2006). *The definitive book of body language: The hidden meaning behind people's gestures and expressions.* New York, NY: Bantam Dell.

Pressly, P. K., & Heesacker, M. (2001). The physical environment and counseling: A review of theory and research. *Journal of Counseling and Development, 79*(2), 148–160 Retrieved from https://search.proquest.com/docview/218955658?accountid=14779

Pugh, C. A. (1999). *Affirmation in psychotherapy: The specific operation of common therapy process.* Unpublished doctoral dissertation, The University of Utah, Utah.

Pulvino, C. J., & Pulvino, C. A. (2010). *Financial counseling: A strategic approach*. Sarasota, FL: Instructional Enterprises.

Reber, A. S., Allen, R. & Reber, E. S. (2009). *The Penguin dictionary of psychology* (4th ed.), London, England: Penguin.

Sharpe, D. L., Anderson, C., White, A., Galvan, S., & Siesta, M. (2007). Specific elements of communication that affect trust and commitment in the financial planning process. *Journal of Financial Counseling and Planning, 18*(1), 2–17.

Velasquez, M. M., Maurer, G. G., Crouch, C., & DiClemente, C. C. (2001). *Group treatment for substance abuse: A stage of change manual*. New York, Guilford.

Vozza, S. (2016, September 16). How music can make your office more (or less) productive. *Fast Company*. Retrieved from https://www.fastcompany.com/3063730/work-smart/how-music-can-make-your-office-more-or-less-productive

Woodward, W. (2013, July 29). Why frigid office temperatures can be bad for business. *Fox Business*. Retrieved from http://www.foxbusiness.com/features/2013/07/29/frigid-offices-bad-for-business.html

Yalom, I. D. (2002). *The gift of therapy*. New York, NY: HarperCollins Publishers.

Chapter 9
Frameworks for Financial Decision Making

Benjamin F. Cummings and Sarah Newcomb

Making decisions is a part of daily life, and making financial decisions is no exception. As society has advanced over the last few hundred years, making effective financial decisions is now a key part of modern life in developed countries. Having a firm understanding of the motivations that are involved in making financial decisions can greatly benefit financial counselors who work to enhance the financial decision making abilities of their clients.

To set the stage for this discussion about making financial decisions, keep in mind that humans are rationalizing beings. Unlike most other animals, humans have an incredibly developed brain that allows them to reason, to align behaviors with intentions, and to plan future actions beyond mere instinctive behaviors. Humans generally have a rationale behind what they do—albeit sometimes that rationale may be questioned by others. Even decisions makers that may appear incredibly irrational can often provide seemingly rational explanations for their behavior.

Sometimes what seems like irrational behavior is motivated by emotion, like fear or greed. Emotions are very real to the person who is experiencing them and responding to those emotions can be a very rational response. Other seemingly irrational behavior is the result of flawed reasoning. A problem with flawed or biased reasoning is that individuals are probably not aware of the flaws or biases in their thought processes. Financial counselors can provide objectivity and help clients

B. F. Cummings (✉)
The American College of Financial Services, Bryn Mawr, PA, USA
e-mail: benjamin.cummings@theamericancollege.edu

S. Newcomb
Morningstar, Inc., Washington, DC, USA
e-mail: sarah.newcomb@morningstar.com

© Springer Nature Switzerland AG 2019
D. B. Durband et al. (eds.), *Financial Counseling*,
https://doi.org/10.1007/978-3-319-72586-4_9

explore the motivations behind their financial decisions and behavior, and—as appropriate—raise awareness about potentially concerning emotional motivations or potentially flawed reasoning.

Social scientists do their best to explore the rationale behind human behavior, and practitioners can benefit from what they have learned. However, human beings—and the decisions they make—are incredibly complex, which often results in models of human behavior that fall short of reality. For example, to develop a generalizable model of how a person may act in a particular situation is incredibly difficult, if not impossible. Similarly, developing a model which fully accounts for the emotional responses, personal narrative, and individual biases that someone may have is extremely challenging. However, learning about the prevalent decision making models can inform financial counselors about the possible motivations that their clients may have. Ideally, counselors can also identify areas where clients may be able to alter their motivations or their decision making process in order to arrive at more desirable outcomes.

Bernoulli and the St. Petersburg Paradox

Although behavioral economics seems like a relatively new field, the exploration of the interaction between psychology and financial decisions dates back at least a few centuries. One of the world's earliest behavioral economists, Daniel Bernoulli, proposed a solution to what is known as the *St. Petersburg Paradox* (Bernoulli, 1738). As conceived by Daniel's brother, Nicolas Bernoulli, the paradox works like this (Bernoulli, 1713). Using a fair coin, a $2 wager is made. If the coin lands on heads, the stakes double to $4, but if the coin lands on tails, the gamble ends with a $2 payout. Each time the coin lands on heads, the stakes double and continue to double until the coin lands on tails, at which point the payout is made. What is a fair price for the gamble?

A fair price naturally depends on the potential payout. On the low end, the gamble could pay out as little as $2. On the high end, however, there is a very small probability that the wager could go on infinitely. In addition, since the gamble doubles each round, it does not take very long before the payout on the high end becomes quite substantial.

Even though the payout is potentially very large, few people are willing to pay very much for this gamble. Why? The heart of Bernoulli's explanation about this gamble is that money or wealth provides *utility*, or satisfaction (Bernoulli, 1738). However, the impact of incremental increases in wealth, called the *marginal utility of wealth*, diminishes at higher levels of wealth (Bernoulli, 1738). In other words, receiving an additional dollar means much more to someone with only $100 than it does to someone with $1 million. A key part of utility theory is making financial decisions that have uncertain outcomes, as in the case of the St. Petersburg Paradox.

Expected Utility Model

After Bernoulli, there was scant development of utility theory for quite some time. With the emergence of social sciences, like psychology and economics, as their own disciplines of study in the nineteenth and early twentieth centuries, many researchers felt a need to develop these new sciences with the same level of rigor as the hard sciences, like physics and chemistry. To many, this rigor meant researchers needed to develop mathematical models that could be tested empirically. In what might be viewed as equation envy, researchers in the soft sciences around the time of World War II sought mathematical models that could be used to explain human behavior and motivation (e.g., see Simon, 1978). Although the debate to enhance the rigor and efficacy of the "soft" sciences continues today (e.g., see Simms, 2010), many mathematical methods and models—often called econometric or psychometric methods and models—have been developed over the years and are used to provide insight about human behavior. Some of these models are discussed in the following sections, especially those most relevant to financial decision making.

Although Bernoulli introduced the world to the theory of utility in the 1700s, von Neumann and Morgenstern (1944) further developed this theory in the 1940s as part of their attempt to better explain the outcomes of economic games. The basic premise of the *expected utility model* is that individuals seek to maximize their utility, or satisfaction. This satisfaction is largely derived from individuals maximizing their utility of consumption, which is made possible because of wealth. Maximizing utility, however, is not the same as maximizing wealth. Individuals tend to be risk averse, and maximizing wealth typically involves taking financial risks. People prefer certain outcomes over risky or uncertain outcomes, which is part of the expected utility model or theory.

Income and Satisfaction

Expected utility theory places considerable weight on the role that wealth or income plays in providing satisfaction, and this relation between financial status and satisfaction has been the subject of considerable research. For example, Kahneman and Deaton (2010) looked the impact of income on two subjective measures of well-being. One measure of well-being is *emotional well-being*, which is described as the emotional quality of everyday experiences. Another measure of well-being is *life evaluation*, which is described as the way one thinks about one's life. Kahneman and Deaton (2010) found that emotional well-being has a positive relation with income, but only up to about $75,000 USD. Beyond that, income does not have a significant impact on emotional well-being. However, life evaluation steadily increases with income, even beyond $75,000 of income. This research can be helpful to know in that increases in income up to about $75,000 (in 2010 dollars) can increase emotional well-being, in part because additional income can alleviate some of the stress associated with limited financial resources. However, increases beyond $75,000 may not have as much of an impact on emotional well-being, although additional income may enhance one's evaluation of one's life as a whole.

Dunn, Aknin, and Norton (2008) explored how income is spent, and they found that spending more income on others increases one's own happiness. However, in another study, Hill and Howell (2014) found that spending on others increased happiness only for those with greater self-transcendent value, meaning that they have a greater concern for others. Most recently, Matz, Gladstone, and Stillwell (2016) found evidence that aligning spending with one's personality traits may increase life satisfaction. Based on these findings, financial counselors may want to consider how their clients spend their income and whether their spending actually enhances their life satisfaction. Counselors may even consider including personality assessments to better understand their clients and how their spending may or may not be enhancing their life satisfaction.

Spending decisions can also impact marital satisfaction for married couples. Rick, Small, and Finkel (2011) find evidence that individuals often marry people with complementary or opposing spending habits (e.g., a tightwad marrying a spendthrift). Couples with opposing spending habits tend to have more financial conflict in their marriages, which in turn tends to drive down marital satisfaction. These findings suggest that financial counselors may benefit by discussing the spending habits of their married clients. Doing so would allow a counselor to assess the extent to which their clients' spending habits align. Counselors can also explore how much financial conflict their clients are experiencing in their marriage. These findings can also be helpful in premarital planning. A financial counselor working with an engaged couple can help them assess their spending habits and can provide guidance on how to handle financial conflicts that arise in their marriage.

Rational Choice Models

The expected utility theory advanced by von Neumann and Morgenstern (1944) is part of a larger collection of decision making models that can be described as *rational choice models*. These models are based on the idea that individuals tend to be rational in their decision making. As a result, many economists have taken the approach that human behavior can be modeled based on this premise of rationality.

Rational choice models, like utility theory, tend to have a number of assumptions (von Neumann & Morgenstern, 1944; Simon, 1955). Although these assumptions often fall short of reality, identifying their importance can also help financial counselors recognize what individuals need to make sound financial decisions.

For example, in order to make a rational decision to maximize utility, an individual needs to have adequate, if not complete, knowledge about the available options. In addition, information needs to be symmetric, meaning that the parties on both sides of a transaction should have access to the same information, and one party (usually the seller) cannot have more information about the good or service than the other (usually the buyer). Another common assumption is that all choice options are known to the individual and can be evaluated. These options need to be unambiguous, and individuals are assumed to have a clear preference structure, where they know which options they prefer over others. Finally, individuals are assumed to have adequate numeracy and computational skills to adequately evaluate all available options. In summary, some of the components that are necessary to make sound financial decisions include:

- Adequate knowledge
- Symmetric knowledge
- Adequate evaluation of all choice options
- Adequate numeracy and computational skills

Although it may be difficult to fully achieve all these components, identifying and addressing considerable deficiencies can help them make better financial decisions. For example, if clients seem to be operating on the basis of limited information about a financial decision, they obviously need more information before they can make a better decision. If they are considering buying something, and the other party is considerably more knowledgeable about the item, then they may benefit by doing more research in order to reduce the information asymmetry. Clearly, this will be a challenge when making a decision that involves complex knowledge, like a medical procedure. Doctors almost always know more about a procedure than a patient, but the patient should learn as much as possible before making a decision about the procedure. Likewise, with financial decisions, if a client has considered only a few of the available options before them, then perhaps they need some guidance on what other options might be available to them. Lastly, clients may simply need help performing complex financial calculations before they can adequately understand the results of their decisions.

Bounded Rationality

Although rational choice models are quite aspirational, they provide helpful insight about how individuals may be—and possibly should be—making financial decisions. Herbert Simon (1955) tried to bring these models closer to reality when he introduced the concept of *bounded rationality*, meaning that individuals seek to make rational decisions, but they face natural limitations. In other words, their capability to act rationally has bounds. Some of these natural limitations include:

- Limited attention
- Limited cognitive resources
- Limited processing power and energy
- Limited information
- Limited time

Simon (1955) argued that these limitations may result from internal or external constraints, which can inhibit the ability of an individual to make rational decisions.

Internal constraints exist within a person, and external constraints come from their external environment. Each of these limitations highlighted in Simon (1955) are discussed in the following paragraphs. Particular attention is given to the way in which these constraints play out internally.

Limited Attention

Humans simply cannot pay attention to all aspects of a decision at one time. As a result, some features of a decision receive more weight in the outcome than others, not because they necessarily have greater importance or deserve more weight, but merely because they dominate the attention of the decision maker. Not surprisingly, features with more salience tend to play larger roles in financial decisions. Financial counselors can help clients evaluate the characteristics or features of a particular choice to determine which features should carry the most weight in the decision. Counselors can then help clients focus on those features.

Limited Cognitive Resources

Regardless of one's intelligence, cognitive ability is limited by nature. Even incredibly smart people may have a difficult time performing complex mathematical calculations. Financial decisions often involve difficult calculations, particularly for decisions that involve moving financial resources across time, either in the form of borrowing future resources to use today or investing today in order to increase financial resources available in the future. Because financial calculations can be difficult, counselors can help their clients perform complex calculations, which can in turn help them make more informed decisions.

Limited Processing Power and Energy

One's ability to process financial information is limited in part by what else our brain is being asked to process. An additional limitation is the energy that a person is willing and able to put towards making a sound financial decision. Personal worries and stress can put a toll on processing power. For example, Evans and Schamberg (2009) found that the chronic stress associated with childhood poverty led to reduced working memory as young adults. Sleep deprivation can also inhibit effective decision making (Harrison & Horne, 2000). Even making choices can impair subsequent decision making (Vohs et al., 2014). Regardless of whether these limitations come from external factors (e.g., childhood poverty) or internal factors (e.g., stress, sleep deprivation), limited processing power and limited energy are natural constraints on optimal decision making.

Financial counselors can help clients consider their stress and energy levels, and if either of these aspects are a concern, they can explore ways to reduce their stress and/or increase their energy. At the same time, financial counselors should be aware of the stress that their clients may be experiencing during their sessions together, especially because clients are typically unable to assess how much financial stress they are experiencing (Grable & Britt, 2012). Britt, Lawson, and Haselwood (2016) find that clients under stress express less readiness to make financial changes. However, Ford, Grable, Kruger, and DeGraff (2017) find that joint physiological arousal within a couple during financial discussions can increase the couple's intention of seeking professional financial advice. The InCharge Financial Distress/ Financial Well-Being Scale (Prawitz et al., 2006) is a publicly available scale that counselors can use to assess the financial stress their clients are experiencing.

Financial counselors can raise awareness among clients that stress and energy levels can impact their ability to make decisions. Counselors can also help clients consider the timing and setting in which they make impactful financial decisions as well as the frame of mind they should have going into these decisions. In short, counselors can teach clients not to make important decisions when they are *HALT*: *H*ungry, *A*ngry, *L*onely, or *T*ired.

Limited Information

As mentioned previously, information asymmetry exists when counterparties to a transaction have unequal information. Akerlof (1970) explores this imbalance in information as it exists in the used car market, since the seller of a used car has more information about the quality of the car than a potential buyer would have. Information is also limited simply by the lack of knowledge. Individuals with low financial literacy have limited knowledge, yet they still must make financial decisions. Constraints due to limited information are especially relevant to financial decisions, as indicated by the relatively low levels of financial literacy in the USA (Lusardi & Mitchell, 2014).

Limited Time

Increasing the amount of time allocated to making a decision can lead to better decisions. Ordonez and Benson (1997) find that putting participants under a time constraint reduces the likelihood that they will perform additional cognitive tasks when making a decision. Although allocating significant time to financial decisions may not be ideal, either, financial counselors can encourage clients to spend an appropriate amount of time evaluating a decision they need to make.

Constraints on time and other resources can make it difficult for individuals to gather relevant information. Some information is easier to acquire, but other information can take substantial amounts of time to learn and integrate into making financial decisions. Financial counselors can be a great resource and provide relevant information that can provide helpful context for making important financial decisions.

Understanding expected utility theory as well as its limitations can provide value for financial counselors as they consider the extent to which a client may be operating under a utility theory framework. Counselors can also consider the limitations to those models, and how those limitations might be rectified in order to enhance the decision making abilities of their clients.

Decisions Involving Uncertain Outcomes

In addition to discussing some of the potential limitations to rational choice models, Simon (1955) also described some of the common approaches employed when making a decision with an uncertain outcome. Many financial decisions involve uncertainty or risk because we simply do not know the future, and a mental framework can help those who are facing decisions with uncertain outcomes. An example of such a mental framework is to minimize or eliminate the worst possible outcome, where the choice with the best of the worst possibilities is selected. An application of this framework could be used if someone is facing the possibility of losing their house or being late on a number of credit card payments, the best of the worst possibilities is to make only the house payment and forego making any payments on the other debts.

Another mental framework is to maximize the expected value, which involves considering the potential payoffs and the respective probabilities of those payoffs. For example, a couple who views bankruptcy as their only option may benefit by considering the probability that a judge may instead restructure their debts, especially if their primary debts are student loans. In this case, there might be a low probability that the debt will be fully forgiven and a high probability that it will remain. These outcomes ought to be weighed against any legal fees that they may need to incur in order to file for bankruptcy.

A final mental framework is that someone might focus merely on the option with the largest possible payoff regardless of the probability, although this approach often overlooks the risks associated with each of the alternatives. For example, someone may choose to purchase a lottery ticket because of the possibility of a very large payoff, even though the probability of winning is incredibly remote. Because only the *size* and not the *probability* of the largest payoff is considered in this mental framework, it is not usually an advisable framework to use for financial decisions, yet it is commonly employed.

Descriptive and Normative Models of Decision Making

Although Simon (1955) challenged the assumptions of the rational choice models, these models were and are commonly used to explain how individuals make financial decisions. However, now there is a general sense that because of the unrealistic assumptions, rational choice models are not effective *descriptive* or *positive models.* Instead, now they are more commonly used as *normative models*, where they are used to explain how individuals *should* behave. In this sense, counselors can better understand the potentially optimal decisions a person could make, keeping in mind that all models are flawed because they simplify reality. But they can be useful and provide helpful insights. In the development of models of financial decision making, an effective descriptive model was still needed.

Prospect Theory

Prospect theory, developed by Kahneman and Tversky (1979), attempts to reconcile utility theory with bounded rationality. One of the central tenets of prospect theory is that individuals make financial decisions by comparing outcomes to an arbitrary reference point. In this sense, outcomes are viewed either as gains or losses, relative to the reference point. Another important concept in prospect theory is that losses hurt, meaning they create something of a *dis*utility, and gains feel good, suggesting that utility can come from the mere acquisition of a monetary gain rather than from consuming a good or service. In addition, losses hurt twice as much as a similar gain feels good, as shown in Fig. 9.1. An important concept introduced by prospect theory is that individuals are loss averse, meaning we try to avoid losses.

Keep in mind that the reference point in prospect theory is completely arbitrary and can vary person by person, even for a nearly identical decision. Each individual determines their own reference points, but they can be influenced. For example, changing the framing of a decision can influence the outcome. Since losses hurt

Fig. 9.1 Gains and losses modeled in prospect theory

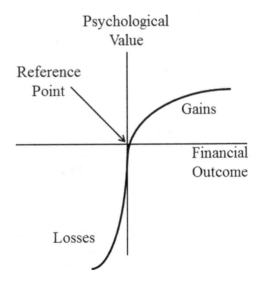

more than gains feel good, individuals may respond differently if a choice is framed as avoiding a loss as opposed to seeking a gain.

By changing the way a decision is framed, the arbitrary reference point is often changed as well. As a result, an individual may approach the same decision differently, depending on the revised reference point. In this sense, a possibility exists that the reference point may change every time a similar decision is made. At the same time, because reference points can be influenced, outcomes can be perceived as more positive based on a changed reference point. In this way, individuals can be guided towards more optimal outcomes by adjusting the influential reference point of a particular decision.

Financial counselors can have a powerful influence on a client's reference point in financial decisions. As an example, a client who likes to gamble may use the initial amount brought to the casino as the reference point and that leaving with any less than that would be a loss, which individuals try to avoid. However, because gambling establishments are built on probabilities in favor of the house, perhaps a better reference point is to set a specific budget that can be used to gamble, as an entertainment activity. Once the budget is exhausted, the client needs to leave the casino. As a second example, a client who likes shopping may believe that purchasing items on sale actually saves money. This perspective uses the retail purchase price as the reference point, and as such, savings are indeed achieved. However, a counselor can help such a client adjust to a more accurate reference point, such as the balance in the bank account or a budgeted category, either of which would show a decrease or loss when a purchase is made.

Tversky and Kahneman (1981) explored decisions with uncertain outcomes, and they discovered that people tend to overweight very unlikely events, and underweight moderately and very likely events. For example, individuals may be willing to spend considerable sums on lottery tickets, in part because they overweight the extremely unlikely probability that they might win. On the other hand, many individuals drive without adequate auto insurance protection, or forego purchasing disability insurance, because they underweight the much more likely probability of experiencing a serious accident. Financial counselors can play an important role in helping their clients consider the actual probabilities of these uncertain events so that they can make decisions that are more in line with what might actually happen.

Biases and Heuristics

Shortly after the development of prospect theory, behavioral economists started identifying *anomalies*, or instances in which observed financial behaviors differed from what might be predicted using rational choice models (Thaler, 1987). These researchers also started studying *biases* that may exist in our reasoning. Biases are systematic and predictable errors in judgment. An example of a bias is loss aversion, since individuals systematically treat losses differently than gains (Kahneman, Knetsch, & Thaler, 1991). Interest in behavioral biases corresponded with an interest in *heuristics*, or mental shortcuts. These shortcuts can be beneficial, especially when they compensate for biases; however, they can also lead to poor financial decisions. Although heuristics are not always helpful, these mental shortcuts can make some decision making easier, and they can lead to somewhat optimal outcomes. What follows is a discussion of some common behavioral biases and heuristics.

Two common examples of biases are the *endowment effect* and the *status quo bias* (Kahneman et al., 1991). The endowment effect suggests that people value things they own or possess more than things they do not own. The endowment effect may just be another example of loss aversion; in other words, "the disutility of giving up an object is greater that the utility associated with acquiring it" (p. 194). More recent research suggests that owning something creates a bond between the item and oneself (Dommer & Swaminathan, 2013). This bond has actual value, thereby increasing the value of owning the item. In financial counseling, the endowment effect can help strengthen a client's commitment if he or she can create a bond with a desired objective or goal. By helping clients "own" the outcomes they desire, financial counselors can increase the likelihood that their clients will achieve their objectives.

The status quo bias is when an individual gives preference for maintaining the status quo, even when it makes financial sense to make a change. Much like inertia, individuals tend to continue behaving as they have in the past unless acted upon by some external force. Financial counselors can explore potential forces that can help clients change negative behaviors that are part of their status quo. Although making a change may require considerable effort, the benefit is that once a new behavior becomes a new habit, it becomes part of a client's status quo, thereby making it difficult to change back to the previous behavior. The obvious caveat is that new behaviors need to be practiced long enough that they become a habit; otherwise, the former status quo may likely return.

In contrast to a behavioral bias as a predictable judgment error, a heuristic is a mental shortcut that can be used to make quicker financial decisions. An example of a heuristic is a shortcut to identify how much someone should be saving for retirement. A common heuristic in this domain is the recommendation to save a certain percentage of income. Another heuristic is to save enough of one's salary to fully benefit from an employer's matching contribution within a retirement plan (Benartzi & Thaler, 2007). These heuristics can be helpful in making financial decisions quickly, but they can also oversimplify those decisions. In the case of saving for retirement, the simple heuristics mentioned previously may result in saving less than is needed for retirement, especially for older individuals who have little or no retirement savings. Alternatively, these heuristics could also generate excess savings, which would reduce one's available financial resources earlier in life.

In general, biases and heuristics in financial decision making are not just fascinating findings; rather, they can lead to suboptimal decisions if individuals are not aware of them and their consequences. Financial counselors who have an awareness of common biases and heuristics are better equipped to identify problematic financial beliefs and behaviors in their clients and help their clients make appropriate adjustments in order to improve financial outcomes.

Two Decision Making Systems

Some of the most recent models of financial decision making have focused on the idea that individuals actually have two mental systems that are involved in making decisions. Kahneman (2011) describes these two systems as System 1 and System 2. System 1 refers to a decision making process that is rather quick, intuitive, and instinctive. System 2 refers to the slow, thoughtful, deliberate, and logical process of making decisions. Both of these systems work in tandem, where System 2 stands by in case System 1 faces a decision to which it is not equipped to respond.

James (2011) describes a two-system model originally proposed by Buddha and further promoted by Haidt (2006). This two-system model is represented visually by an elephant and a rider. The rider has the perception of control, but in truth, the strength of the elephant can dominate the rider's attempts at control. The elephant is also quick to react to emotional responses and innate desires, whereas the rider is much more thoughtful and slow in processing information and decisions.

Other two-system models exist, although they have arguably received less attention. For example, Fudenberg and Levine (2006) and others describe a model of a short-term self and a long-term self who have competing interests. When making decisions in the short run, impatience tends to dominate, where we prefer things now instead of tomorrow. But when decisions involve the future, we do not mind waiting an extra day for a reward. Hershfield (2011) takes a slightly different approach by looking at how we tend to view our present self and our future self. When we view our future self to be similar to our present self, then we make decisions consistent with the interests of our future self. However, because our future self is more *psychologically distant* from our current self, we tend to view our future self differently. We may even view our future self as someone else, which may help explain why some people have a hard time saving for retirement. If they view their future self as someone else, it would be like contributing money towards their neighbor's retirement, not their own. Counselors interested in exploring how a client views their present and future selves can ask them to draw circles to represent these two selves and to draw them in relation to one another as they feel they are (Hershfield, Garton, Ballard, Samanez-Larkin, & Knutson, 2009). Clients with circles that are far apart are more likely to view their future self separately from their present self.

Chen (2013) suggests that language may exacerbate this separation between one's present and future self. Some languages have a different verb conjugation for present tense and future tense, but other languages do not. An example from Chen (2013) shows that the German language tends to have a weak differentiation between the present and future tense. An appropriate way to predict the weather for tomorrow would be to say something like, "It *rains* tomorrow." (Chen, 2013, p. 690, emphasis in original). Conversely, English has a strong future-time reference (FTR), which "would require the use of a future marker like 'will' or 'is going to,' as in: 'It *will* rain tomorrow.'" (Chen, 2013, p. 690, emphasis in original).

Chen (2013) found that speakers of languages that do not require future markers (like German) tend to be more future-oriented. Specifically, Chen (2013) found that speakers of languages with weak FTR (like German) tend to save at a higher rate and retire with relatively higher net worth than speakers of languages with strong FTR. These findings suggest that when people speak without a strong differentiation between the present and the future, they tend to make financial decisions that are focused more on future outcomes. Although changing one's native language is beyond the scope of a financial counselor, using language with clients that strengthens the connection between present behavior and future results may enhance the future orientation of clients and thereby improve financial behaviors and outcomes.

The competing interests, strengths, and weaknesses of the two selves in each of these models create interesting opposition within each individual. They may be acting rationally within the limited perspective of one of the selves while at the same time downplaying the interests of the opposing self. Helping clients grasp an understanding of these opposing selves can be helpful in making more informed decisions that are aligned with the interests of both selves.

Conclusion

The models and frameworks for decision making discussed in this chapter can help financial counselors better understand the approaches that clients may be using when they make financial decisions. As such, counselors who understand these various approaches can potentially have an easier time meeting their clients where they are in their decision making process, and—when needed—guide them to a more appropriate decision making framework.

References

Akerlof, G. A. (1970). The market for "lemons": Quality uncertainty and the market mechanism. *Quarterly Journal of Economics, 84*(3), 488–500.

Benartzi, S., & Thaler, R. H. (2007). Heuristics and biases in retirement savings behavior. *Journal of Economic Perspectives, 21*(3), 81–104.

Bernoulli, D. (1738). Specimen theoriae novae de mensura sortis. Translated from Latin into English by Sommer, L. (1954). Exposition of a new theory on the measurement of risk. *Econometrica, 22*(1), 22–36. https://doi.org/10.2307/1909829

Bernoulli, N. (1713). *Essay d'analyse sur les jeux de hazard [Essays on the analysis of games of chance]* (2nd ed.). Providence, RI: American Mathematical Society Reprinted in 2006 (in French). Translated by Pulskamp, R. J. (2013). Correspondence of Nicolas Bernoulli concerning the St. Petersburg Game.

Britt, S. L., Lawson, D. R., & Haselwood, C. A. (2016). A descriptive analysis of physiological stress and readiness to change. *Journal of Financial Planning, 29*(12), 45–51.

Chen, M. K. (2013). The effect of language on economic behavior: Evidence from savings rates, health behaviors, and retirement assets. *American Economic Review, 103*(2), 690–731.

Dommer, S. L., & Swaminathan, V. (2013). Explaining the endowment effect through ownership: The role of identity, gender, and self-threat. *Journal of Consumer Research, 39*(5), 1034–1050.

Dunn, E. W., Aknin, L. B., & Norton, M. I. (2008). Spending money on others promotes happiness. *Science, 319*, 1687–1688.

Evans, G. W., & Schamberg, M. A. (2009). Childhood poverty, chronic stress, and adult working memory. *Proceedings of the National Academy of Sciences, 106*(16), 6545–6549.

Ford, M. R., Grable, J., Kruger, M., & DeGraff, A. (2017). Physiological arousal during couple financial discussions as a precursor to seeking financial planning help. *Journal of Financial Therapy, 8*(1), 1–20. https://doi.org/10.4148/1944-9771.1131

Fudenberg, D., & Levine, D. K. (2006). A dual-self model of impulse control. *The American Economic Review, 96*(5), 1449–1476.

Grable, J. E., & Britt, S. L. (2012). Assessing client stress and why it matters to financial advisors. *Journal of Financial Service Professionals, 66*(2), 39–45.

Haidt, J. (2006). *The happiness hypothesis: Finding modern truth in ancient wisdom*. New York, NY: Basic Books.

Harrison, Y., & Horne, J. A. (2000). The impact of sleep deprivation on decision making: A review. *Journal of Experimental Psychology: Applied, 6*(3), 236–249.

Hershfield, H. E. (2011). Future self-continuity: How conceptions of the future self transform intertemporal choice. *Annals of the New York Academy of Sciences, 1235*(1), 30–43.

Hershfield, H. E., Garton, M. T., Ballard, K., Samanez-Larkin, G. R., & Knutson, B. (2009). Don't stop thinking about tomorrow: Individual differences in future self-continuity account for saving. *Judgment and Decision Making, 4*(4), 280–286.

Hill, G., & Howell, R. T. (2014). Moderators and mediators of pro-social spending and well-being: The influence of values and psychological need satisfaction. *Personality and Individual Differences, 69*, 69–74.

James, R. (2011). Applying neuroscience to financial planning practice: A framework and review. *Journal of Personal Finance, 10*(2), 10–65.

Kahneman, D. (2011). *Thinking, fast and slow*. New York, NY: Farrar, Straus and Giroux.

Kahneman, D., & Deaton, A. (2010). High income improves evaluation of life but not emotional well-being. *Proceedings of the National Academy of Sciences, 107*(38), 16489–16493.

Kahneman, D., Knetsch, J. L., & Thaler, R. H. (1991). The endowment effect, loss aversion, and status quo bias. *American Economic Review, 5*(1), 193–206.

Kahneman, D., & Tversky, A. (1979). Prospect theory: An analysis of decision under risk. *Econometrica: Journal of the Econometric Society, 47*, 263–291.

Lusardi, A., & Mitchell, O. S. (2014). The economic importance of financial literacy: Theory and evidence. *Journal of Economic Literature, 52*(1), 5–44.

Matz, S. C., Gladstone, J. J., & Stillwell, D. (2016). Money buys happiness when spending fits our personality. *Psychological Science, 27*(5), 715–725.

Ordonez, L., & Benson, L. (1997). Decisions under time pressure: How time constraint affects risky decision making. *Organizational Behavior and Human Decision Processes, 71*(2), 121–140.

Prawitz, A. D., Garman, E. T., Sorhaindo, B., O'Neill, B., Kim, J., & Drentea, P. (2006). InCharge Financial Distress/Financial Well-Being Scale: Development, administration, and score interpretation. *Financial Counseling and Planning, 17*(1), 34–50.

Rick, S. I., Small, D. A., & Finkel, E. J. (2011). Fatal (fiscal) attraction: Spendthrifts and tightwads in marriage. *Journal of Marketing Research, 48*(2), 228–237.

Simms, J. R. (2010). Making the soft sciences hard: The Newton model. *Systems Research and Behavioral Science, 28*(1), 40–50.

Simon, H. A. (1955). A behavioral model of rational choice. *Quarterly Journal of Economics, 69*(1), 99–118.

Simon, H. A. (1978). The uses of mathematics in the social sciences. *Mathematics and Computers in Simulation, 20*, 159–166.

Thaler, R. H. (1987). Anomalies: The january effect. *The Journal of Economic Perspectives, 1*(1), 197–201.

Tversky, A., & Kahneman, D. (1981). The framing of decisions and the psychology of choice. *Science, 211*(4481), 453–458.

Vohs, K. D., Baumeister, R. F., Schmeichel, B. J., Twenge, J. M., Nelson, N. M., & Tice, D. M. (2014). Making choices impairs subsequent self-control: A limited-resource account of decision making, self-regulation, and active initiative. *Motivation Science, 1*(S), 19–42.

Von Neumann, J., & Morgenstern, O. (1944). *Theory of games and economic behavior*. Princeton, NJ: Princeton University Press.

Chapter 10
Making the Science Practical: Behavioral Interventions in Practice

Sarah Newcomb and Benjamin F. Cummings

> *In theory, theory and practice are the same. In practice, they are not.*
>
> —*Albert Einstein*

Outside the small circle of economic theorists, the idea that people make financial decisions based on highly personal reference points is not exactly revolutionary. It is merely common knowledge that social, cultural, and emotional factors play a role in daily financial decisions. Luxury and niche brands exist to capitalize on this fact, as do the experience and entertainment economies. In fact, considerable work on psychology and financial decision making has been published in research journals aimed at marketing professionals (e.g., Kahnx, Ratner, & Kahneman, 1997; Novemsky & Kahneman, 2005; Thaler, 1985).

Clearly, there are non-financial aspects to purchases, and the field of economics is rightly evolving to better measure and model these factors. The more subjective and psychological factors that predict poor financial decisions are understood, the closer financial professionals get to finding ways to help their clients overcome them. However, creating workable mathematical models of human behavior based on subjective variables like emotional or social utility is extremely difficult, and often painfully slow.

From a practitioner's perspective, the important question is not "Why do people make seemingly irrational decisions?" but rather "What can financial counselors do about it?" It is not difficult to understand the benefit of learning about the motives that drive irrational financial decisions. What is difficult is putting this knowledge to use in a practical and efficient way. While behavioral science continues to add more revealed biases to an already enormous list, and new ways we harm ourselves

S. Newcomb (✉)
Morningstar, Inc., Washington, DC, USA
e-mail: Sarah.newcomb@morningstar.com

B. F. Cummings
The American College of Financial Services, Bryn Mawr, PA, USA

© Springer Nature Switzerland AG 2019
D. B. Durband et al. (eds.), *Financial Counseling*,
https://doi.org/10.1007/978-3-319-72586-4_10

financially are continuously being discovered, advisors and coaches are left to make sense of this glut of information without a guide. How do financial counselors create actionable solutions to the myriad behavioral risks clients face? This is where the work on behavioral *interventions* becomes important.

Interventions are attempts to intervene in the decision-making process in order to minimize the effect of behavioral biases. Interventions can be as simple as sending a reminder email about an upcoming counseling appointment to reduce program dropout, or as intensive as talking through and deconstructing a person's early childhood experiences with money.

Unfortunately, the body of work on financial interventions is much smaller than the research that reveals irrational behaviors. In addition, much of the work that has been published thus far was performed in the confines of research laboratories with limited populations. Financial decisions are fraught with irrational biases, and while some clues exist about how individuals might overcome or reduce the effects of these biases, no definitive order exists that maps symptoms to causes to cures. The field is simply too young.

Armed with the understanding that this burgeoning field is likely to bring more changes and surprises in the coming years, this article has arranged the plethora of current behavioral interventions into three broad categories: Nudges, education, and high-touch coaching. The following sections provide a brief overview of each type of intervention and examples of how they can be employed. A simple decision tree is also included, which can be helpful for determining when to use which kind of intervention in a financial counseling practice.

Nudges: Small Changes with Big Results

Most people who are familiar with behavioral economics have heard the term *nudge* in the context of behavioral change. The term was coined by Cass Sunstein and Richard Thaler in their *New York Times* bestselling book by the same name (Thaler & Sunstein, 2008). In this book, which aims to explain the concept of nudges to the layman, the authors argue the merits of making small changes in choice environments in order to help people make decisions that are better aligned with their long-term best interest. The act of nudging is more formally referred to as *choice architecture*.

Choice Architecture

Human beings are sensitive to the way in which options are presented. For example, explaining the benefits of preventive surgery in terms of increased *survival* rates rather than decreased *death* rates can increase interest in treatment (Armstrong, Schwartz, Fitzgerald, Putt, & Ubel, 2002). Choice architecture is the practice of strategically designing the way in which options will be presented to people. A nudge is a choice architecture that has been designed to subtly push, or nudge, decision-makers toward a particular choice. Perhaps the most famous example of a successful nudge is the practice of defaulting employees into a company retirement plan rather than requiring them to enroll on their own. When a company employs this tactic, employees have full freedom to decline participation in the program, but if they do not indicate otherwise, they will be enrolled in the savings plan. This approach replaced the previous procedure requiring people to indicate that they wanted to participate; otherwise, they were not enrolled. This nudge has been adopted by many employers and has resulted in a dramatic increase in retirement plan participation rates (Choi, Laibson, Madrian, & Metrick, 2001), although some measures show that contribution amounts under auto-enrollment are lower (Butricia & Karamcheva, 2015).

Choice architecture is used in many places. Menus, store layouts, websites, and voting ballots are all examples of places where choice architecture is involved. Any time we are presented with options, there is a structure to those options; whether the design is intentional or not is irrelevant. Even cafeteria workers who decide if they will put healthy foods or desserts first in the display have an effect on the choices that kids make when filling their trays (Thaler & Sunstein, 2008). For this reason, anyone who is responsible for presenting others with options is a *choice architect*. By nature of the work they do, financial counselors are choice architects for their clients. This fact is unavoidable, so it is best to understand some best practices for presenting options to clients.

In general, automation is the easiest option for nudging follow through on financial behaviors that people *intend* to do but have difficulty actually doing. If a client is able to have money deposited automatically from a paycheck into a savings account, he or she does not need to perform this kind of transaction after every paycheck. Automation removes friction, complexity, and resistance. The advent of automatic bill payment can be a boon to many people's credit scores and help avoid late fees and interest charges that would otherwise be incurred due to simple forgetfulness or disorganization. Automation uses the phenomenon of inertia to benefit rather than to harm. However, automation is not always ideal due to logistical factors, and some people may consider it an imposition on their personal freedoms. Still, many people find automating financial transactions to be a great organization aid, reducing the cognitive load they need to carry on a daily basis.

A few more financial nudges that show promise include:

One study run by the US government's behavioral sciences unit found a significant increase in college enrollment for low-income citizens by having tax preparers offer to help complete FAFSA applications at the same time. Since the two forms require the same information, combining the tasks reduced friction, perceived complexity, and inertia (Social and Behavioral Sciences Team, 2015)

The Save More Tomorrow program automatically increases employees' savings rates when they receive a raise. A randomized control trial of this technique showed that the average savings rates of people in the program increased from 3.5 to 13.6% over the course of 3.5 years. By comparison, the savings rates of those in the control group did not rise (Thaler & Benartzi, 2004)

Texts with goal-specific reminders of the reasons for saving helped increase savings rates compared to a control group. Reminders that were not goal-specific also increased savings, but not to the extent that goal-specific reminders did (Karlan, McConnell, Mullainathan, & Zinman, 2010)

Some of these methods may be feasible within a financial counseling practice, and others will not. For example, financial counselors who are involved with the Volunteer Income Tax Assistance (VITA) program may be able to help clients with Free Application for Federal Student Aid (FAFSA) forms while also helping with their tax preparation. They may be able to offer timely reminders to increase savings when they are anticipating a raise or bonus, and in some circumstances to set up automatic text reminders for important financial tasks. There are thousands of possible ways to nudge financial behavior. These are only a few that have been tested using randomized control trials and show positive results.

The Paradox of Choice

As helpful as automation and reminders can be, many financial choices require active decision-making on the part of the consumer. Investment allocation decisions, choosing between lenders and financial product offerings, and deciding between consumer product options are just a few. Today, consumers enjoy more access to information and more freedom of choice than at any other time in history. With the internet came the ability to access boundless information on nearly any topic, but this has posed problems as well as opportunities. Rather than ease the decision-making process, having so much freedom, and so many options from which to choose, can increase selection difficulty, which has been shown to be a key driver of decision avoidance. This phenomenon, often called *choice paralysis*, describes the fact that many people freeze when they are faced with a choice that has myriad possible solutions. Because they fear doing the wrong thing, they do nothing, often to their own detriment.

For example, imagine Steven, a new employee at Ace, Inc. On his first day of work, he is presented with a packet of forms and information about the company's health, dental, and vision plans, his automatic deposit and savings options, and the company's 401(k) program. This choice environment is overwhelming to him, since he is simultaneously thinking about his new role, responsibilities, office and colleagues, as well as what to do with his 401(k) from his previous employer. He feels pressed for time and confused by all the options. He does not know whether to enroll in the HSA or the FSA, let alone which of the 20 investment options available would best suit his long-term needs. Simply having information and freedom of choice is not enough. We often need direction and guidance as well.

Decision Aids

To ease the perceived complexity of decision-making in choice environments, decision aids are helpful. Calorie counts on menus, star ratings on investment funds, and side-by-side comparisons of product features are all examples of decision aids that can help reduce perceived complexity and increase confidence when making a choice. Decision aids can take many forms, but they tend to focus on key attributes that are important to the decision-maker.

In the financial counseling environment, it may be especially useful to develop decision aids for clients that compare the key factors of financial products, services, and tradeoffs for complex choices. To aid clients, financial counselors may find it useful to develop comparison charts for various types of financial products such as auto loans, payday loans, rent-to-own vs. save-to-own options, and for other decisions that can have a long-term impact on a client's financial stability if key attributes are not known or carefully considered.

Decision aids help people make choices because they reduce the perceived complexity of the task, and thereby help to overcome choice paralysis and improve confidence in one's decision-making ability (Broniarczyk & Griffin, 2014). This may be especially important for those who do not have high levels of financial literacy. A study of employees faced with several options for their company retirement funds found that offering star ratings for the fund choices improved decision satisfaction among low-knowledge investors by making the task seem less complex (Morrin, Broniarczyk, & Inman, 2012).

Policy, Paternalism, and the Importance of Ethics

While some financial choices can be automated, and the world of financial technology is making this easier and more cost-effective every day, there are limitations on how much power a financial counselor has to change a person's choice environment. It may be very effective to nudge FAFSA applications at a tax preparer's office, but if a financial counselor does not have the resources or opportunity to organize that kind of intervention, then its potential effectiveness is somewhat irrelevant. The difficult reality may be that a financial counselor may not be able to implement nudges beyond emails and text reminders. For many of these interventions to be truly effective, a much larger, societal effort is required.

On a national scale, policymakers have taken note of the potential of nudges to improve the financial lives of Americans. In 2015, President Obama issued an executive order advising government agencies to incorporate the findings from behavioral economics into their communications and policies (Executive Order No. 13707, 2015). This was a direct implementation of what Thaler and Sunstein called *libertarian paternalism*: Libertarian because it preserves the autonomy and freedom of those being nudged, and paternalism because the method takes a stance that those nudging know best.

The challenge for choice architects lies in earnestly considering the ethics involved. Any time professionals present others with choices, they are in fact influencing those choices by the way in which the information is presented. As such, the decision-maker must be treated with respect while also preserving their autonomy. Ethics are paramount. Financial counselors serve to aid people in their financial choices. The insights from behavioral economics can help increase the sense of responsibility that accompanies such a role, and to avoid, or work against, any unintended negative consequences of the choice environments presented to others.

Knowledge: The Value of Financial Education in Advice

In some cases, policymakers have begun to put pressure on private businesses to include consumer-focused nudges in their product literature. Credit card statements have, in recent years, begun to simplify their language, and now include comparison charts that show how a consumer can save significantly on interest by making additional or larger monthly payments. These types of interventions are similar to nudges, but they aim to influence behavior by increasing knowledge and improving comprehension. Education, or improving knowledge, is another form of intervention. Many financial professionals find that their role requires them to be an educator to clients, but the value of financial education is another issue of heated debate. Hundreds of follow-up studies have been performed to measure the effects of financial education. Some report that financial education programs have a significant effect on savings rates and improve financial decisions, while others show little or no impact. A meta-analysis of more than 200 individual studies showed that the effect size of education, while often significant, was small, and knowledge gained was rapidly forgotten (Fernandes, Lynch, & Netemeyer, 2014). Due to the rapid decay of new knowledge observed in these studies, some advocate for a method of teaching known as just-in-time education, which offers hope by intervening with information close to the moment of decision, in order to avoid the knowledge being forgotten before it can be put to use.

Just-In-Time Education

Just-in-time education enjoys the benefits of two behavioral factors. First, when one actively seeks information on a topic, he or she is more engaged, and as a result, is a better student. Second, when one learns something just before needing the knowledge, he or she is less likely to forget it because of the ability to quickly apply what was learned. The problem with just-in-time education is that the responsibility for seeking out knowledge is in the hands of the unknowing individual, who may be vulnerable to the unscrupulous who would like to take advantage of their lack of understanding.

This problem can in part be overcome in practice because financial counselors are in an ideal role to offer just-in-time education to clients. Financial counselors see when clients are facing major decisions and can offer specific advice in the moment of greatest relevance.

Rules-of-Thumb

Another approach to education that shows some promise is a rule-of-thumb approach. Heuristics can impede good decisions, but many scholars believe that they can help as well. Gerd Gigerenzer and his team of researchers at the Max Planck Institute advocate for what are called *smart heuristics* (Gigerenzer, Todd, and ABC Research Group, 1999). These are rules-of-thumb that make decision-making easier. The idea is that, while some mental shortcuts lead to bad decisions because they ignore important information or focus on the wrong things, cognitive shortcuts can be an adaptive trait to help individuals make good decisions when they don't have all the necessary information, or time to consider all of it. The same "follow-the-herd" instinct that may cause a person to invest in an overvalued stock could save their life if the crowd is running away from a true physical threat. The idea of smart heuristics is simple: the right rule-of-thumb in the right situation can help make decisions easier and faster. It is matching the rule to the circumstance that is important (Gigerenzer, Todd, and ABC Research Group, 1999).

When it comes to teaching financial concepts, some work with small business owners shows promise. In the Dominican Republic, researchers split business owners with limited financial knowledge into two groups. The first group took an accounting course, and the second group learned simple rules-of-thumb. Over the next year, those who had the accounting class showed no change in business or accounting practices, but those who had been taught rules-of-thumb showed significant improvement in both (Drexler, Fischer, & Schoar, 2014).

Rules-of-thumb work with our natural tendency to reduce complex ideas to simple heuristics. They are easy to remember, can apply to many situations, and they do not require a heavy cognitive load. For this reason, they can be beneficial teaching tools.

Decision aids can also be used as discussion starters. Consider a chart comparing save-to-own vs. rent-to-own strategies for a new living room set, an example of which is in Table 10.1.

This decision aid can help foster a conversation about the tradeoffs clients face between saving for 9 months to purchase something at retail value or borrowing and paying for twice as long for something that is only worth half of what they would pay in total. While some clients may still value immediate acquisition more than reason, drawing attention to the true dollar cost of impatience may convince a few. Adding a general rule-of-thumb may also be useful here: "If you pay more than retail value, you end up poorer as a result of the trade." This could also be an opportunity to discuss how assets should maintain resale value over time.

Like nudges, there are thousands of rules-of-thumb. Table 10.2 offers a few that may be of use for financial counseling clients.

Table 10.1 Couch and loveseat set: purchase option comparison

Retail value	$1330	
	Save-to-own	*Rent-to-own*
Amount per week	$35	$35
Number of weeks	38	78
Total spent	$1330	$2730
Difference		*$1400*

Table 10.2 Potential rules-of-thumb for a variety of financial topics

Topic	Rule-of-thumb
Saving	Strive for 20% of earnings (including employer match)
	Try to have 3 months of expenses saved in case disaster strikes
Debt	Keep balances to 20% or less of available credit
	Always pay more than the minimum due on credit cards
	Borrow less for school than what income is expected to be in the first year after graduation
Investment	Invest in a broadly diversified portfolio throughout life
	Indexes are less risky than individual stocks
	ETFs tend to have lower fees than mutual funds
	When interest rates rise, bond prices fall
Economics	Prices on everything double just about every 25 years
	Assets earn more than they cost
	Liabilities cost more than they earn
	Land, labor, and capital are the three ways of earning money

High-Touch Interventions

In some cases, there is simply no easy fix. Nudges and rules-of-thumb can pale in comparison with the influential power of social pressure, family culture, and other human factors. If financial counselors find themselves working with clients with behaviors that are resistant to simple cures, they may want to try behavioral coaching. If a client is willing, simple assessment tools can be used to determine which, if any, of their mental frameworks might be sabotaging their financial health. This approach can help counselors work with clients over time to change the underlying issue. This is not psychotherapy, but it does draw on lessons from psychology.

For example, many people unwittingly damage their financial security because of unhealthy personal narratives in which they cast money as a villain or as the "root of all evil."[1] Others have an insatiable hunger for the freedom and status that money can

---

[1] This biblical reference is often misquoted. 1 Timothy 6:10, which is often cited as the source for this belief, actually specifies "the *love* of money" to be the root of all evil, not money itself. This clarifying distinction can have important implications for some Christian clients.

buy. Some people feel that the world of money is not open to them because of their upbringing, or their lack of knowledge. These personal narratives—sometimes called money scripts (Klontz & Klontz, 2009)—can be limiting, and even destructive, if left unexamined. Tips and tools for uncovering and working with personal financial narratives are addressed in greater detail in Chap. 11 of this book.

Time perspective can be another handicap. Studies focusing on future self-continuity suggest that "When the future self shares similarities with the present self, when it is viewed in vivid and realistic terms, and when it is seen in a positive light, people are more willing to make choices today that may benefit them at some point in the years to come" (Hershfield, 2011, p. 30). In a study performed by Morningstar, Inc., people who had planned 20 or more years into the future had, on average, 20 times more money saved for retirement than those who had only planned about a year ahead (Newcomb, 2017). Clients who are living hand-to-mouth may struggle to think further ahead than a week at a time. While this is perfectly understandable, the "propensity to plan" has been shown to be a key factor in financial success (Lynch, Netemeyer, Spiller, & Zammit, 2010). Helping people to stretch their planning horizon, little by little, can build a foundation for future security. Running a marathon is out of the question until one can first run around the block. Likewise, to a person who cannot plan past their next paycheck, planning for retirement feels irrelevant. Mental time horizon and the propensity to plan are crucial for developing long-term financial stability, but these often take concerted effort to develop.

Visualization exercises can help people to elongate their mental time horizon and shrink the psychological distance between the present and the future. When thinking of things that are far away in time, individuals tend to picture them in vague, abstract terms. By adding detail and clarity to the mental picture of the future, the abstract becomes more concrete, which may help clients care more about that future and about making it a good one. In tests with undergraduate students, those who interacted with an age-progressed version of their own faces reported higher intentions to save than those who did not (Hershfield, 2011). By picturing the future clearly, imagining it in detail, and picturing what it will be like to enjoy the fruits of financial stability, clients can increase their concern for their future self, which can help motivate future-oriented behaviors.

Helping people to develop a long-term mindset, and build a propensity to plan, as well as countering damaging financial beliefs can take time. Behavioral financial coaching is a very new field, and there is little in the way of definitive, best-practice advice. Recognizing that financial decisions are not made in a vacuum, but are affected by one's hopes, dreams, identities, beliefs, and cultural norms is an important step. Helping clients to recognize this for themselves is another. Changing behavior at its root requires a level of self-awareness at which not all clients will be willing to engage. Behavioral coaching requires mutual effort on the part of financial counselor and client, or it will not be effective.

With so many options and no clearly prescribed path, it can be daunting for financial counselors to try to adopt behavioral techniques in practice. To help, Fig. 10.1 offers a simple decision aid for coaches to assist in choosing which type of intervention may be best suited to their needs in a particular instance.

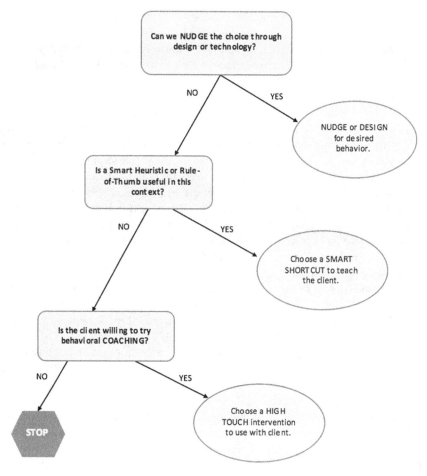

Fig. 10.1 Fast and frugal intervention selection. Source: Morningstar, Inc.

Conclusion

The science of decision-making is offering insight into the roots of financial behavior. In the past few decades, hundreds of heuristics and biases have been discovered that describe ways in which humans veer from rational behavior in financial decisions. Still, the science is very young, and few methods have been proven for reversing the effects of these biases. Nudges, technological assistance, decision aids, timely rules-of-thumb, and conscious perspective changes are all tools that financial counselors can use to try to improve their client's chances of building long-term financial security.

References

Armstrong, K., Schwartz, J. S., Fitzgerald, G., Putt, M., & Ubel, P. A. (2002). Effect of framing as gain versus loss on understanding and hypothetical treatment choices: Survival and mortality curves. *Medical Decision Making, 22*(1), 76–83.

Broniarczyk, S. M., & Griffin, J. G. (2014). Decision difficulty in the age of consumer empowerment. *Journal of Consumer Psychology, 24*(4), 608–625. Retrieved from https://pdfs.semanticscholar.org/6504/2c35457c8894e383ca19ac16d8f7aaad4434.pdf

Butricia, B., & Karamcheva, N. (2015). The relationship between automatic enrollment and DC plan contributions: Evidence from a national survey of older workers. *Center for Retirement Research,* Working Paper 2015-14.

Choi, J. J., Laibson, D., Madrian, B. C., & Metrick, A. (2001). Defined contribution pensions: *Plan rules, participant decisions, and the path of least resistance.* NBER Working Paper No. 8655. Retrieved from: http://www.nber.org/papers/w8655.pdf

Drexler, A., Fischer, G., & Schoar, A. (2014). Keeping it simple: Financial literacy and rules of thumb. *American Economic Journal: Applied Economics, 6*(2), 1–31.

Fernandes, D., Lynch, J., & Netemeyer, R. (2014). Financial literacy, financial education, and downstream financial behaviors. *Management Science, 60*(8), 1861–1883.

Gigerenzer, G., Todd, P. M., & ABC Research Group. (1999). *Simple heuristics that make us smart.* New York: Oxford University Press.

Hershfield, H. E. (2011). Future self-continuity: How conceptions of the future self transform intertemporal choice. *Annals of the New York Academy of Sciences, 1235*(1), 30–43.

Kahnx, B., Ratner, R., & Kahneman, D. (1997). Patterns of hedonic consumption over time. *Marketing Letters, 8*(1), 85–96.

Karlan, D., McConnell, M., Mullainathan, S., & Zinman, J. (2010). *Getting to the top of mind: How reminders increase saving.* NBER Working Paper 16205. Retrieved from http://www.nber.org/papers/w16205.pdf

Klontz, B., & Klontz, T. (2009). *Mind over money: Overcoming the money disorders that threaten our financial health.* New York: Crown Business.

Lynch Jr., J., Netemeyer, R., Spiller, S., & Zammit, A. (2010). A generalizable scale of propensity to plan: The long and the short of planning for time and for money. *Journal of Consumer Research, 37*(1), 108–128.

Morrin, M., Broniarczyk, S. M., & Inman, J. J. (2012). Plan format and participation in 401(k) plans: The moderating role of investor knowledge. *Journal of Public Policy & Marketing, 31*(2), 254–268.

Newcomb, S. (2017). *When more is less: Rethinking financial health.* Chicago, IL: Morningstar, Inc.

Novemsky, N., & Kahneman, D. (2005). The boundaries of loss aversion. *Journal of Marketing Research, 42*(2), 119–128.

Office of the President. (2015, September 15). *Using behavioral science insights to better serve the american people* (E.O. 13707, pp. 56365–56367, Document No. 2015-23630).

Social and Behavioral Sciences Team. (2015). *Social and behavioral sciences team annual report.* Retrieved from https://sbst.gov/download/2015%20SBST%20Annual%20Report.pdf

Thaler, R. (1985). Mental accounting and consumer choice. *Marketing Science, 4*(3), 199–214.

Thaler, R. H., & Benartzi, S. (2004). Save More Tomorrow™: Using behavioral economics to increase employee saving. *Journal of Political Economy, 112*(S1), S164–S187.

Thaler, R. H., & Sunstein, C. R. (2008). *Nudge: Improving decisions about health, wealth, and happiness.* New York: Penguin Books.

Chapter 11
Identifying Problematic Financial Behaviors and Money Disorders

Bradley T. Klontz and Derek R. Lawson

Introduction

The majority of Americans cite money as one of the top stressors in their lives, and those with lower incomes report experiencing the highest levels of stress (American Psychological Association, 2016). Often, financial stress drives clients to seek the assistance of financial counselors and other professionals. Sometimes, a client's financial stress is due to not only a lack of financial resources but a lack of financial literacy (for a discussion on financial literacy, please refer to Chap. 2). In these cases, financial counselors are well equipped to offer the financial information, tools, and strategies to help clients better navigate their financial lives. This can include helping clients analyze cash flow, set up a budget and track spending, establish savings goals, and develop a plan to service debt. After providing their expert advice, financial counselors often consult with clients to help keep them on track and navigate changes and challenges to their plans.

However, it is not uncommon for financial professionals to work with clients who do not seem to benefit from their education and encouragement. Even when financial counselors offer their best analysis and advice, some clients are not able to initiate action, maintain momentum, and execute lasting change. A lack of readiness for change has been identified as a common roadblock to counseling effectiveness across a range of professions, including medical, mental health, and personal finance. In their development of the transtheoretical model, Prochaska, Norcross, and DiClemente (1994) identified a six-stage change process. They identified the fourth stage as the "action" phase, wherein clients are ready to implement and carry out change. They note that only 20% of clients are in the action phase around a given challenge at a

B. T. Klontz (✉)
Heider College of Business, Creighton University, Omaha, NE, USA

D. R. Lawson
Institute of Personal Financial Planning, Kansas State University, Manhattan, KS, USA

© Springer Nature Switzerland AG 2019
D. B. Durband et al. (eds.), *Financial Counseling*,
https://doi.org/10.1007/978-3-319-72586-4_11

given time (please refer to Chap. 7 for more information on the transtheoretical model). The application of tools and techniques that financial counselors can use to help clients navigate through these stages of change in their financial lives has been explored in recent years (Horwitz & Klontz, 2013; Klontz, Horwitz, & Klontz, 2015; Klontz, Kahler, & Klontz, 2016), some of which are discussed below.

At times, the skillful use of counseling techniques designed to motivate clients towards action is effective in initiating and maintaining client change. In other cases, counselor interventions are not successful in facilitating change. This lack of success could be due to myriad of client and counselor factors. In some cases, however, clients appear to be engaging in chronic, self-destructive financial behaviors. Despite the counselor's best efforts, some clients are either unable or unwilling to change. For these individuals, their financial problems are not due to a lack of information or strategies. Instead, they may be suffering from a money disorder.

Money Scripts and Disordered Money Behaviors

The close link between beliefs and behaviors is the hallmark of psychological treatment approaches, including cognitive-behavioral therapy (CBT). At the heart of CBT, there is the understanding that distorted beliefs are the cause of self-defeating behaviors (Beck, 2011). As such, a primary approach to treatment is to identify, challenge, and change these problematic beliefs. Research has linked money beliefs to financial behaviors. For example, money status beliefs, such as believing that one's self-worth equals their net worth (Klontz, Britt, Mentzer, & Klontz, 2011), have been found to predict disordered money behaviors including compulsive buying disorder, gambling disorder, and financial dependence (Klontz & Britt, 2012). Accordingly, the following sections review each of the four money scripts that have been identified. These include money avoidance, money worship, money status, and money vigilance.

Money Avoidance

Money avoidance can be defined as a belief that money is bad or evil and that wealthy people are corrupt and greedy (Klontz et al., 2011; Klontz & Britt, 2012). Individuals with money avoidance beliefs may blame others for their financial behaviors, avoid spending money on necessary items, or unconsciously spend money (Klontz et al. 2011; Klontz & Britt, 2012). As a result, individuals with money avoidance beliefs might reject their financial responsibility and attempt to avoid dealing with money altogether (Klontz & Klontz, 2009). Money avoidance beliefs might also increase anxiety, induce fear, and can bring about feelings of disgust around money (Klontz et al. 2011; Klontz & Britt, 2012; Taylor, Klontz, & Britt, 2016).

Research has indicated that individuals who hold money avoidant beliefs tend to have lower levels of income and net worth, and that these individuals may not even know how much they earn or what their net worth is (Klontz et al., 2011; Klontz & Britt, 2012). Other research has supported the notion that money avoidant beliefs are negatively associated with income (Klontz, Seay, Sullivan, & Canale, 2014; Klontz, Sullivan, Seay, & Canale, 2015). Single people and young adults were most likely to endorse money avoidance beliefs, and money avoidance beliefs tend to decrease with age (Klontz et al., 2011). Klontz and Britt (2012) found that money avoidance beliefs positively predicted financial enabling, financial denial, hoarding and compulsive buying, and workaholism. Profession may also be associated with money beliefs. Research has found that mental health professionals, when compared to other professionals such as financial advisors and other business men and women, are more likely to hold money avoidance beliefs (Britt, Klontz, Tibbetts, & Leitz, 2015; Klontz & Britt, 2012).

Money Worship

The belief that more money will result in more happiness is the basic premise of money worship (Klontz et al., 2016). Individuals who endorse money worship beliefs are obsessed with the notion that the acquisition of more money will help them advance in life (Britt et al., 2015). Money worshippers believe that they can never have enough money, and that they will not be able to afford what they want (Klontz & Britt, 2012). That is, they perceive that their needs will never be met resulting in a viscous cycle in which there will always be some dollar amount or physical item they believe will make them happier (Lawson, Klontz, & Britt, 2015).

Klontz et al. (2011) found individuals who were younger, single, and had lower (or unknown) levels of net worth were most likely to have money worship beliefs. Additionally, their research indicated that money worshippers were more likely to carry credit card debt from month-to-month. Money worship beliefs were found to be negatively associated with income (Klontz et al., 2014) and risk planning (Britt et al., 2015). Klontz and Britt (2012) found money worship beliefs positively predicted financial enabling and financial denial. Similar to money avoidance, Klontz and Britt (2012) found that individuals with money worship beliefs were more likely to exhibit hoarding and compulsive buying, and that money worship beliefs positively predict workaholism. Additionally, they found money worship beliefs to be positively associated with financial dependence.

Money Status

Individuals with money status beliefs endorse a tendency to buy the newest, most expensive things, and equate their self-worth with their net worth (Klontz & Britt, 2012). These individuals believe that money gives them status and they relate their money with their socioeconomic status, seeing clear distinctions between the classes

(Klontz et al., 2011). They tend to be materialistic, and therefore, competitive in terms of wanting to acquire more than those around them (Klontz et al., 2011). Money status differs from money worship in that money worshippers are concerned with the positive feelings money can give them, whereas those with money status beliefs are overly focused on an outward display of their money to garner the respect of others (Lawson et al., 2015).

Research on money status has shown that the individuals who endorse these beliefs tend to be younger, non-married, and have lower levels of income and education (Klontz et al., 2011; Klontz & Britt, 2012). Additionally, they are more likely to have been raised in a lower socioeconomic class (Klontz & Britt, 2012). However, more recent research found that very high income earners (those earning greater than $154,000 per year), were 9.9 times more likely to hold money status beliefs (Klontz et al., 2014). Money status beliefs have been found to be positively associated with compulsive buying, gambling disorder, financial dependence, and financial infidelity, or lying to one's partner or spouse regarding spending behaviors (Klontz & Britt, 2012).

Money Vigilance

The money vigilant are typically more alert and watchful of their finances and strongly believe it is important to save for the future. Money vigilance beliefs appear to have a protective effect, minimizing the likelihood of negative financial outcomes (Klontz & Britt, 2012). These individuals tend to not like financial gifts and/or handouts as they believe that one should work for their money (Klontz & Britt, 2012). They are more likely to pay with cash and thus, less likely to have credit card debt (Klontz & Britt, 2012). However, individuals who hold money vigilance beliefs may also be anxious around money and more secretive about their financial status; that is, they are less trustful around others regarding their financial affairs (Klontz et al., 2011; Klontz & Britt, 2012).

The research on money vigilance has indicated that it is associated with positive financial outcomes. The money vigilant tend to be high income earners with higher net worth (Klontz & Britt, 2012; Klontz, Horwitz, et al., 2015). Klontz and Britt (2012) found money vigilance beliefs to be negatively associated with the compulsive buying, gambling disorder, financial enabling, financial denial, and financial infidelity. Individuals who hold money vigilance scripts are also more likely to engage in risk planning and have higher levels of financial health (Britt et al., 2015). However, the money vigilant can be overly anxious around money with negative money behaviors ensuing. This could include hiding money under the mattress or using only savings accounts, which would guarantee an erosion of net worth due to inflation. Klontz et al. (2011) mention that excessive wariness and/or anxiety around money may lead these individuals to have less positive experiences with their money and end up not providing the "sense of security that money can provide" (p. 17).

Money Disorders

Disordered money behaviors have been defined as "maladaptive patterns of financial beliefs and behaviors that lead to clinically significant distress, impairment in social or occupational functioning, undue financial strain or an inability to appropriately enjoy one's financial resources… These maladaptive behaviors persist despite their emotional, relational, and financial consequences" (Klontz, Bivens, Klontz, Wada, & Kahler, 2008, p. 295–296).

A distinction has been made between problematic financial behaviors and money disorders (Klontz et al., 2016). Money disorders are recognized by the medical field as formal mental disorders, can be diagnosed using the *Diagnostic and Statistical Manual of Mental Disorders*, Fifth Edition (DSM-5™), and are treated by mental health professionals (Klontz et al., 2016). In contrast, Klontz et al. describe problematic financial behaviors as clusters of symptoms associated with money disorders or unique syndromes in themselves that have not yet been classified as distinct mental disorders but may require treatment from a mental health professional. Money disorders are distinctly different than problematic financial behaviors and the following sections will help identify those differences as descriptions of commonly seen money disorders and other problematic financial behaviors are presented. When a financial counselor sees these disordered money behaviors in clients and their typical advice and suggestions are not effective in helping a client change his or her behaviors, further assessment may be needed and a referral to a mental health provider may be warranted.

As mentioned above, money disorders are distinct mental disorders that can be diagnosed and treated by qualified mental health professionals. In many cases, these disorders qualify for insurance reimbursement. They include hoarding disorder, gambling disorder, compulsive buying disorder, and financial dependence.

Hoarding Disorder

Historically, hoarding disorder was a symptom of obsessive compulsive disorder (OCD) and obsessive-compulsive personality disorder (OCPD). In the most recent edition of the DSM-5, Hoarding Disorder (HD) was identified as a distinct mental disorder. HD is characterized by: (a) difficulty parting with possessions regardless of their monetary value, (b) the desire to save items and emotional distress when getting rid of them, (c) the accumulation of items compromising the individual's use of their living area, with (d) the hoarding behaviors causing significant distress or impairment (American Psychiatric Association, 2013). Miserliness, the hoarding of money, and an inability to enjoy one's financial resources have also been linked with HD (Canale & Klontz, 2013). Approximately 2–6% of the population currently exhibit HD, with symptoms often emerging in the teenage years, starting to interfere with life functioning in their mid-20s and causing clinically significant impairments

by their mid-30s (American Psychiatric Association, 2013). It has been hypothesized that HD could be a response to early financial trauma or poverty in one's early
life (Klontz & Klontz, 2009).

Research has shown that the money scripts of money worship and/or money
avoidance are predictive of HD (Klontz & Britt, 2012). Additionally, there is some
evidence to suggest that males are more likely than females to exhibit hoarding
behaviors, and that hoarding is negatively associated with net worth (Klontz, Britt,
Archuleta, & Klontz, 2012). King and Devasagayam (2017) found that a fear of
uncertainty about a future item was strongly and positively associated with all hoarding disorder behaviors. They also found that when shown advertisements about a
shortage of an item, purchase rates of said items increased for the consumers with
HD. Later in this chapter we provide information about assessments that are currently available for counselors to implement with their financial counseling clients.

Gambling Disorder

Gambling disorder involves pathological gambling that leads to functional impairments. Individuals with a gambling disorder exhibit: (a) preoccupation with gambling,
(b) the need to gamble with more and more money to feel excited, (c) irritability or
restlessness when trying to reduce or stop gambling, (d) unsuccessful attempts to control gambling, (e) gambling to improve one's mood, (f) trying to conceal gambling
behaviors from others, (g) chasing losses, which involves continuing to gamble in an
attempt to recoup one's losses, (h) jeopardizing or losing relationships, educational, or
career opportunities due to gambling, and (i) relying on others to relieve financial difficulties caused by gambling (American Psychiatric Association, 2013). Gambling
disorder is the most studied money disorder (Klontz et al., 2011). Approximately 1%
of individuals will develop this disorder during their lifetime, with males historically
exhibiting it more often than females, although the gender gap appears to be narrowing
(American Psychiatric Association, 2013; Klontz & Britt, 2012). Specifically, single
males who grew up in a high net worth family were found to be most likely to identify
with gambling disorder (Klontz & Britt, 2012).

Money scripts have also been linked with gambling disorder. Previous research
has indicated that money status is positively associated with gambling disorder
while those with money vigilance scripts are less likely to engage in these behaviors
(Klontz & Britt, 2012).

Compulsive Buying Disorder

Compulsive buying disorder has been defined by Faber and O'Guinn (1989, 1992)
as a chronic and repetitive purchasing behavior that is brought on by negative events
and/or emotional feelings in the person's life resulting in detrimental consequences.

It is characterized by an irresistible urge to shop and purchase items that may not be needed, thus creating negative financial outcomes and potentially negative emotional issues (Klontz & Britt, 2012). While first introduced in 1915, compulsive buying disorder remained mostly ignored until the 1980s when two main events occurred: (a) the widening of the wealth disparity between the poor and wealthy, and (b) prevalent advertisements started to bring the "Joneses" into our homes through our televisions (Benson, 2015). Since the turn of the millennium, an explosion of online retail shopping has only further enhanced the growth of compulsive buying disorder (Benson, 2015; Dittmar, Long, & Bond, 2007).

Research on the financial effects of compulsive buying disorder is becoming more prevalent. Klontz and Britt (2012) found that compulsive buying was associated with specific money beliefs. In particular, they found the money scripts of money avoidance, money worship, and money status to be positively associated with compulsive buying behaviors and that individuals who hold money vigilance scripts were negatively associated with compulsive buying behaviors. Compulsive buying behaviors have also been found to be negatively associated with age, education levels, income, and net worth (Klontz et al., 2012). On the other hand, recent research has shown that females, non-Whites, and those that are not married have higher odds of engaging in compulsive buying behaviors (Klontz et al.). Those who have revolving credit cards were also positively associated with financial behaviors related to compulsive buying (Klontz et al.). Klontz and Britt (2012) showed that individuals who are compulsive buyers also tend to engage in other destructive financial behaviors such as financial denial and financial enabling. In the examination of a control group of non-compulsive buyers versus a group of compulsive buyers, Frost, Steketee, and Williams (2002) observed that compulsive buyers were more likely to have grown up in families with a history of depression and anxiety. Furthermore, the authors found the compulsive buyers to be more likely to suffer from compulsive hoarding, matching findings by Klontz and Britt (2012). Assessments that can help financial counselors differentiate between compulsive buying disorder and overspending are described below.

Financial Dependence

Financial dependence is characterized by the need for non-work income (e.g., gifts, windfalls, trusts, financial support from parents) that is associated with resentment, fear, and amotivation (Klontz & Britt, 2012). It is theorized to be caused by financial enabling (described in more detail below) and has been shown to be correlated with financial denial (Klontz & Britt, 2012). Individuals who exhibit financial dependence behaviors have a reliance on others for their financial resources, which creates a lack of motivation to succeed and a fear of being cut off from financial resources (Klontz & Canale, 2016). While prior research posits that women are more likely to be raised to think that financial dependence is okay (Newcomb & Rabow, 1999), Taylor et al. (2016) found that men had higher levels of financial dependence than did women, perhaps suggesting that men are becoming increasingly vulnerable to this disorder. Research has shown that people who hold money worship and/or money status beliefs are more likely to be financially dependent upon others (Klontz & Britt, 2012). Financially dependent individuals are more likely to be single, have lower levels of education, and to have grown up in more affluent households (Klontz et al., 2012). Financial dependence on other can have significant negative consequences. For example, research has shown that 46% of victims of domestic abuse cite financial dependence as one of the main reasons they returned to their abusers (Anderson et al., 2003).

Other Problematic Financial Behaviors

Problematic financial behaviors include subclinical symptoms of the money disorders described above but may manifest themselves as other unique syndromes. However, these syndromes have not yet been identified by the mental health field as distinct mental disorders (Klontz et al., 2016). They include behaviors such as financial denial, financial enabling, and financial enmeshment.

Financial Denial   Financial denial has been defined as the "attempt to cope by simply not thinking about money or trying not to deal with it" (Klontz, Kahler, & Klontz, 2008, p. 97). Individuals with financial denial deal with their anxiety around money by avoiding and/or rejecting their current financial state (Klontz & Britt, 2012). Financial denial has been described as a defense mechanism to help individuals avoid dealing with money problems and/or to escape psychological distress because of money (Canale, Archuleta, & Klontz, 2015; Klontz & Klontz, 2009). Specific behaviors of clients in financial denial include: (a) avoiding looking at financial statements, (b) trying to forget about their financial situation, and (c) avoiding thinking about money (Klontz et al., 2012).

Klontz and Britt (2012) found that financial denial is strongly correlated with compulsive buying disorder and moderately correlated with financial dependence and financial enabling behaviors. Other research has shown financial denial to be negatively associated with age, education, income, and net worth (Klontz et al., 2012). Non-married individuals and those with revolving credit card debt are also more likely to engage in financial denial than those who are married and do not have a revolving credit card balance (Klontz et al., 2012). As is the case with other problematic money behaviors, financial denial has been found to be associated with money beliefs. Specifically, financial denial is positively associated with money avoidance and money worship beliefs and is negatively associated with money vigilance beliefs (Klontz & Britt, 2012). Research has also found that mental health professionals are more vulnerable to exhibit financial denial behaviors than some other professions (Klontz & Britt, 2012). As such, it might be beneficial for financial counselors to examine their own relationship with money and take steps to enhance their own financial health so that they can maximize their ability to help their clients.

Financial Enabling When someone attempts to "help" another person financially but inadvertently causes financial harm to either themselves or those they tried to help, they have engaged in financial enabling (Klontz & Britt, 2012). One common example of this is a parent who cannot say no to their adult child when the child continually asks for money or financial support, leading to both parties having increased shame, guilt, or resentment because of the poor financial behavior (Klontz & Klontz, 2009). Klontz, Kahler, et al. (2008) hypothesize that financial enabling may be one of the most common problematic financial behaviors that financial planners face when working with their clients. This is likely because financial enabling is often done in an attempt to bring family members close together (Klontz et al., 2016; Klontz & Klontz, 2009), but the enabling typically leads to relationships that "are so tangled up in money that they confuse emotional investments with money" (Canale et al., 2015, p. 52). Signs of financial enabling include: (a) giving money to others even when the individual cannot afford it, (b) sacrificing their own well-being for the benefit of others, (c) having difficulty saying no to other people's requests for money, and (d) having perceptions that the individual has been taken advantage of financially (Klontz et al., 2012).

Limited research exists around financial enabling, but progress is being made. For example, Klontz et al. (2012) has found that financial enabling tends to become less problematic as individuals age. Financial enabling is negatively associated with education, net worth, and childhood socioeconomic status (Klontz et al., 2012; Klontz & Britt, 2012). Additionally, non-married individuals and those with revolving credit card debt are also likely to exhibit financial enabling behaviors.

Financial Enmeshment Individuals who inappropriately involve minor children in financial matters have committed financial enmeshment (Klontz & Britt, 2012). For example, financial enmeshment occurs when a parent manipulates a child through the use of money (Canale et al., 2015). Sixty-five percent of teenagers have expressed stress or anxiety related to concerns around family financial matters (American Psychological Association, 2013). This is likely because when parents involve children with age-inappropriate financial household information, anxiety and stress typically follow (Klontz et al., 2012). Signs of financial enmeshment include: (a) feeling better after talking to a minor child about financial stress or (b) having children pass along financial information to other adults (e.g., the child acts as an intermediary between the parents; Klontz et al.). In turn, financial enmeshment is likely to cause strained relational dynamics between the parent and child (Canale et al., 2015), and blurred boundaries and roles within the family, hindering the child's development and coping skills (Kemnitz, Klontz, & Archuleta, 2015). Financial enmeshment occurs when adults share intimate financial problems with children who are not developmentally able to help. In essence, financial enmeshment is a sharing of information with children for the exclusive emotional benefit of the adult. In so doing, the adult is transferring his or her emotional distress to the child in an effort to enlist their help or emotional support. This is very different than sharing developmentally appropriate information, such as teaching children about budgeting, saving, or debt.

Financial enmeshment is positively associated with income and males are more likely than females to report engaging in the behavior (Klontz et al., 2012; Klontz & Britt, 2012). Money scripts and other disordered financial behaviors have been found to be associated with financial enmeshment. Specifically, financial enmeshment is positively associated with money status beliefs and negatively associated with money vigilance scripts, and has been linked to hoarding disorder, compulsive gambling, compulsive buying, financial dependence, financial denial, and financial enabling (Klontz & Britt, 2012).

Helping Clients in Financial Counseling

When meeting with a client who does not seem to benefit from traditional financial counseling efforts, consideration of money disorders and related interventions may be helpful. Assessments and interventions have been created to help identify and work with money disorders. It is important to note that while these assessments and interventions can help identify a potential problem, treating a money disorder would be outside the scope of traditional financial counseling. As such, a referral to a trained mental health professional may be necessary.

Even if a client seems to be benefiting from the financial counseling relationship, it may be helpful to consider using one or more of the following inventories. Helping clients better understand their weaknesses can help them improve their money habits and better achieve their goals. Formal, research-based assessments can assist financial professionals better access a holistic view of their client's financial life, allowing the financial professional quick identification of potential problems, and a way to monitor client progress (Britt et al., 2015).

Assessment of Money Disorders

Klontz Money Behavior Inventory (KMBI) Understanding the money behaviors of clients is paramount to the financial professional so that they can best determine how to move forward with the client. When significant behavioral problems are identified, this could include a referral to, or consultation with, a mental health professional (Klontz et al., 2012). The Klontz Money Behavior Inventory (KMBI; Klontz et al., 2012) can provide financial professionals with an awareness of the extent to which their clients exhibit a wide range of dysfunctional money behaviors. The KMBI is a 68-item assessment designed to measure eight different money behaviors: (a) compulsive buying, (b) gambling disorder, (c) hoarding, (d) workaholism, (e) financial dependence, (f) financial enabling, (g) financial denial, and (h) financial enmeshment.

Klontz Money Script Inventory (KMSI) The Klontz Money Script Inventory (KMSI; Klontz et al., 2011) and Klontz Money Script Inventory-Revised (KMSI-R; Taylor et al., 2016) are designed for financial professionals. These assessments can be part of the data gathering process to help better understand how clients' beliefs around money may be influencing their financial behaviors and financial outcomes. The KMSIs can be used to have in-depth conversations with clients regarding their money scripts and to help determine the extent to which clients endorse four categories of scripts: (a) money avoidance, (b) money worship, (c) money status, and (d) money vigilance (Klontz & Britt, 2012; Lawson et al., 2015).

Klontz-Britt Financial Health Scale (K-BFHS) The Klontz-Britt Financial Health Scale (K-BFHS; Britt et al., 2015) is a 49-item assessment that measures a client's overall financial health. Specifically, the K-BFHS scores four distinct areas of financial health: (a) global financial health, (b) money disorders, (c) risk planning, and (d) self-care. These four areas have been found to be associated with a variety of factors including income, net worth, financial and life satisfaction, gender, race, and money scripts (Britt et al., 2015).

Research by Britt et al. (2015) reviewed the financial health of mental health practitioners compared to other business-related professionals. In doing so, they also examined how money scripts, life satisfaction, and socioeconomic factors were associated with the four areas of financial health. In particular, mental health professionals had significantly lower levels of global financial health, while net worth and financial knowledge were positively associated with global financial knowledge. Additionally, money scripts influenced the financial health sub-scales. Specifically, money status beliefs were positively associated with money disorders, money worship was negatively associated with risk planning, and money vigilance was positively associated with risk planning.

Financial Anxiety Scale (FAS) The Financial Anxiety Scale (FAS; Archuleta, Dale, & Spann, 2013) was designed to measure an individual's financial anxiety, wherein higher scores indicate increasing levels of financial anxiety. Individuals with higher levels of financial anxiety have more difficulty managing their personal finances and typically have lower levels of financial literacy (Shapiro & Burchell, 2012). Clients with high levels of anxiety around money have been found to make financial decisions that were not well aligned with their goals, leading to negative financial outcomes, and, in turn, increased financial anxiety (Sages, Griesdorn, Gudmunson, & Archuleta, 2015). The FAS enables financial professionals to quickly identify clients with high financial anxiety, who may be in need for a referral for mental health support.

Archuleta et al. (2013) first utilized the FAS to better understand the financial anxiety of college students. They found financial satisfaction to be the most significant predictor of a college student's financial anxiety, even when accounting for student loan debt, other debts, and demographic characteristics. Bell et al. (2014) utilized a shortened version of the FAS when examining the impact of financial resources on soldier's financial well-being. They found emergency funds, net worth, and perceived financial knowledge to be positively associated with financial well-being, while having credit card debt about $2500 and having automobile debt from $10,001 to $20,000 to be negatively associated with a soldier's financial well-being. Further research using the FAS has examined similarities and differences in financial behaviors between soldiers and college students (Bell Carlson, Britt, Nelson Goff, & Archuleta, 2015). Specifically, the researchers found financial anxiety was negatively associated with financial behaviors for the overall sample, as well as for soldiers and college students when analyzed separately.

Interventions for Money Disorders

When faced with a client suffering from a money disorder, such as gambling disorder, financial counselors should consider making a referral to a financial therapist. These conditions often require the assessment and diagnosis of a qualified mental health professional. Financial counselors can continue to work with the client within their normal scope of practice; however, they should not attempt to treat a money disorder, or any other mental health disorder, unless they are licensed therapists. However, financial counselors are well positioned to use techniques and theories borrowed from psychology to help motivate a client to take appropriate action and to help clients overcome problematic financial behaviors. For example, a financial counselor should not attempt to treat a person suffering from compulsive buying disorder, which may require a combination of medication and cognitive-behavioral therapy. However, the financial counselor may be in a position to encourage the client to seek out the help of a mental health professional to begin with, and if appropriate, help the client set up a budget and plan to track spending behaviors. The financial counselor could also work in collaboration with the mental health provider, where the therapist provides the psychological treatment and the financial counselor provides the financial life management expertise. With the client's permission, the financial counselor and therapist could share information with each other regarding their various roles and progress. There is a growing interest in the financial planning profession with regard to integrating psychological theory and techniques into work with clients (Klontz & Horwitz, 2017). These schools of thought include motivational interviewing, cognitive behavior therapy, solution-focused therapy, and positive psychology.

Motivational Interviewing Motivational Interviewing (MI) is a counseling technique designed to encourage change (Miller & Rollnick, 2002). It uses research-based methods for having change-inspiring conversations with clients. The focus is on interacting with clients in ways that encourage them to contemplate and talk about the benefits to change versus arguments in favor of the status quo. In recent years, MI techniques have been applied to financial planning, to help clients overcome ambivalence to change (Horwitz & Klontz, 2013; Klontz et al., 2016). See Chap. 7 for more information on MI.

Cognitive Behavior Techniques Cognitive-Behavioral Therapy (CBT) is a "present-oriented psychotherapy directed towards solving current problems and teaching clients skills to modify dysfunctional thinking and behavior" (Beck Institute for Cognitive Behavior Therapy, 2017). Clients often present with dysfunctional financial beliefs and behaviors and in order to effectively help them, financial counselors may need to address these beliefs and behaviors. CBT provides a framework for understanding the etiology and maintenance of problematic beliefs and behaviors and provides tools that counselors can use to help clients modify their thoughts and behaviors. Many of these tools can be adapted for use by financial counselors to help clients with self-defeating financial beliefs and behaviors, which may not have risen to the severity of a full blown money disorder requiring the help of a mental health professional. Research has shown that CBT can be effective in improving the financial behaviors of clients with self-defeating financial beliefs and behaviors. For example, there is strong evidence that CBT can be helpful in addressing hoarding disorder, gambling disorder, and compulsive buying disorder (Nabeshima & Klontz, 2015). CBT exercises adapted for use in the area of financial health include the *money script log* (Klontz et al., 2016), which is used to help clients discover, evaluate, and modify their financial beliefs. Other CBT techniques that can be of use to financial professionals include *mindfulness strategies*, *relaxation techniques* such as breathing exercises and imagery, and *exposure strategies* (Nabeshima & Klontz, 2015). See Chap. 6 for more information on CBT.

Solution-Focused Therapy Rather than focusing on problems, Solution-Focused Therapy (SFT) is a future and goal-oriented therapy approach that focuses on solutions. SFT has recently been adapted for use by financial professionals with their clients (Archuleta, Grable, & Burr, 2015). The major assumptions of SFT include: (a) if it is not broken, don't fix it, (b) if it works, do more of it, (c) if it is not working, do something different, (d) small steps lead to big changes, and (e) problems don't happen all the time and these exceptions to the problem can be identified and utilized (de Shazer et al., 2007). SFT techniques that can be adapted for use by financial professionals include asking the *miracle question* and using *scaling questions* (Archuleta et al., 2015). See Chap. 7 for more information on SFT.

Positive Psychology Traditional psychology has its origins in the medical model, with a focus on diagnosing and treating mental illness. In contrast, positive psychology describes the growing body of theory and research that is focused instead on optimizing human functioning and well-being. Positive psychology has been described as "the scientific study of the strengths that enable individuals and communities to flourish" (Positive Psychology Center, 2017). Many positive psychology techniques and activities such as the *what-went-well*, the *gratitude visit*, and *signature strengths* exercises can be adapted for use with financial planning and counseling clients (Asebedo & Seay, 2015). See Chap. 7 for more information on positive psychology.

Conclusion

Financial counselors offer financial education and tools to help clients improve their financial lives. Despite the counselor's best efforts, some clients do not benefit from standard financial counseling approaches. Even though they may report a desire to change their financial behaviors and improve their financial status, some clients are unable to initiate or sustain change. In these cases, financial counselors would benefit from considering whether or not the client is exhibiting a money disorder or other problematic financial behavior. Potential money disorders and problematic financial behaviors that might be encountered by financial counselors include hoarding disorder, gambling disorder, compulsive buying disorder, financial dependence, financial enabling, financial denial, and financial enmeshment. In severe cases, such as with hoarding disorder, gambling disorder, or compulsive buying disorder, clients may need the help of a mental health professional in addition to financial counseling.

Financial counselors could benefit from an understanding of the signs and symptoms of money disorders. Additionally, an understanding of the specific money scripts that have been found to be associated with these behaviors, such as money avoidance, money worship, and money status, can help financial counselors identify clients at risk for these behaviors. Lastly, financial counselors can borrow intervention techniques from the emerging fields of financial psychology, financial therapy, and behavioral finance to help motivate clients towards taking action and help them initiate and sustain financial behavior change.

References

American Psychiatric Association. (2013). *Diagnostic and statistical manual of mental disorders* (5th ed.). Arlington, VA: American Psychiatric Association.

American Psychiatric Association (2013). *Diagnostic and statistical manual of mental disorders* (5th ed.). American Psychiatric Publishing: Washington, D.C.: Author.

American Psychological Association. (2016). *Stress in America: Coping with change.* Retrieved from http://www.apa.org/news/press/releases/stress/2016/coping-with-change.pdf

Anderson, M. A., Gillig, P. M., Sitaker, M., McCloskey, K., Malloy, K., & Grigsby, N. (2003). Why doesn't she just leave? A descriptive study of victim reported impediments to her safety. *Journal of Family Violence, 18*(3), 151–155.

Archuleta, K. L., Dale, A., & Spann, S. M. (2013). College students and financial distress: Exploring debt, financial satisfaction, and financial anxiety. *Journal of Financial Counseling and Planning, 24*(2), 50–62.

Archuleta, K. L., Grable, J. E., & Burr, E. (2015). Solution focused financial therapy. In B. T. Klontz, S. L. Britt, & K. L. Archuleta (Eds.), *Financial therapy: Theory, research & practice* (pp. 347–362). New York, NY: Springer.

Asebedo, S. D., & Seay, M. C. (2015). From functioning to flourishing: Applying positive psychology to financial planning. *Journal of Financial Planning, 28*(11), 50–58.

Beck, J. S. (2011). *Cognitive behavior therapy: Basics and beyond* (2nd ed.). New York: Guilford Press.

Beck Institute for Cognitive Behavior Therapy. (2017). *What is cognitive behavior therapy (CBT).* Retrieved from https://www.beckinstitute.org/get-informed/what-is-cognitive-therapy/

Bell Carlson, M., Britt, S. L., Nelson Goff, B. S., & Archuleta, K. L. (2015). Similarities and differ-
    ences in financial behaviors of students and soldiers. *College Student Journal, 49*(4), 542–552.
Bell, M. M., Nelson, J. S., Spann, S. M., Molloy, C. J., Britt, S. L., & Nelson Goff, B. S. (2014).
    *The impact of financial resources on soldiers' well-being (SSRN Scholarly Paper No. ID
    2466556)*. Rochester, NY: Social Science Research Network Retrieved from https://papers.
    ssrn.com/abstract=2466556
Benson, A. L. (2015). Stopping overshopping model. In B. T. Klontz, S. L. Britt, & K. L. Archuleta
    (Eds.), *Financial therapy: Theory, research & practice* (pp. 191–214). New York, NY: Springer.
Britt, S., Klontz, B., Tibbetts, R., & Leitz, L. (2015). The financial health of mental health profes-
    sionals. *Journal of Financial Therapy, 6*(1), 17–32. https://doi.org/10.4148/1944-9771.1076
Canale, A., Archuleta, K. L., & Klontz, B. T. (2015). Money disorders. In B. T. Klontz, S. L.
    Britt, & K. L. Archuleta (Eds.), *Financial therapy: Theory, research & practice* (pp. 35–67).
    New York, NY: Springer.
Canale, A., & Klontz, B. T. (2013). Hoarding disorder: It's more than just an obsession—
    Implications for financial therapists and planners. *Journal of Financial Therapy, 4*(2), 43–63.
de Shazer, S., Dolan, Y., Korman, H., McCollum, E., Trepper, T., & Berg, I. K. (2007). *More than
    miracles: The state of the art of solution-focused brief therapy.* New York, NY: Taylor and
    Francis Group.
Dittmar, H., Long, K., & Bond, R. (2007). When a better self is only a button click away:
    Associations between materialistic values, emotional and identity-related buying motives,
    and compulsive buying tendency online. *Journal of Social and Clinical Psychology, 26*(3),
    334–361.
Faber, R. J., & O'Guinn, T. C. (1989). Classifying compulsive consumers: Advances in develop-
    ment of diagnostic tool. *Advances in Consumer Research, 16*, 738–744.
Faber, R. J., & O'Guinn, T. C. (1992). A clinical screener for compulsive buying. *Journal of
    Consumer Research, 19*(3), 459–469.
Frost, R. O., Steketee, G., & Williams, L. (2002). Compulsive buying, compulsive hoarding, and
    obsessive-compulsive disorder. *Behavior Therapy, 33*(2), 201–214.
Horwitz, E., & Klontz, B. T. (2013). Understanding and dealing with client resistance to change.
    Journal of Financial Planning, 26(11), 27–31.
Kemnitz, R. Klontz, B. T., & Archuleta, K. L. (2015). Financial enmeshment: Untangling the web.
    Journal of Financial Therapy, 6(2), 32–48.
King, D., & Devasagayam, R. (2017). An endowment, commodity, and prospect theory perspective
    on consumer hoarding behavior. *Journal of Business Theory and Practice, 5*(2), 77–88.
Klontz, B. T., Bivens, A., Klontz, P. T., Wada, J., & Kahler, R. (2008). The treatment of disordered
    money behaviors: Results of an open clinical trial. *Psychological Services, 5*(3), 295–308.
Klontz, B. T., & Britt, S. L. (2012). How clients' money scripts predict their financial behaviors.
    Journal of Financial Planning, 25(11), 33–43.
Klontz, B., Britt, S., Archuleta, K., & Klontz, T. (2012). Disordered money behaviors: Development
    of the Klontz money behavior inventory. *Journal of Financial Therapy, 3*(1), 17–42. https://doi.
    org/10.4148/jft.v3i1.1485
Klontz, B., Britt, S., Mentzer, J., & Klontz, T. (2011). Money beliefs and financial behaviors:
    Development of the Klontz money script inventory. *Journal of Financial Therapy, 2*(1), 1–22.
    https://doi.org/10.4148/jft.v2i1.451
Klontz, B. T. & Canale, A. (2016). When helping hurts: 5 recommendations for planners with
    financial-enabling clients. *Journal of Financial Planning, 29*(3), 25–28.
Klontz, B. T., & Horwitz, E. J. (2017). Behavioral finance 2.0: Financial psychology. *Journal of
    Financial Planning, 30*(5), 28–29.
Klontz, B. T., Horwitz, E. J., & Klontz, P. T. (2015). Stages of change and motivational inter-
    viewing in financial therapy. In B. T. Klontz, S. L. Britt, & K. L. Archuleta (Eds.), *Financial
    therapy: Theory, research & practice* (pp. 347–362). New York, NY: Springer.
Klontz, B., Kahler, R., & Klontz, T. (2008). *Facilitating financial health: Tools for financial plan-
    ners, coaches, and therapists.* Cincinnati, OH: The National Underwriter Company.
Klontz, B., Kahler, R., & Klontz, T. (2016). *Facilitating financial health: Tools for financial plan-
    ners, coaches, and therapists* (2nd ed.). Cincinnati, OH: The National Underwriter Company.

Klontz, B., & Klontz, T. (2009). *Mind over money: Overcoming the money disorders that threaten our financial health.* New York, NY: Broadway Press.

Klontz, B. T., Seay, M. C., Sullivan, P., & Canale, A. (2014). The psychology of wealth: Psychological factors associated with high income. *Journal of Financial Planning, 27*(12), 46–53.

Klontz, B. T., Sullivan, P., Seay, M. C., & Canale, A. (2015). The wealthy: A financial psychological profile. *Consulting Psychology Journal: Practice and Research, 67*(2), 127–143. https://doi.org/10.1037/cpb0000027

Lawson, D. R., Klontz, B. T., & Britt, S. L. (2015). Money scripts. In B. T. Klontz, S. L. Britt, & K. L. Archuleta (Eds.), *Financial therapy: Theory, research & practice* (pp. 23–34). New York, NY: Springer.

Miller, W. R., & Rollnick, S. (2002). *Motivational interviewing: Preparing people of change.* New York, NY: Guilford Press.

Nabeshima, G., & Klontz, B. T. (2015). Cognitive behavioral financial therapy. In B. T. Klontz, S. L. Britt, & K. L. Archuleta (Eds.), *Financial therapy: Theory, research & practice* (pp. 347–362). New York, NY: Springer.

Newcomb, M. D., & Rabow, J. (1999). Gender, socialization, and money. *Journal of Applied Social Psychology, 29*(4), 852–869. https://doi.org/10.1111/j.1559-1816.1999.tb02029.x

Positive Psychology Center. (2017). *PositivePsychology.org.* Retrieved from http://ppc.sas.upenn.edu/

Prochaska, J. O., Norcross, J. C., & DiClemente, C. C. (1994). *Changing for good: A revolutionary six-stage program for overcoming bad habits and moving your life positively forward.* New York, NY: William Morrow and Company, Inc.

Sages, R. A., Griesdorn, T. S., Gudmunson, C. G., & Archuleta, K. L. (2015). Assessment in financial therapy. In B. T. Klontz, S. L. Britt, & K. L. Archuleta (Eds.), *Financial therapy: Theory, research, and practice* (pp. 69–85). New York, NY: Springer.

Shapiro, G. K., & Burchell, B. J. (2012). Measuring financial anxiety. *Journal of Neuroscience, Psychology, and Economics, 5*(2), 92–103. https://doi.org/10.1037/a0027647

Taylor, C., Klontz, B., & Britt, S. (2016). Reliability and convergent validity of the Klontz money script inventory-revised (KMSI-R). *Journal of Financial Therapy, 6*(2), 1–13. https://doi.org/10.4148/1944-9771.1100

Chapter 12
Managing Challenging Conversations with Financial Counseling Clients

Sonya Britt-Lutter and Sarah D. Asebedo

Introduction

Seeking financial counseling implies some intention to alter one's current financial situation, which could stem from dissatisfaction to a desire to maximize financial resources or life satisfaction. Reasons for seeking financial counseling due to dissatisfaction could range from personal control issues (such as overspending) to financial crisis (such as job loss or bankruptcy) to couple-related issues (such as divorce or dispute over spending). Alternatively, individuals may seek financial counseling to improve or take preventive measures toward a neutral or even positive situation. In any case, revealing personal financial information is generally considered a private affair and can induce stress. Having a set of tools to manage challenging conversations with clients will assist with more productive meetings and attaining better client outcomes.

Managing client conversations can be particularly challenging when individuals see no reason to change their behavior. For instance, the Transtheoretical Model of Change (TTM) suggests that people in the pre-contemplation stage see no reason to change their current situation or behaviors, as they often do not recognize a problem exists (Prochaska, Redding, & Evers, 2013); thus, in the client's view there is no problem to address or preventive action to take. Consequently, significant progress is not typically made until the contemplation, preparation, and action stages when the client recognizes undesirable behavior and is motivated to learn more about the behavior and how to modify behaviors. Encouraging movement from the earlier stages of readiness to change to later stages should aid in managing

S. Britt-Lutter (✉)
Institute of Personal Financial Planning, Kansas State University, Manhattan, KS, USA
e-mail: lutter@ksu.edu

S. D. Asebedo
Department of Personal Financial Planning, Texas Tech University, Lubbock, TX, USA

© Springer Nature Switzerland AG 2019
D. B. Durband et al. (eds.), *Financial Counseling*,
https://doi.org/10.1007/978-3-319-72586-4_12

private and possibly difficult client conversations. (For more information about TTM, please refer to Chap. 7 of this book.)

In the sections that follow, challenges are grouped by external and internal challenges. External challenges are contextual in nature; the client is in a challenging position based on circumstances at that particular point in time. External challenges describe feelings associated with the context. Internal challenges account for the client's emotional reaction to the external challenges.

External Challenges

Individuals are all part of larger systems. We are constantly influenced by a range of external factors including families' opinions, comments of friends, and messaging from media. Considering the role those messages play on clients' ultimate behaviors is essential or the counselor is unlikely to see any change. It is very difficult for financial enablers to change their behaviors, for instance. Enablers may recognize undesirable behavior of lack of personal savings for retirement, for instance, and providing continued financial support to adult children. The adult child(ren) could feel offended and express feelings of being unloved by the parent who stops providing financial support. This, in turn, encourages the enabler to continue providing financial support because their behavior is only hurting him or her and is "doing good" for others. The enabler's perception of help is distorted by other members of the system, so behavior change is unlikely without considering and possibly bringing the larger system into financial counseling meetings. The whole system needs to shift to make room for new positions.

The way individuals operate as part of a system is especially apparent when working with couples (for a further discussion on systems, refer to Chaps. 4 and 6). Counselors who have had the experience of working with an individual and then are introduced to the couple system may have seen changes in the way the client talks or behaves. By incorporating some therapeutic skills and strategies into financial counseling, counselors can identify some of the system patterns and help with couple and other dyadic interactions.

Conflict Resolution

When it comes to money, arguments abound (Britt & Huston, 2012; Dew, Britt, & Huston, 2012)—making conflict resolution an essential skill for financial counselors. Drawing from conflict theory, money arguments are a naturally occurring event due to differences in power (e.g., income differences, financial knowledge, financial management), scarce resources (e.g., money, goods), and self-oriented human nature (Smith & Hamon, 2012). Conflict, however, may be positive and a catalyst for change and relationship growth. Resolving conflict within families can be particularly challenging as families attempt to persevere through intense conflict situations to protect the family structure (Smith & Hamon, 2012). Financial counselors might feel uncomfortable initially, but can learn and develop specialized conflict resolution skills designed to resolve money arguments within couples and the family unit.

Based upon conflict theory and widely used mediation principles, a conflict resolution framework has been proposed within the literature for use in financial planning, counseling, and therapy situations (Asebedo, 2016). First, financial counselors must be cognizant of setting the stage for constructive conflict resolution in three basic ways (informed by conflict theory): (a) expect money arguments, (b), see conflict as opportunity, and (c) balance power.

Framing conflict as a normal process that promotes growth and change can encourage clients to be open and willing to discuss the situation; clients tend to avoid conflict they view as rare and destructive. Moreover, power imbalances can be substantial when one client makes more or is more knowledgeable about the family finances. In these situations, power might be balanced by educating the less financially knowledgeable spouse, facilitating an open conversation that ensures the spouse who makes less has a voice at the table, or changing the meeting to a neutral location. From a conflict resolution perspective, it is important for the power differential to be balanced so that a mutually beneficial solution can be reached. It is important to note that "power" refers to each party feeling as though they have influence and a voice in the conflict discussion; it does not mean that each party needs to be equally involved in the day-to-day management of the finances. The counselor should recognize the couple's existing financial management structure and how this structure might create an imbalance of power (e.g., the more involved partner having more knowledge of the couple's financial situation). The ten steps to resolving conflict is a common strategy found within couple enrichment programs (e.g., PREPARE-ENRICH®, 2017).

Financial counselors could benefit from encouraging couples to work through the conflict resolution steps between sessions when progress is hindered by unmet expectations. The first step is for couples to set a time and place for discussion. It is easy to say that a problem will be talked about later and to never return to the subject. It is also easy for one partner to bombard the other with the dozen reasons why he or she is upset without giving fair warning that there was even a problem. Second, couples should each define the problem from their perspective. Third, each partner lists ways in which they contribute to the problem to illustrate that it is not one person causing the issue. This is followed by each partner contributing to the list of ways in which the couple has attempted to resolve the issue in the past that were not successful. This leads into Step 5 of brainstorming ten new ways of solving the problem. The goal is to list no less than ten options to open the communication lines. There is no judging or eliminating of options in this stage of the conflict resolution process. After ten possibilities have been identified, the couple discusses and evaluates each of these possible solutions. Step seven is for the couple to agree on one solution to try. Followed by identification of how each partner will contribute to the solution. Again, the problem should never be seen as one-sided. The last two steps are to agree on a time to re-evaluate progress toward the solution and finally to reward one another for marking progress on the solution (see PREPARE-ENRICH®, 2017).

Second, drawing from widely used mediation principles (Fisher, Ury, & Patton, 1991), financial counselors can help clients resolve conflicts by separating the people from the problem; focusing on interests, not positions; generating options for mutual gain; and establishing objective criteria. By focusing on the problem and not the people (Fisher, Ury, & Patton, 1991), financial counselors can create a more positive and aligned atmosphere that minimizes destructive criticism and blaming, which keeps the conversation forward-focused. Positions typically represent fixed ideas each party holds (e.g., I want to spend money on "a," and you want to spend it on "b"); interests, on the other hand, focus on the underlying values and goals held by both parties—e.g., "we" want to accomplish (or care about "c"). Resolving conflict based upon interests ensures a sustainable resolution is reached that meets both party's needs; whereas, the typical "compromise" solution often results in both parties giving up a piece of their closely held interests. Conflict resolution entails generating multiple options that are built upon interests resulting in mutual gain. In this step, it is often helpful for each party to generate solutions from the other spouse's perspective. Lastly, effective conflict resolution is based on objective criteria. For example, a couple that decides to retire earlier should ensure that an earlier retirement is feasible. An objective third party that brings financial analytics to the table can be highly influential and impactful within the conflict resolution process because they can demonstrate which generated options are financially feasible and can produce a variety of practical solutions (e.g., alternative retirement dates or saving amounts).

Crises and Loss

Some crises may result *in* a loss and some crises may be the result *of* a loss. A crisis in financial counseling is a sudden change or turn of events that is related to individual or family finances. Crisis could be thought of as the event that forces a change in direction. A crisis is a time when counseling might be sought for the first time, for instance, filing for bankruptcy. Some crises, such as bankruptcy, require mandated financial counseling (Federal Trade Commission, 2012) which presents additional complications of client readiness to change (Britt, Lawson, & Haselwood, 2016). The financial counselor must carefully assess the situation to determine if the client is receptive to change. If not, the counselor may want to start with general education about the crisis at hand. For instance, providing context and normalizing the situation could help the client feel more comfortable and open to discussing his or her situation. Next, the financial counselor should continuously repeat him or herself in case the client is not in a position to hear what is being said at the particular point in time. Providing follow-up communication is especially important in times of crisis.

In the reverse order, a crisis could also be the result of a loss like the loss of a job or the loss of a spouse through divorce or death. Losses may not be associated with an immediate crisis, but brought upon more gradually such as becoming empty nesters or transitioning to retirement. Ambiguous loss, or unsolved grief, can happen at any point in a loss or crisis situation. The uncertainty or confusion about the loss (e.g., are we really going to divorce or just live apart) can paralyze individuals to the point of inability to make decisions (Ambiguous Loss, n.d.). The same principles in handling crisis situations presented above apply here, as well. Most importantly, financial counselors should approach crisis situations with caution and carefully assess where the client is with willingness to address the situation. Approaching change too quickly could result in loss of communication with the client whereas giving too much space may result in lack of change and continued negative financial behaviors and/or outcomes.

Internal Challenges

Client internal challenges may arise due to an emotional reaction to external challenges. Internal challenges are often observed during the change process. Thus, the Transtheoretical Model of Change (TTM) provides a useful framework within which to explore four common internal challenges that can inhibit the change process: ambivalence, reluctance, resistance, and overconfidence/overoptimism. See Chap. 7 for a description of each stage of change within the TTM.

Ambivalence and Reluctance

Clients may fail to follow through with financial counseling advice due to ambivalence and reluctance. Ambivalence is defined as "the coexistence of opposing attitudes or feelings, such as love and hate, toward a person, object, or idea" (American Heritage® Dictionary of the English Language, 2011, para. 1). Clients may make an appointment to review their credit report only to make excuses for not inputting their information to get the credit report once they meet with the financial counselor. Ambivalent clients want to learn but do not want to know at the same time. Reluctance, a closely related concept, is when the unwilling side of ambivalence is ongoing. Ambivalence and reluctance often arise in the contemplation stage of TTM as clients evaluate the costs and benefits resulting from behavior change, with severe ambivalence and reluctance resulting in a chronic state of contemplation or procrastination (Prochaska et al., 2013). In this stage, clients tend to weigh the costs of behavior change relative to the potential gains. For example, the psychological costs associated with saving (i.e., eliminating fun expenditures) might seem more significant in the short-term relative to the long-term benefits of financial security in retirement. The client recognizes the long-term benefits of saving but these benefits seem insignificant compared to the short-term loss of an experience or material good (e.g., vacation, sporting event, or a new car). The client would be ambivalent about change and reluctant to follow advice.

Responses to Ambivalent and Reluctant Clients Kerkmann (1998) stated that a key task of the financial counselor is to convince ambivalent and reluctant clients that the benefits of change outweigh the costs. Kerkmann suggested that financial counselors work with clients to explore their values and identify where current financial behavior might deviate from these values. Bringing forth the discrepancy between where the client is today and where the client wants to be in the future may help them find the motivation to change. Moreover, it may be useful to focus on the consequences of failing to change to create client awareness about the risks associated with continuing along the current financial trajectory. Using the saving example from above, a financial projection can be completed to demonstrate the extent to which the client's retirement goals will be underfunded if saving is not increased.

Resistance

Where reluctance results in a general unwillingness to change, resistance results in direct opposition to change. Resistant clients are often in the pre-contemplation stage and are unaware a problem exists, appear unmotivated, and seem impervious to advice (Prochaska et al., 2013). Being silent, making excuses, and missing appointments could all be signs of resistance in a client. A financial counselor is less likely to come across a new client who is resistant to change because someone in this stage is unlikely to initiate financial counseling. A financial counselor will most likely find resistance when identifying a new problem an existing client is unaware of, or they may find resistance in working with couples: one spouse may be open and ready for change, whereas the other spouse is not yet ready to acknowledge a problem exists and is resistant to any advice offered.

Responses to Resistant Clients A key task of the financial counselor is to raise the client's awareness of the problem. Kerkmann (1998) suggested that a financial counselor provide a thorough overview and assessment of the client's financial situation. Kerkmann stressed that this assessment must remain focused on the objective facts and circumstances. Consequently, it is useful to use analytical tools that demonstrate the client's current strengths and weaknesses based on the numbers (e.g., balance sheet, income and expense statement, financial ratios). Problem-solving is very ineffective with resistant clients (Kerkmann, 1998). Rather, as outlined in Chap. 8, financial counselors can take a motivational interviewing approach to resistance and "roll" with it rather than engage directly in the resistance. Rolling with resistance suggests that the financial counselor is a facilitator helping the client generate solutions rather than an advisor offering prescriptive recommendations (Levensky, Forcehimes, O'Donohue, & Beitz, 2007). It is important to spend enough time "with" the client in their resistance, as moving on too quickly can further entrench the client in their resistant state (see Chap. 8 for further details about motivational interviewing). Creating a comfortable environment for the client to share and genuinely being interested in hearing the client's perspective are other techniques to apply with all clients, but especially resistant clients (Wall, 2002).

Overconfidence

Optimism is a key psychological characteristic that facilitates positive financial behavior and a future-oriented perspective (Puri & Robinson, 2007). Extreme optimism or overconfidence, on the other hand, has been linked to less prudent financial attributes—a short planning horizon, not saving, less self-control, highly concentrated individual stock positions, and less liquid wealth (Puri & Robinson, 2007). While optimism can and should be cultivated (Seligman, 2011), financial counselors must be aware of the need to temper this positive psychological characteristic. It is most likely that an overconfident client is unaware of the financial risks they are facing, possibly indicating pre-contemplation.

Responses to Overconfident Clients Working with an overconfident client requires the financial counselor to carefully analyze and communicate the associated risks if the current financial behavior continues. This can be accomplished through traditional financial analytical techniques; such as a life insurance needs analysis, retirement projection, portfolio depletion analysis, or longevity risk assessment. Once analyses are completed, it is critical for the financial counselor to have an open and honest conversation with the client about the results and risks the client is facing, possibly resulting in increased awareness and a desire to change. Moreover, what a financial counselor interprets as overconfidence or overoptimism could actually be a reflection of the client's values or religious beliefs. For example, a retiree may be withdrawing a significant portion of their investment portfolio each year without concern because their values or religious beliefs support the notion that "everything will work out." Thus, it is important for the financial counselor to identify the beliefs underlying the observed behavior so an effective intervention can be applied. It should be noted that a referral to another professional might be appropriate (e.g., a clergy member) depending on the situation.

Stress

Entire book chapters and books have been dedicated to the topic of financial stress. For purposes of this chapter, it is relevant to understand that people perceive stressors differently based on resources and prior experiences resulting in different levels and perceptions of stress. People who perceive more stress in their lives may develop immune deficiencies and/or other physical diseases as a result (Uchino, Smith, Holt-Lunstad, Campo, & Reblin, 2007). Aside from the long-term negative effects of stress, acute and chronic stress limits the brain's ability to make rational decisions leaving the process to habit, instinct, or emotion (Pham, 2007). Stress in general, and financial stress, in particular, takes a toll on personal and marital satisfaction (Kim, Garman, & Sorhaindo, 2003; Randall & Bodenmann, 2009). To a certain degree, financial stress has even been linked with suicide (Holub, 2002), making the conversation with clients that much more challenging and important. According to the American Psychological Association (2015), financial issues consistently top the list of stressors for Americans across the country and women tend to report higher levels of overall stress in their lives when compared to men.

Responses to Clients with Stress Getting an indication of client's subjective and/or objective stress is critical in understanding their ability and willingness to hear what the financial counselor is communicating. Although a bit dated, the Holmes and Rahe (1967) social readjustment scale is still widely used today as a basis for the measurement of 43 stressor events. Some of these events can have a positive outcome, such as marriage or retirement, while others may produce a negative reaction, such as death of a loved one or being fired from work. Financial counselors could incorporate the social readjustment scale or other scale into the intake process to get a more holistic view of the client's situation. Abbreviated versions of the scale have been used in a vast array of recent literature exploring the impact of financial strain and parental stress on adolescent outcomes (Camacho-Thompson, Gillen-O'Neel, Gonzales, & Fuligni, 2016) to depression in older Chinese women (Ho, Liang, Yu, & Sham, 2017).

Recent research within the health psychology literature suggests that how people view their stress has a more significant impact on their physical and psychological health than the presence of stress alone (Keller et al., 2012). When clients experience stress that cannot be immediately eliminated, financial counselors can have a significant impact by helping clients adjust how they perceive and respond to that stress. For instance, a client who has been faced with job loss may feel less financial stress simply by reframing the situation. Brainstorming responses to the job loss (e.g., evaluating support systems available to bridge the financial gap during brief periods of income volatility) is also likely to be associated with reduced stress. The financial counselor can help the individual think of the situation as an opportunity for re-evaluation of life goals versus the termination of employment. The financial counselor can assist by brainstorming alternative job environments that would produce higher satisfaction and possibly even higher income. By identifying the positives and negatives of the old job and the current situation, individuals will feel in more control of their situation and feel less stress.

Grief

Grief is very personally defined and could be very brief or chronic in length. It could run an expected process (e.g., disbelief-anger-depression-resolution) or could be more complicated and non-linear in nature. The most commonly cited way of understanding grief is through Kübler-Ross's stages of grief originally published in 1969 (Kübler-Ross, 2009). The stages consist of denial, anger, bargaining, depression, and acceptance. While these are good benchmarks to understand how a person *might* experience grief, they are not absolute. In fact, Friedman and James (2008) pointed out that the stages of grief are not empirically based and are simply reflections of feelings felt by terminally ill clients. Friedman and James provided several examples of how the stages of grief have inadvertently harmed grieving individuals by the outward expectation that they should be feeling a certain way. Spiritual beliefs, personal motivation, and context all frame how grief is perceived and resolved. To expect clients to react in a certain way is dangerous to their personal well-being.

Responding to Clients with Grief If grief is so individual-specific, how does a financial counselor know what to do when faced with grieving clients? The answer is relatively simple—listen and seek to understand. Do not make broad statements about how they must be feeling. What could commonly be perceived as sad for outsiders may actually be a relief to the griever. It is impossible to understand without full information, so seek to understand as appropriate and as the individual is willing to share. It is not necessary for financial counselors to become mental health counselors, but they do need to be diligent about their efforts. Applying commonly held beliefs, such as the stages of grief, to client's situation could cause them to turn further away from help.

Conclusion

The purpose of this chapter was to highlight some of the difficult conversations that may arise during financial counseling. The general areas of conflict resolution, crises, ambivalence, resistance, overconfidence, stress, and grief were summarized and ideas for how to respond to conversations with clients around these areas were presented throughout the chapter. It is important to remember that seeking help from a financial counselor can be a difficult decision for clients to make. The reasons clients seek financial counseling can vary widely, with topics such as personal control issues (such as overspending), financial crisis (such as job loss or bankruptcy), couple-related issues (such as divorce or dispute over spending), or personal-improvement issues (such as planning for a future goal). Clients feel vulnerable and outside of their comfort zone, while counselors can feel uncomfortable. Thus, the financial counselor must exercise caution and care when broaching these topics so that trust can be built within the counselor–client relationship. In all areas, it is important that financial counselors do not overstep their knowledge and capability limits. To learn more, see Chap. 3 on making effective referrals.

References

Ambiguous Loss. (n.d.). *Four questions about ambiguous loss*. Retrieved from https://www.ambiguousloss.com/four_questions.php

American Heritage® Dictionary of the English Language, Fifth Edition. (2011). *Ambivalence*. Retrieved from http://www.thefreedictionary.com/ambivalence

American Psychological Association. (2015). *Stress in America™: Paying with our health*. Retrieved from https://www.apa.org/news/press/releases/stress/2014/stress-report.pdf

Asebedo, S. D. (2016). Building financial peace: A conflict resolution framework for money arguments. *Journal of Financial Therapy, 7*(2), 1–15. https://doi.org/10.4148/1944-9771.1119

Britt, S. L., & Huston, S. J. (2012). The role of money arguments in marriage. *Journal of Family and Economic Issues, 33*(4), 464–476. https://doi.org/10.1007/s10834-012-9304-5

Britt, S. L., Lawson, D. R., & Haselwood, C. A. (2016). A descriptive analysis of physiological stress and readiness to change. *Journal of Financial Planning, 29*(11), 45–51.

Camacho-Thompson, D. E., Gillen-O'Neel, C., Gonzales, N. A., & Fuligni, A. J. (2016). Financial strain, major family life events, and parental academic involvement during adolescence. *Journal of Youth and Adolescence, 45*(6), 1065–1074. https://doi.org/10.1007/s10964-016-0443-0

Dew, J., Britt, S. L., & Huston, S. J. (2012). Examining the relationship between financial issues and divorce. *Family Relations, 61*(4), 615–628. https://doi.org/10.1111/j.1741-3729.2012.00715.x

Federal Trade Commission. (2012). *Filing for bankruptcy: What to know*. Retrieved from https://www.consumer.ftc.gov/articles/0224-filing-bankruptcy-what-to-know

Fisher, R., Ury, W., & Patton, B. (1991). *Getting to yes: Negotiating agreement without giving in* (2nd ed). New York: Penguin Books.

Friedman, R., & James, J. W. (2008). The myth of the stages of dying, death and grief. *Skeptic, 14*(2), 37–41.

Ho, S. C., Liang, Z., Yu, R., & Sham, A. (2017). Association of life events and depressive symptoms among early postmenopausal Chinese women in Hong Kong. *Menopause, 24*(2), 180–186. https://doi.org/10.1097/GME.0000000000000734

Holmes, T. H., & Rahe, R. H. (1967). The social readjustment rating scale. *Journal of Psychosomatic Research, 11*(2), 213–218. https://doi.org/10.1016/0022-3999(67)90010-4

Holub, T. (2002). *Credit card usage and debt among college and university students*. Retrieved from http://www.eriche.org/digests/2002-1.pdf

Keller, A., Litzelman, K., Wisk, L. E., Maddox, T., Cheng, E. R., Creswell, P. D., & Witt, W. P. (2012). Does the perception that stress affects health matter? The association with health and mortality. *Health Psychology, 31*(5), 577–684. https://doi.org/10.1037/a0026743

Kerkmann, B. C. (1998). Motivation and stages of change in financial counseling: An application of a transtheoretical model from counseling psychology. *Journal of Financial Counseling and Planning, 9*(1), 13–20.

Kim, J., Garman, E. T., & Sorhaindo, B. (2003). Relationships among credit counseling clients' financial well-being, financial behaviors, financial stressor events, and health. *Financial Counseling and Planning, 14*(1), 75–87.

Kübler-Ross, E. (2009). *On death and dying: What the dying have to teach doctors, nurses, clergy and their own families*. Abingdon, Oxon: Routledge.

Levensky, E. R., Forcehimes, A., O'Donohue, W. T., & Beitz, K. (2007). Motivational interviewing: An evidence-based approach to counseling helps patients follow treatment recommendations. *The American Journal of Nursing, 107*(10), 50–58. https://doi.org/10.1097/01.NAJ.0000292202.06571.24

Pham, M. T. (2007). Emotion and rationality: A critical review and interpretation of empirical evidence. *Review of General Psychology, 11*(2), 155–178. https://doi.org/10.1037/1089-2680.11.2.155

PREPARE-ENRICH®. (2017). *Workbook for couples*. Retrieved from https://www.prepare-enrich.com/prepare_enrich_content/reference/couples_workbook.pdf

Prochaska, J. O., Redding, C. A., & Evers, K. E. (2013). The transtheoretical model and stages of change. In K. Glanz, B. K. Rimer, & K. Viswanath (Eds.), *Health behavior and health education* (4th ed., pp. 97–122).

Puri, M., & Robinson, D. T. (2007). Optimism and economic choice. *Journal of Financial Economics, 86*, 71–99. https://doi.org/10.1016/j.jfineco.2006.09.003

Randall, A. K., & Bodenmann, G. (2009). The role of stress on close relationships and marital satisfaction. *Clinical Psychology Review, 29*, 105–115. https://doi.org/10.1016/j.cpr.2008.10.004

Seligman, M. (2011). *Learned optimism: How to change your mind and your life*. New York: Random House Digital, Inc.

Smith, S. R., & Hamon, R. R. (2012). *Exploring family theories* (3rd ed.). New York: Oxford University Press.

Uchino, B. N., Smith, T. W., Holt-Lunstad, J., Campo, R., & Reblin, M. (2007). Stress and illness. In J. Caciopp, L. G. Tassinary, & G. G. Berntson (Eds.), *Handbook of psychophysiology* (pp. 608–632). New York: Cambridge University Press.

Wall, R. W. (2002). *Financial counseling in practice*. Honolulu: Financial Wellness Associates.

Chapter 13
Resources and Tools for Use in Financial Counseling

Ryan H. Law, Ann C. House, and Thomas A. Duffany

There are online tools to help one with practically every task, from tracking when an oil change is needed to when the milk is going to expire. The right tools can make life easier. For example, a person might have a grocery shopping "app" that syncs with a partner's list. Each person can add items to the shopping list, and next time one of them is heading by the store they can check the app and see if anything needs to be picked up. It is efficient (items can be added as they are remembered) and helpful in getting errands completed.

Financial counseling is no exception to this idea. There are numerous tools and resources that the counselor and/or client can use to improve the counseling experience. Criteria for tools and resources recommended in this chapter include clinical experience of the authors, cost, ease of use, and implementation in a counseling setting, availability of instructions or training, and reviews or testimonials. It is important to note that while there is limited academic research about the effectiveness of these tools, there are anecdotal success stories and field experience suggesting that there is value in using them.

The structure of the chapter will include an overview of each resource, use in the counseling relationship, and how to access the resource. The tools and resources discussed include the Consumer Financial Protection Bureau (CFPB) Financial Well-Being Scale and CFPB's Your Money, Your Goals; Money Habitudes; The Financial Checkup, Financial Remedies & Financial First Aid booklets; budgeting

R. H. Law (✉)
Money Management Resource Center, Personal Financial Planning program,
Utah Valley University, Orem, UT, USA
e-mail: Ryan.law@uvu.edu

A. C. House
Personal Money Management Center, University of Utah, Salt Lake City, UT, USA

T. A. Duffany
Brightside, Chandler, AZ, USA

© Springer Nature Switzerland AG 2019
D. B. Durband et al. (eds.), *Financial Counseling*,
https://doi.org/10.1007/978-3-319-72586-4_13

tools; debt elimination software PowerPay; credit score tracking including Credit Karma, Credit Sesame and Quizzle; slide calculators; America Saves and the federal student aid website.

Consumer Financial Protection Bureau (CFPB) Financial Well-Being Scale

The Financial Well-Being Scale was developed to provide a standardized form of measurement for financial well-being. It was determined by a research team with the Consumer Financial Protection Bureau (2015), that financial wellness includes having control over one's finances, having a cushion for emergencies and other financial shocks, having financial goals and being on track to meet those goals, and being able to make choices that allow you to enjoy life. The scale includes ten questions (or five for an abbreviated version) and gives the user a score between 0 and 100. The CFPB conducted extensive testing and validation of the scale to ensure its quality and reliability.

In 2016, a survey was conducted by the CFPB on more than 6000 US adults (CFPB, 2017). Each individual completed the Financial Well-Being Scale and answered a number of other questions about their individual, household, and family characteristics, income, employment status, savings levels, financial experiences and financial behaviors, skills, and attitudes. The survey determined that the average score of US adults is 54. Those age 65 and older have the highest average score, at 61, and those age 34 and under have the lowest score at 51. Those with liquid savings of $250 of less had an average score of 41, while those with $75,000 or more in liquid savings had an average score of 68. Three strong factors relating to scores include employment status, income level, and educational attainment. Along with the report, the CFPB released the dataset from this survey to encourage future research.

Using the Resource in the Counseling Relationship

The CFPB (2015) recommends that the scale be used at the initial appointment, to track an individual's progress, to assess program outcomes and for research. It is recommended that the client completes the scale at each appointment so their score can be tracked over time. The counselor may review the score with the client, but it is mainly for the counselor to keep track of progress. It is anticipated that the score the client gets each time they complete the assessment will be retained in client files, either digitally or in a paper file. If the score is going up over time, there is evidence that the client is making progress and is increasing their financial well-being. If the score goes down, the financial counselor should review which areas of the scale have gone down so those areas can be addressed. For example, one of the statements on the scale is, "I have money left over at the end of the month." If a client had been selecting "sometimes" but they now marked it "never" this opens the door to a conversation about what changed in this area.

Accessing the CFPB Financial Well-Being Scale

The scale is free and publicly available and can be accessed online at http://www.consumerfinance.gov/. The scale can be downloaded and printed or taken online. On the CFPB website users can find the User Guide, which provides more information about the research behind the tool and provides instructions for administering and scoring the scale, the paper and digital versions of the scale, and a scoring sheet to interpret the score.

Your Money, Your Goals

According to the Consumer Financial Protection Bureau (2016), Your Money, Your Goals is a toolkit of financial resources designed for individuals who work with low and moderate-income individuals. The modules within the toolkit cover the following topics: (1) understanding the client's situation; (2) starting the conversation about money; (3) emotions, values, and culture; (4) setting goals and planning for large purchases; (5) savings for emergencies, bills, and goals; (6) tracking and managing income and benefits; (7) paying bills and other expenses; (8) getting through the month; (9) dealing with debt; (10) understanding credit reports and scores; (11) money services, cards, accounts, and loans; and (12) protecting your money.

Using the Resource in the Counseling Relationship

Your Money, Your Goals is not meant to be used in full from beginning to end with each client. Financial counselors or others who use the toolkit are encouraged to do a full assessment of their client's financial state in the first meeting, then utilize whichever module would be most helpful for that particular client in future meetings. For example, a financial counselor might have a client who is budgeting their money and paying off debt, but they need to know how to save for a large purchase, such as a home. In this instance, the module about making large purchases could be utilized without necessarily utilizing the other content.

While the modules are meant to be used at financial counseling appointments, clients could do some reading on their own to reinforce the lessons. While it is likely that financial counselors who have been working in the profession will have developed many tools and teaching methods for these topics, this toolkit can reinforce what the counselor is already doing.

Accessing Your Money, Your Goals

Your Money, Your Goals can be accessed on the CFPB website (http://www.consumerfinance.gov). The guide is more than 300 pages. On the website, financial counselors can find training and implementation guides. An organization who uses the toolkit on a regular basis should consider ordering or printing copies for the office.

Money Habitudes®

Money Habitudes® (a combination of money habits and attitudes) is a tool developed by Syble Solomon (Our story, n.d.). Solomon explains that otherwise rational men and women would share their stories with her about irrational money decisions, and she wanted to come up with a way to help people talk about money honestly and openly in an interactive and engaging solution. From these experiences, the Money Habitudes card game was created. The game consists of statements on cards that the user determines whether or not fits them. The cards that the user identifies with are sorted into piles based on categories. The six categories are spontaneous, carefree, giving, status, security, and planning. Research by Delgadillo and Bushman (2015) found, utilizing Cronbach's alpha, that all six domains met the minimum standards for reliability and therefore, financial counselors can utilize Money Habitudes as a reliable tool.

Using the Resource in the Counseling Relationship

Money Habitudes can help both the client and financial counselor understand more about how their money habits and attitudes are reflected in how they manage their finances. For example, if a client is strong in the spontaneous category, the importance of a budget and planning could be stressed. The game includes instructions for how to play, but also has cards about each Habitude including advantages, challenges, and suggestions. A financial counselor can learn how to play the game utilizing the instructions included with each deck, or a facilitator guide may be purchased that will help guide them.

If Money Habitudes is played as part of a counseling session, the financial counselor may want to excuse him or herself from the room while the client is sorting the cards. Based on the author's experiences, it takes most clients 10–15 min to sort the cards and, if the counselor is watching them, the silence could be awkward and it could also influence the results. If the client is a couple, they should each complete the game. The results may provide a platform to discuss each partner's strengths and potential weaknesses and open a conversation about understanding each other's money habits and attitudes.

Accessing Money Habitudes

Money Habitudes is available as a physical deck of cards or as an online sorting game. The cards are a one-time purchase while the online version is paid for each time it is used. The online version includes a detailed report that will be automatically generated that explores that particular user's results. If Money Habitudes is used as part of a presentation or workshop, each participant will need their own deck. More information about Money Habitudes can be found at http://www.moneyhabitudes.com/.

The Financial Check Up, Financial Remedies, and Financial First Aid

The Financial Check Up, Financial Remedies, and *Financial First Aid* are booklets by educator Alena Johnson to provide practical resources for those who work with individuals seeking personal financial help and guidance. The delivery method is designed to help take an overall look at finances on an annual basis, just as one may get a yearly physical checkup.

The Financial Checkup is geared to look at one's current financial situation, assess needs and risks, and then to evaluate progress toward goals. It is meant to be a quick assessment to measure one's financial health. Johnson (2001) noted that *The Financial Checkup* will help a client recognize where they are right now, where they want to be, and how to get there. The booklet is divided into 11 chapters: Introduction, Net-Worth Statement, Income & Expense Statement, Financial Ratios, Savings, Retirement, Taxes, Insurance, Goals, Budgeting, and Conclusion. Each chapter includes information, terms and definitions, a worksheet, and instructions.

Johnson (2001) conducted a study which evaluated *The Financial Checkup* program using the stages of change model. The findings of the study indicated that individuals advanced along the stages of change especially in the areas of debt, saving, taxes, homeowners' insurance, auto insurance, and retirement, as well as gained an understanding of net worth and income and expenses.

Financial Remedies, a companion book to *The Financial Checkup,* is designed to help solve the problems uncovered in *The Financial Checkup.* It gives strategies for creating and staying on a budget, reducing debt, which debt to pay off first, saving and investing, avoiding identity theft, and includes a chapter for teaching children wise money management. *Financial First Aid* is a resource for laypeople, such as clergy, who find themselves helping people who have financial problems. It outlines strategies for dealing with emergencies, living within one's means, debt, budgeting, savings, and goal setting. It also includes a chapter on counseling techniques.

Using the Resource in the Counseling Relationship

Copies of these booklets can be purchased online. Permission is given by the author to print all worksheets in *The Financial Checkup* which can be helpful in a counseling situation, especially in assessing the client's progress. *Financial Remedies* gives best practices and tips for helping clients through the process of becoming better money managers, such as how the "step-down principle" works. Though *Financial First Aid* is written for non-professionals, it is a good resource to recommend to individuals, such as clerics, who may be first-in-line to hear of those who struggle with personal finances. The booklets can be purchased on https://exemplarpress. com/collections/textbooks.

Budgeting Tools

Setting up a budget with a client will often be a key component of a financial counseling appointment. Budgets can be set up with clients using a number of tools, including a paper-based budget, spreadsheets (such as Excel or Google Sheets), specialized software programs (such as Microsoft Money or Quicken), or online budgeting apps (such as Mint or You Need a Budget). Budgeting tools can support the counseling relationship in one of the most challenging areas—implementation. The functionality in these tools can provide the framework that can help reinforce the principles discussed in counseling sessions. Additionally, this can support a core objective: helping the client develop confidence and become self-sufficient.

When a client is looking for a software program or app to help manage their budget, there are several key factors to look for, with the foremost being the security of their data. If the software can connect to the user's bank account, it should only be able to view and import account information—not transfer funds or access accounts in any other way. Additionally, the software should be certified by prominent third-party providers such as TrustArc or VeriSign. To better understand how budgeting apps can serve clients, the authors have chosen to review two popular budgeting apps—Mint and You Need a Budget.

Mint

Mint is a money management app that was acquired by Intuit in 2009—the same company that owns Quickbooks and Turbotax. Mint allows users to have a comprehensive overview of their finances by connecting to a user's financial accounts (including checking, savings, and retirement accounts), credit cards, student loans, and bills. According to Prince (2016) on the Mintlife blog, the software has over 20 million registered users. Mint is free for the consumer. Mint receives their funding through companies who offer deals such as car insurance, investments, loans, and other offers on Mint in the form of advertisements.

Mint keeps all financial data in one place. It acts as a financial dashboard where one can get a complete overview of their finances. With it all in one place there is no need to go to each bank, loan, or credit card website separately to view balances and payments. Mint has more than 20 types of alerts so the user can be notified of fees, be warned if they are going over budget, or let them know if something seems suspicious. Mint Bills is a feature of Mint where users can pay credit cards or car payments in one place. Mint has comprehensive reports where the user can see the average amount spent each month throughout the entire year, or multiple years, which gives a clear idea on the actual amount of money that is spent on different categories each month. Mint can be accessed online at https://www.mint.com.

You Need a Budget

You Need a Budget (YNAB) is web-based budgeting software designed to help users gain total control of their money, stop living paycheck-to-paycheck, get out of debt, and increase savings. It features an expense tracking system that flows into a customizable budgeting tool that allows users to forecast expenses/income and adapt as life happens. YNAB hosts live, interactive classes to support users in customizing the use of the app to meet their individual needs and life circumstances.

YNAB encourages a zero-sum or zero-based budget system where users "give every dollar a job" by assigning it to a spending category. In this system, expenses (including saving and paying down debt) equal income. One focus of this system is to embrace true expenses by planning for infrequent or irregular expenses (holidays, insurance, registrations, etc.). Any surplus should be allocated to a spending category—usually savings or paying down debt. The user is encouraged to change their perspective from checking their account balances to checking their category balances. If something unexpected arises, or a category balance does not have sufficient funds, the user has the option of moving money from another category as appropriate based on their priorities.

YNAB provides goal setting options and reports, including net worth and average spending in a category that can help initiate or guide conversations with a client. YNAB offers web-based and mobile apps allowing users to access the software anywhere and from any device. There is an annual cost to using YNAB, and while some users will feel they can meet their needs with other free tools, those who use it report that the savings exceed the cost. The cost also means that users will not have advertisements in the app to sell them products. YNAB offers a 34-day free trial which allows users time to test the software and still have a full month to see if the software fits their needs. Students can get a free YNAB account by contacting customer service. YNAB can be accessed online at https://www.youneedabudget.com.

PowerPay©

The snowball method is a tried-and-true concept for debt reduction. This method helps clients reduce debt by paying off debt with one of two methods, starting with either the highest interest rate or the lowest balance, while paying the minimum on all other debt. Once this first account is paid off, the monthly payment is rolled to the next highest interest rate debt or lowest balance and added to the minimum payment. This continues until all debt is paid. The process starts small, but gains momentum as more and more debt is paid off.

A software program, PowerPay (Miner, Harris, & Bond, 1993), developed by Utah Cooperative Extension, assists users with this snowball method thereby saving months of payments and hundreds, even thousands, of dollars of interest. This program was first offered on computer software and sold to financial professionals. Later this debt-reduction tool, PowerPay 5.0, was presented free and online for consumers.

Using PowerPay in the Counseling Relationship

PowerPay offers a personalized, self-directed plan. A client begins with setting up a free account. The client then enters creditor information, including creditor name, outstanding balance, minimum monthly payment, and interest rate. Once all debt is entered, the user clicks on the payment calendar. The program then calculates the payoff time in years and months. The consumer can run several different scenarios including highest interest balance, lowest balance, or shortest term first. PowerPay calls the rolled-over payment from each debt "Power Payments." The benefit of using Power Payments is defined in terms of time and money saved. The consumer can download and print a detailed calendar which they can use to know how much to pay to which debt each month. Someone struggling to get out of debt can feel that their monthly payments are not making a dent in their overall situation. By utilizing PowerPay they can see their progress and maintain momentum, which can give the debtor the confidence to be successful.

Research by O'Neill (1998), with Extension clients showed that when PowerPay was used and a printout provided to the client 74% managed debt with increased confidence, 52% made changes in spending habits, 43% referred others to Extension for a PowerPay analysis, 34% started paying bills on time, and 30% incurred no new debt.

Accessing PowerPay

The PowerPay website offers a guide with step-by-step instructions along with questions and answers. Other features the online tool presents is a spending plan, an education center, savings tools and calculators for consolidation or qualifying for loans. There is also an iPhone/iPad app that can be downloaded from the main PowerPay website, which can be accessed at https://powerpay.org/.

Credit Score Tracking

It has become increasingly important for consumers to understand their credit score as scores have become more widely used not just by lenders but also by landlords, employers, and other parties. As such financial counselors should be aware of the benefits and challenges of services that allow consumers to track their scores. Several credit card companies have started offering credit score monitoring where clients (and sometimes non-clients) can set up an account with the company and get a free score and some monitoring on a regular basis. In addition, popular websites or mobile apps that clients can use to track their credit include Credit Karma, Credit Sesame, and Quizzle. These companies are able to offer their services for free to consumers by generating revenue from advertisements for financial products.

Each of these companies allows consumers to view their credit score for free. While many people believe they have a single score that is their "credit score," that is not the case. The FICO scoring model has been in use since 1956 and is perhaps the most well-known, but the VantageScore model, which was developed in 2006 by the three major credit bureaus (Transunion, Equifax, and Experian), is an alternative scoring model. While the major categories used to calculate the score are similar between the FICO and VantageScore models, there are differences in how certain criteria are weighted which can result in differences in scores depending on an individual's specific circumstances. Additionally, consumers have more than one FICO credit score and more than one VantageScore credit score. Lenders use the formula that best fits their needs (i.e., many lenders will use a different formula for a mortgage loan than a car loan because there are different risk factors associated with those loans). It is important to keep these differences in mind when using these services and recognize that the score reported through these services may or may not reflect the exact score a lender will use.

Each of these services reports the score using the VantageScore scoring model rather than a FICO score. Credit Sesame and Quizzle each report the score provided by TransUnion while Credit Karma reports the scores provided by both TransUnion and Equifax. A brief description of the services offered by each of these companies is provided below.

Credit Karma provides weekly updates of credit scores and the TransUnion and Equifax credit reports. They also send updates and alerts, such as when a new line of credit is added, or a negative item, such as a late payment, has been added to your report. Credit Karma provides credit tools, including a Credit Score Simulator, which estimates the effect of potential financial decisions on the user's credit score (i.e., putting extra funds toward a credit card versus an auto loan). Other services that Credit Karma offers include the My Spending Tool, which allows users to track their credit card and bank transactions, and Credit Karma Tax, which allows users to file their federal and state taxes for free. In addition, Credit Karma has forums, reviews of products, and informational platforms.

Credit Sesame provides daily updates of a user's credit score and TransUnion credit report. Additionally, members get free credit monitoring (including real-time alerts to credit file changes), a free credit report card (including analysis and actionable tips for improvement), and free identity theft protection. While Credit Sesame offers their basic services for free, users can pay to receive added functionality. Paid memberships provide daily monitoring of credit reports from all three bureaus (the free version only provides monitoring of the TransUnion report), and monitoring of a user's Social Security number, public records, and black-market websites.

Quizzle offers a credit score to the user and a free TransUnion credit report every 3 months. Quizzle focuses its services on education about credit, helping users to understand credit reports and credit scores including information on what actions cause credit scores to go up or down. Paid membership offers monthly credit reports and scores as well as credit monitoring and identity protection.

Using the Resource in the Counseling Relationship

While the popular draw of these tools is for a user to see their credit score, this can be misleading as the scores provided may not be the same as the score a lender will use. Using services from multiple sources (including some credit card companies that also provide a free credit score with the monthly statement) can provide a more complete understanding of what each credit bureau is reporting and the general range of an individual's credit score. While the scores reported through these services may not match what a lender sees, they can be used as a benchmark to help clients learn how different actions increase or decrease their credit scores (i.e., carrying a higher credit card balance may result in a lower credit score). Tracking the factors that influence the score can be more helpful than simply monitoring the three-digit number. Additionally, these sites offer alerts that can indicate identity theft and fraud to the user so the user can take more immediate remedial action.

None of these programs or scores is a substitute for professional help. Financial counselors can play a key role in assisting people understand how to put the numbers in context and use the tools to move toward lifetime financial wellness.

Accessing the Resource

Consumers can set up an account with Credit Karma, Credit Sesame, or Quizzle through their respective websites or through free mobile apps available for both Android and Apple devices. Their respective websites are listed below:

- Credit Karma: https://www.creditkarma.com/
- Credit Sesame: https://creditsesame.com/
- Quizzle: https://www.quizzle.com/

Slide Calculators

Slide calculators are a handheld tool used to demonstrate personal financial concepts. The calculators are on laminated cards, where the user pulls the slide up or down and the answers appear in the boxes. The calculators cover topics such as retirement, saving, and paying down debt. They are simple to use and no explanation is needed to engage the consumer.

These calculators are intended to bring awareness to the end user and can motivate action. For example, one calculator shows the value of saving and investing early. Another calculator shows ways to find money to save and invest, such as going without a $1.00 snack from the vending machine will save someone $365 per year or $1826 in 5 years.

Using the Resource in the Counseling Relationship

This tool could be used effectively in individual counseling sessions, workshops and classes, special events, part of materials packets, handouts, inserts and other mailings, and would be especially useful for a client who learns kinesthetically. The tools are generally priced by quantity; the more that are purchased the lower the price for each card. They can often be customized (in content and design) and personalized (with company's name, logo, and contact information) for additional costs. Slide calculators are available through a variety of vendors including Advantage Publications, American Slide Charts, and Datalizer Slide Charts.

America Saves

America Saves, based on a successful campaign by Cooperative Extension called MONEY 2000™, is a nationwide campaign that uses the principles of social marketing and behavioral change to motive and support low to moderate income households to save money, reduce debt, and build wealth. MONEY 2000 was designed to help American households save and/or reduce debt by a specific dollar amount by the year 2000. Many households in the US struggle to save for emergencies and many Americans are coming up short in saving for retirement, however, research by O'Neill, Xiao, Bristow, Brennan, and Kerbel (2000) found that when people set a specific goal and receive periodic reminders the majority of participants (three out of four) increased savings and decreased debt. Based on the positive impact of MONEY 2000, when MONEY 2000 concluded the Consumer Federation of

America (CFA) picked up the movement, named it America Saves, and expanded it by adding resources such as quizzes, videos, printable worksheets, tweets and chats, and photo contests. The nonprofit group Consumer Federation of America seeks to advance consumer interest through research, advocacy, and education. It has a long history of informing the public and news media about consumer issues and advocating pro-consumer policy. Their website contains a range of resources and has current updates on issues such as banking, housing, insurance, and fraud.

America Saves strives to enable households and individuals to save by having consumers make a "savings pledge," or goal, and then with motivation, encouragement and support, assist the new saver with their savings goal. The aim of the pledge is that one makes a written commitment to save, sets a practical goal and makes a plan to stay connected with the campaign. "Savers," as one is called after making a commitment, are also encouraged to reach out to other savers and to get their family, friends, and peers to join the campaign by making a pledge. The idea is that a person does not have to go it alone. For example, if co-workers in the office decide to save money by bringing lunches from home, one is likely to join in making it a group effort to spend less. The campaign utilizes motivational exercises, such as learning from each other, sharing experiences, and having a personal support system.

Using America Saves in the Counseling Relationship

Both MONEY 2000 and America Saves are based on theory about how best to facilitate change in human beings, or the Transtheoretical Model of Change (see Chap. 7 for more details about the Transtheoretical Model of Change). According to the theory, one must be ready to make changes. If a client is not ready to make changes in their savings or debt levels, America Saves offers abundant resources to help savers move to the next step. This is how it works:

Precontemplation—In this stage, an individual is not thinking about changing their financial habits. They may not even know there is a problem. With the America Saves program, people are introduced to personal financial management in a non-threatening setting and in a timely manner so individuals can begin thinking about changing their habits.

Contemplation—When hearing about a program that assists and motivates one to take a look at their own finances, they become more aware of their behavior. Individuals at this stage may consider the possibilities of the successes they could have by changing negative financial behaviors.

Preparation—At this point, an individual is getting ready to change and sets a savings goal.

Action—With America Saves there are many resources and tools for savers to draw on to help them succeed with their goal. A saver is connected with social media and direct emails with tips and reminders.

Maintenance—Research by America Saves (n.d.-a) indicates that large national programs are not as effective as local efforts, therefore cities and states are encouraged to connect with a campaign of their own. Local campaigns may offer events, advice, support, and one-on-one financial counseling.

Counselors may encourage clients to make an America Saves pledge. This will remind and, perhaps, influence clients between appointments and even after financial counseling ends. America Saves can be found at www.americasaves.org and www.consumerfed.org

Supporting Research

America Saves and C + R Research Services study, *Impact of the America Saves Program on Low-Income Youth Workers* (America Saves, n.d.-b), explores the effect of America Saves Youth Workers (ASYW) on summer youth employment participants from August 2015–March 2016. It measured the impact of their use of savings tools, savings attitudes, and savings behaviors. Findings indicated that when low-income urban youth are given access to savings accounts, direct deposit and goal setting, they will save consistently. Following their summer employment program, and their corresponding involvement in the America Saves program, 80% of the young workers had established a savings pattern, an increase of 54%.

An independent study conducted in 2016–2017 (America Saves, 2017) revealed that while lack of income is a barrier to saving, roughly the same number of survey participants reported that poor spending habits and social influence factor into why they do not save. Of those surveyed who had taken the America Saves pledge, nearly two-fifths (39%) said that taking the pledge was "the main factor for me starting to save more." Nearly one-fifth of respondents (18%) indicated that, while they had already started to save, taking the pledge "improved your success at saving." For more than one-quarter (28%), taking the pledge "helped you maintain the success you were already having."

Federal Student Aid Website

Federal Student Aid, which is an Office of the U.S. Department of Education and is the largest provider of student financial aid, has put together a comprehensive website about federal student aid that is intended to be the go-to resource for questions about student aid. The website has sections on preparing for college, different types of financial aid, how to qualify and apply for financial aid, and how to manage student loans. The website features comprehensive articles and videos, a glossary of financial aid terms, current interest rates for student loans, certification forms for

Public Service Loan Forgiveness and the ability to fill out the FAFSA directly from the website.

A very useful part of the website is the Repayment Estimator, which connects directly with the National Student Loan Data System (NSLDS) and brings all federal student loans and interest rates into the calculator. Different scenarios can then be run based on family size, tax-filing status and income. The calculator will then show which repayment plans the user is eligible for and how much the payment will be.

Using Federal Student Aid in the Counseling Relationship

The Student Aid website is a great resource for future students, current students and those repaying their loans. It is also a great information resource for financial counselors who deal with student aid in any form, including those in repayment. A financial counselor might pull up, e-mail and/or print an article to send to or review with a client, help them fill out the FAFSA or review which repayment plans are available. It can be accessed online at https://studentaid.ed.gov/.

Conclusion

This chapter reports on tools to assist with visualization, motivation, convenience, and efficiency. These tools can add to a feeling of security, enable quick access or provide an evaluation of one's current situation. However, this is by no means an exhaustive list of resources and tools available to financial counselors. There are thousands of free and fee-based resources, as an internet search will confirm, and new apps and other tools become available regularly. While some of these new apps may provide additional functionality or other benefits that may be helpful for a client, there will be questions around ongoing maintenance, necessary improvements, and security of information (if applicable). As a financial counselor it is important to find a balance between new functionality and time-tested solutions and to have discussions with clients around the tradeoffs as they select tools to use. The resources and tools that are featured in this chapter were selected because of their importance in the field of personal financial management and their success rate with financial counselors. Furthermore, it is essential to have more than one strategy in your toolbox when working with clients. Different strategies are needed to be able to match appropriate tools to client's needs, personalities, and level of capability. Ultimately, counselors' aim to help clients to wisely assume responsibility for their own financial well-being. Tools and resources can help clients navigate the complex financial world for themselves and set them on the path to financial independence.

References

America Saves. (2017). *Survey indicates that America Saves pledge facilitates savings.* Retrieved from https://americasaves.org/survey-indicates-that-america-saves-pledge-facilitates-saving

America Saves. (n.d.-a). *America Saves local campaign organizing guide.* Retrieved from https://americasaves.org/images/organizing_guide_for_web_with_live_links_final.pdf

America Saves. (n.d.-b). *Impact of the America Saves program on low-income youth workers.* Retrieved from https://americasaves.org/images/Impact-of-the-America-Saves-Program-on-Low-Income-Youth-Workers.pdf

Consumer Financial Protection Bureau. (2015). *Measuring financial well-being: A guide to using the CFPB financial well-being scale.* Retrieved from http://files.consumerfinance.gov/f/201512_cfpb_financial-well-being-user-guide-scale.pdf

Consumer Financial Protection Bureau. (2016). *Your money, your goals: A financial empowerment toolkit.* Retrieved from https://s3.amazonaws.com/files.consumerfinance.gov/f/documents/201701_cfpb_YMYG-Toolkit.pdf

Consumer Financial Protection Bureau. (2017). *Financial well-being in America.* Retrieved from http://files.consumerfinance.gov/f/documents/201709_cfpb_financial-well-being-in-America.pdf

Delgadillo, L. M., & Bushman, B. S. (2015). Reliability analysis of Money Habitudes. *Journal of Extension, 53*(2). Retrieved from https://www.joe.org/joe/2015april/tt2.php

Johnson, A. C. (2001). *Evaluating a financial assessment tool: The financial checkup* (Master's thesis). Retrieved from http://digitalcommons.usu.edu/cgi/viewcontent.cgi?article=3536&context=etd

Miner, F. D., Harris, J., & Bond, L. (1993). PowerPay Version 3.0. Logan, UT: Utah State Cooperative Extension Service.

O'Neill, B. (1998). Money talks: Documenting the economic impact of extension personal finance programs. *Journal of Extension, 36*(5). Retrieved from https://www.joe.org/joe/1998october/a2.php

O'Neill, B., Xiao, J., Bristow, B., Brennan, P., & Kerbel, C. (2000). MONEY 2000™: Feedback from and impact on participants. *Journal of Extension, 38*(6). Retrieved from https://www.joe.org/joe/2000december/rb3.php

Our story. (n.d.). Retrieved from http://www.moneyhabitudes.com/about/history/

Prince, K.T. (2016, April 6). Mint by the numbers: Which user are you? [Blog post]. Retrieved from https://blog.mint.com/credit/mint-by-the-numbers-which-user-are-you-040616/

Chapter 14
Looking Forward: The Future of Financial Counseling

Angela K. Mazzolini, Bryan Ashton, Rebecca Wiggins, and Vicki Jacobson

Throughout this book, the reader has been exposed to a variety of perspectives and approaches in financial counseling. In every profession there are challenges, and financial counseling is no exception. This chapter will explore some of those challenges and explore some possible solutions to overcome them. The authors also wish to cast a vision for the future of financial counseling that includes research to build evidence-based practices, provides services to multiple generations, and strengthens collaboration with multiple disciplines to advance the financial counseling profession. Finally, a call to action will be provided to facilitate involvement in the profession.

Challenges in Financial Counseling

How do financial counselors provide services to people from different backgrounds, a variety of age levels, different educational levels, and all socioeconomic levels? This is indeed a significant challenge that financial counselors face. Another challenge is understanding and developing evaluation processes that will benefit not

Electronic supplementary material: The online version of this chapter (https://doi.org/10.1007/978-3-319-72586-4_14) contains supplementary material, which is available to authorized users.

A. K. Mazzolini (✉)
Financial Counseling Consultant, Lubbock, TX, USA

B. Ashton
Trellis Company, Austin, TX, USA

R. Wiggins
Association for Financial Counseling and Planning Education®, Westerville, OH, USA

V. Jacobson
Center for Excellence in Financial Counseling, University of Missouri-St. Louis, St. Louis, MO, USA

© Springer Nature Switzerland AG 2019
D. B. Durband et al. (eds.), *Financial Counseling*,
https://doi.org/10.1007/978-3-319-72586-4_14

only the individual financial counselor, but also continue to build the profession of financial counseling. Other challenges financial counselors may face are choosing which, if any, professional designations are appropriate to earn and navigating the changing landscape of regulations for the profession to stay current.

Continuum of Care

Money is an integral part of the human culture and life cycle. Throughout a lifetime, people seek financial guidance for a variety of reasons—from overcoming credit card debt, to paying for college, to purchasing a new home, to saving for retirement. Consumers turn to financial professionals for current financial needs, but also to build a foundation for the future that will help them prepare and avoid moments of financial crisis. When it is time to find a financial counselor, where does a person who realizes that they need help begin to look for that help? How do they know where they fit in the continuum of financial services, and are all points along the continuum of care accessible to that individual? There is a general lack of formalized financial education in the K-12 system. As of 2016, only 17 US states required high school students to complete a course in personal finance (Council for Economic Education, 2016). Consequently, many American children are only exposed to financial education through family and personal experience. While there is value in both, not all families are equipped to provide equitable or accurate financial education and awareness, and many would not know how to find a qualified professional if one was needed. These shortcomings further exacerbate an inequality of access and understanding of such imperative life skills. While educators, parents, and financial professionals continue to advocate and work towards a financial education requirement for kindergarten to 12th grade curriculum (JumpStart Coalition, 2015), there are other important steps financial counseling professionals can and should take to ensure that financial education is available through all stages of life. This can occur through building a strong community of practice and providing more integrated services across the financial services industry.

For many individuals, the landscape of personal finance is fraught with misleading messages and confusing marketing. The list of financial designations is exhausting, with more than 150 listed on the Financial Industry Regulatory Authority (FINRA) website (FINRA, n.d.). As a community of professionals, it is our responsibility to work together to help individuals and families navigate financial education and achieve financial well-being, particularly those who are most vulnerable and lack adequate access to services. By building a community of practice, financial counseling professionals bring clarity and definition to this continuum and provide access to high-quality financial education and counseling for consumers from all demographics, income levels, and backgrounds. Organizations like the Association for Financial Counseling and Planning Education® (AFCPE®) bring together financial researchers, educators, and practitioners working in all areas of the profession—government, military, higher education, nonprofits, private practice, banks, and credit unions—to exchange best practices, unify goals and purposes, and create stronger referral networks for consumers. Creating professional communities between individuals and organizations eliminates duplication, increases efficiency, and elevates the rigor of programs. Together, efforts like these, elevate the standards of the financial counseling profession, enhance the value of the profession, increase meaningful career opportunities, and ultimately better serve individuals and families.

As previously discussed, there is a lack of formalized financial education in the K-12 environment. This is a missed opportunity to engage multiple generations and improve older individuals' financial knowledge in the process. Two paths seem to emerge in the search for ways to engage families in financial education. The first is continuing the push for formalized financial education. While much of the recent push has been on engaging high school students in standalone financial education, an alternative school of thought advocates for this education to begin even earlier, integrating it into math and social studies courses during elementary or middle school. For example, the State of Texas has requirements that begin financial literacy programming in Grade 1 (Texas Council on Economic Education, 2012).

Recently, the Consumer Financial Protection Bureau (CFPB) began an initiative to integrate financial education into another avenue, the public library system (CFPB, n.d.-a). These programs provide an opportunity to reach students in a community setting, and also open the door for further intergenerational education; working to provide information to parents around a variety of topics as their children are being educated. Programming ideas from the CFPB include family money night, financial book clubs, and scouting badge days, all targeted at engaging the whole family system in learning more about money management (CFPB, n.d.-b).

Today, many adults struggle to answer basic financial literacy questions (Klapper, Lusardi, & van Oudheusden, 2015). Additionally, the habits and norms that are viewed by children in the home set the tone for their future attitudes and behaviors (Whitebread & Bingham, 2013). In order to break the cycle of financial challenges, a two-generational approach for financial education focused on both children and their parents or guardians is imperative. This will allow for reinforcement of positive behaviors and provide an opportunity to enhance the financial knowledge of the entire family.

Importance of Evaluation in Financial Counseling

Another challenge financial counselors face is how to evaluate financial counseling programs and client success. One reason this is such a challenge is because financial counselors can be found in a variety of organizations, as mentioned in the first chapter. A financial counselor working with single mothers through a non-profit agency will have different assessment and evaluation needs than a financial counselor working in a college or university setting and overseeing peer financial mentors. Another reason evaluation is challenging is that success can be defined differently for different organizations and even for each client. With no federal or state regulations on financial counseling, no data are required to be reported and many financial counselors lack the necessary resources, such as time, money, and knowledge, to implement a program evaluation.

Evaluation is crucial to moving the financial counseling profession forward. Knowing what kinds of programming are effective, understanding the needs of clients, and being able to compare data with other agencies will not only help financial counselors implement best practices, but will also enable financial counselors and agencies to apply for crucial funding to support their programs. Evaluating what works, identifying what does not work, and comparing those data across the profession will better support client financial health, the ultimate goal for financial counselors.

Financial counselors may evaluate both objective and subjective client outcomes. Objective client outcomes are typically based on numeric measurements: decreases in debt, increases in savings, or increases in credit scores. Subjective client outcomes may be client-assessed internal changes such as self-reported levels of financial stress, financial satisfaction, or financial confidence. Approaches to measuring these outcomes vary, with examples ranging from client satisfaction questionnaires, behavioral measures (e.g., client drop out and program completion rates), and self-report inventories. These can indicate to the professional, their employer, or program funder if the financial counseling program or approach is meeting its objectives. The outcomes can also be used to determine if clients are progressing towards goals, as well as serve as a source of feedback for both the counselor and client. A financial education class conducted by a financial counselor may include a pretest and post-test to measure outcomes of interest. For example, a participant's self-reported assessment of financial knowledge may increase in the short term. However, to build ongoing financial literacy that combines both knowledge with action, the financial counselor should assess the long-term impact with a follow-up survey.

Programs that provide training and development for new financial counselors should incorporate the topic of empirically based measurement tools into their educational materials. In addition, current financial counselors can partner with academic programs, professional organizations, and peers to support their service delivery through integrating assessment tools. Academic programs at universities, such as those aligned with the AFCPE, can support practice and client outcome assessment through inclusion of research on the financial counseling profession and dissemination of research findings through publication and presentation at professional conferences. Financial counseling professionals can work with researchers to obtain appropriate measurement strategies for their specific needs or develop measurement tools to assess program effectiveness and client outcomes. The statistical analyses of data received from financial counselors about their counseling model and client outcomes can lead to feedback about financial counseling approaches. This partnership moves the financial counseling approach from being anecdotally based to empirically based.

Professional organizations can connect financial counselors with the latest research and practice applications through multiple avenues: (a) continuing education opportunities that include assessment topics, (b) professional journals that publish research on the financial counseling profession, (c) professional magazines that discuss the importance of assessment and include clear assessment tools, (d) professional conference presentations devoted to helping practitioners learn about and incorporate assessment into their models, and (e) building peer networks to share successful assessment tools and experiences.

The Cities for Financial Empowerment (CFE) Fund noted that one-on-one financial counseling and coaching programs supported by private funders, federal agencies, and local municipalities, have not only grown over the last several years, but have demonstrated that the free services targeting low-income consumers "can be delivered at scale, by trained professionals and with measurable client outcomes" (CFE Fund, email communication, June 1, 2015). The CFE Fund further suggested that rigorous program evaluations that demonstrate value and benefit to stakeholders should be implemented in order to focus financial support for these programs. Program evaluation and consistency in successful service delivery are both integral to sustaining and expanding the future of financial counseling for all career paths and target audiences.

Much of the literature on the effectiveness or benefit of financial counseling often equates financial counseling with financial education and financial literacy with little distinction between counseling and education efforts (Collins & O'Rourke, 2010). Likewise, financial counseling and financial coaching are often presented as very similar, if not interchangeable (Carlson, 2014). Over the years, a few evaluation efforts have focused solely on the outcomes of financial counseling with little examination of the content or process of the counseling and any connection between that process and the outcomes (Elliehausen, Lundquist, & Staten, 2007). Although informative, these efforts conclude that more research and study is required to determine the long-term benefits of financial counseling. Identifying, implementing, and evaluating effective financial counseling processes that achieve intended outcomes will help demonstrate the value of financial counseling efforts.

Development of a financial counseling protocol that utilizes evidenced-based practices to support a program's outcomes for a specific target audience helps form the foundation for conducting the program's evaluation. Archuleta and Grable (2011) offer reasons for empirically based evaluations: to create a baseline for assessing progress or lack of progress, to serve as corrective feedback, and to account for outcome effectiveness or decline. Establishing a specific financial counseling protocol, and a method to monitor counselor performance in delivery of the protocol, assures consistent delivery of the program's intended treatment. Monitoring and measuring the consistent delivery of the program's protocol will help establish that the counseling process is in place, setting the stage to determine any correlation between the counseling program and observed outcomes as well as connections to the program's inputs. Fidelity to program protocol can begin to isolate what works and what does not work in accomplishing desired outcomes as well as identify areas of the program requiring revisions. Such reviews provide a mechanism for accountability that can be used to seek resources to continue or expand services.

Findings from an evidence-based protocol developed and implemented by the Center for Excellence in Financial Counseling for student loan borrower repayment counseling are encouraging and show promise (Jacobson, Ortega, & Tranel, 2015). A solution-focused exploration of a borrower's available repayment options was designed and successfully delivered through a behavior-change counseling model which featured a strong emphasis on post-counseling follow-up and confidence building. The counseling protocol was integrated into an electronic intake form that required counselors to collect specific borrower data to determine the borrower's available federal repayment options as well as perform various behavior-change counseling communication tasks to develop the borrower's repayment action plan steps. Essential checkpoints were identified within the intake and counseling process for monitoring the counselor's performance. These checkpoints assured that all borrowers were exposed to the overall counseling protocol, including properly applying the federal repayment options checklist based on the borrower's repayment status. The protocol established the framework for consistently delivering the program's "treatment" of assuring all borrowers received the same counseling "dosage," to determine his/her best available repayment solution (Jacobson et al., 2015).

Financial Counseling Certification

Financial counselor certification programs, viewed as the keystone to providing quality financial counseling services, vary in their rigor, depth, and scope. A certification designation may serve as an indicator of a designee's financial competencies (Office of Community Services, n.d.), but certification alone does not guarantee the delivery of effective financial counseling. Training in the process of financial counseling needs to be an important component of counselor certification to ensure the effective delivery of financial counseling programs.

Continuing education to maintain counselor certification is often provided to financial counselors on various counseling theories, frameworks, and delivery models for implementation into their practice. Due to the many constraints on a financial counselors' time, implementation of these theories and practices is often voluntary and without support of a knowledgeable professional. In addition, counselor performance is usually not monitored for use of evidence-based practices. A financial counselor's knowledge of counseling theory and evidence-based practices, including counseling models and frameworks to implement into counseling practice is equally as important as financial knowledge to demonstrate financial counselor competency. The future of financial counseling certification efforts must not limit its focus to financial knowledge and competencies, but also include coverage of counseling theories, frameworks, evaluation, and processes that enhance counseling outcomes.

A financial professional without proper education and experience can cause more harm than good. It is important to remember that the profession of financial counseling and education has existed for over 30 years and was founded on decades of research and practice. Awareness of the rigorous standards that already exist and insisting that those who use certification titles be held accountable to those standards is important. Professionals must have education and experience in the field and be committed to upholding a strong code of ethics and acquiring ongoing professional development. This ensures an approach that creates both measurable and meaningful outcomes for their clients in achieving long-term financial well-being.

When financial counselors begin to research the variety of choices available in designations and certifications, it is easy to become overwhelmed. During this process, it is imperative to focus on the value that any certification or designation can provide to the counselor. Certifications should be held to the highest standard, in this case, accreditation. Only two financial certifications are nationally accredited: Certified Financial Planner™ and Accredited Financial Counselor®. Any certifications that are pursued should be rigorous. Just because a certification can be obtained this does not mean it is appropriate nor does it indicate a level of knowledge that a client should demand. As with most things, the more difficult it is to obtain and maintain a particular certification the more likely it is to be worthwhile to your practice. Programs like the Accredited Financial Counselor® (AFC®) prepare a professional to work with a client through their unique financial life cycle, rather than focusing on a one-size fits all approach. The certification communicates to individuals and families that the professional adheres to high standards and is informed of new developments in field updates and research. An AFC professional also adheres to the fiduciary rule, which puts the clients' interests above those of the financial counselor.

Across the financial continuum, consistency, accountability, and regulation are critical. Financial counseling focuses on the goals and needs of each client, which makes standardization across each practice difficult to measure in a unified manner. However, when the profession coalesces around comprehensive standards for financial counseling training, it ensures that professionals have the necessary depth of knowledge to provide personalized life cycle financial education for each consumer. This approach ultimately supports clients in making financial behavior changes to strengthen their families and communities.

Need for Regulation

All consumers, regardless of their income level or background, deserve access to highly trained professionals with education, experience, and ongoing professional development and ethical requirements. By setting necessary regulations and defining the continuum of care, appropriate certification provides consumers with the ability to identify financial professionals who have the knowledge and experience to provide financial expertise and help guide financial behavior change.

There are many questions that are currently outstanding about the financial counseling profession going forward. These include determining the clientele, evaluating the quality of the services rendered, and identifying a sustainable model to facilitate the work that needs to be done. In examining different options for sustainability in the profession, many of the options hinge on the definition of the clientele and the assurance of a quality service that is being delivered. Beyond providing financial education and counseling, some financial counselors may work with clients on a Debt Management Plan (DMP). It is important that financial counselors disclose up front what services they will be providing and what fee structures may be used with the client. Much of the media criticism of financial counseling has been focused on companies that were unethical in their treatment of clients and their debt management, including DMPs.

Defining Clientele

Looking at the competitive landscape of financial support services, it is important that the financial counseling profession take an introspective approach and work to define its clientele. Providers of financial counseling programming must focus on identifying and consistently implementing, monitoring, and evaluating processes that demonstrate effectiveness in order to compete for sustainable funding sources.

In the past, financial support services have traditionally been provided by financial planners, who often have minimums for assets under management, and various non-profit organizations that work with the economically vulnerable. The funding model for these two types of models is vastly different. The wealthy have traditionally been targeted by financial planners, who leverage an individual's assets and develop a plan to reach goals and grow the asset base. Given that the clientele have assets, the financial management program is typically supported by fees and/or commission charged to the individual receiving the service. On the other hand, the model for low-income individuals has been more difficult to fund, with organizations (student funded, private support, and volunteer based) providing services to low-income communities as volunteers or at a reduced or subsidized fee. Such programs offer the hope of providing a framework to grow the financial security of the individuals in the community. This model relies heavily on private support and puts the burden on individuals or agencies who are not receiving the service to fund the support.

As financial counselors work to develop a clientele for the profession, the funding options to support those that are doing this work will likely look vastly different based on the clients being served. It is important for financial counselors to be compensated fairly for their expertise, and such payments contribute to the perception that the work being performed is valuable. It is also important to recognize that clients will vary in their ability to afford the services of a financial counselor, and that those who may need such services the most can least afford to pay for them. Because of the variety of clients who may benefit from financial counseling, there is value in exploring a variety of options to find a sustainable model. Beginning with service delivery, there is an opportunity to look towards differential service delivery, including the use of a variety of technology, to serve certain clients. This can help reduce costs and allow for more flexibility in the clients served. Additionally, a hybrid model for counselor compensation can allow for a more diverse client base as counselors can work with lower income individuals (and explore funding streams to support that), while still working with middle income individuals, that may have some personal expense for services but may have the opportunity for a subsidy as well. Additionally, there is an opportunity to work with recent vocational trade school and college graduates who will eventually have means but may need immediate help with debt management. As a profession, it is important to continually evaluate the standards of professionalism and sustainability of the field of financial counseling. We must be willing and able to address the complexities of our profession by expanding career opportunities and solidifying the business structure for financial counselors who service a wide variety of clients.

Vision for the Future of Financial Counseling

Acknowledging the challenges that financial counselors face is important so that plans can be made by individuals and organizations to overcome those challenges and make improvements to the profession. Using research to build an evidence base for financial counseling is one of the most crucial pieces for the future of the profession. It may also be one of the most daunting. Financial counselors will need to be able to recognize and adapt to the generational differences in clients, including their financial capabilities and their comfort level with using technology in financial counseling. Having clear career pathways to the profession and continuing to collaborate with other disciplines will also continue to advance the profession.

When crafting a title for this book, one of the first ideas was Integrated Evidence-Based Financial Counseling. As the authors begin to write their chapters, it became clear that while the chapters embraced the "integrated" aspect of the profession, the "evidence-based" piece was not quite there. What does it mean to be evidence based and why is it important? The term evidence-based first saw a rise in popularity in the early 1990s and was initially emphasized by medical experts from England, Canada, and the United States. "Evidence based medicine is the conscientious, explicit, and judicious use of current best evidence in making decisions about the care of individual patients. The practice of evidence based medicine means integrating individual clinical expertise with the best available external clinical evidence from systematic research" (Sackett, Rosenberg, Gray, Haynes, & Richardson, 1996, p. 71). In other words, it is the "...partnership among hard scientific evidence, clinical expertise, and individual patient needs and choices" (McKibbon, 1998, p. 396).

What is needed in financial counseling is a partnership between evidence, expertise, and client needs and choices. The challenge facing financial counseling as a new profession is that there needs to be more evidence obtained via research before the practice of financial counseling can be considered evidence based. The profession needs practitioners and researchers who can work together to provide empirical evidence that informs the tools and techniques employed by financial counselors. Not only will this evidence base inform practice for financial counselors, but it also has the potential to inform future regulations to provide best services for clients.

As Millennials, also known as Generation Y, enter the workforce it is important for financial counselors to be aware of the differences in this generation when compared to previous generations. Because current life expectancy is high, younger generations will have to be prepared to support themselves longer than other generations have had to in the past (Klapper, Lusardi, & van Oudheusden, 2014). Transferring the burden of savings to individuals and a decrease in welfare systems also puts Millennials in a precarious position if they are not financially savvy. As a group, Millennials have grown up in a digital world, which means they rely on the Internet and their peers for information, including information about finances. According to the 2014 Standard & Poor's Ratings Services Global Financial Literacy Survey, 57% of Millennials in the United States are financially literate.

While that number sounds promising, it still means that 43% of Millennials are not (Klapper et al., 2014). Accordingly, financial counselors should begin to think about how to reach current and future Millennial clients, keeping in mind that they receive most of their information through digital means. Millennial financial counselors will likewise need to be cognizant of the needs of older clients who are not as technologically driven or who may require proof of content expertise.

Continuing to advance the profession, especially through defining clear career paths, will be important to the future of financial counseling. Educating the public and potential employers on the role of a financial counselor is another key to growing the profession. When a financial counselor seeks employment, it can be challenging to navigate the myriad definitions of what constitutes financial counseling. For example, a job description may be labeled as financial counseling, when in fact, the job may actually be more of a healthcare billing and reconciler position.

Financial counseling is an interdisciplinary profession and one that requires collaboration with other disciplines in order to provide the best care for clients. In order to maintain collaborations, it is imperative that financial counselors stay abreast of important issues in not only financial counseling but in other areas as well. This can be done through professional development opportunities, such as webinars and symposiums, and through building strong resources and professional referrals in one's local community.

Call to Action

As this book concludes, the editors and authors wish to leave the reader with a call to action to get involved. Get involved in education and professional development by attending symposiums, registering for webinars, and taking advantage of local development opportunities. Get involved in local communities by providing pro bono services, working with volunteer centers, and creating professional alliances. Be an advocate for clients by referring them to other professionals when you reach your knowledge limit, supporting them through difficult situations such as divorce, bankruptcy, or working with special needs families.

Financial counselors have the opportunity to empower not only their clients, but also their clients' families and communities. The goal is to help all individuals and families become financially well and stable and when this happens and there will no longer be a need for the profession. Until then, there is much work to be done. The editors hope that this book will be a valuable reference for work in financial counseling and empowering clients in their financial futures.

References

Archuleta, K. L., & Grable, J. E. (2011). The future of financial planning and counseling: An introduction to financial therapy. In J. E. Grable, K. Archuleta, & R. R. Nazarinia. *Financial planning and counseling scales* (pp. 33–59). New York: Springer. doi: 10.1007/978-1-4419-6908-8

Carlson, M. (2014). Financial counselor versus financial coach: What's the difference anyway? *AFCPE® the Standard, 32*(4), 1, 12. Retrieved from http://afcpe.org/assets/publications/newsletter/Q4-2014.pdf

Collins, J. M., & O'Rourke, C. M. (2010). Financial education and counseling-still holding promise. *Journal of Consumer Affairs, 44*(3), 483–498. https://doi.org/10.1111/j.1745-6606.2010.01179.x

Consumer Financial Protection Bureau. (n.d.-a). *Librarian training.* Retrieved from https://www.consumerfinance.gov/practitioner-resources/library-resources/librarian-training/

Consumer Financial Protection Bureau. (n.d.-b). *Program ideas.* Retrieved from http://www.consumerfinance.gov/library-resources/program-ideas/

Council for Economic Education. (2016). *Survey of the states: Economic and personal finance education in our nation's schools.* Retrieved from http://councilforeconed.org/wp/wp-content/uploads/2016/02/sos-16-final.pdf

Elliehausen, G., Lundquist, E. C., & Staten, M. E. (2007) The impact of credit counseling on subsequent borrower behavior. *Journal of Consumer Affairs 41*(1), 1–28.

Financial Industry Regulatory Authority. (n.d.). *Professional designations.* Retrieved from http://www.finra.org/investors/professional-designations

Jacobson, V., Ortega, J., & Tranel, M. (2015). Findings from a student loan debt repayment counseling program pilot. In V. Mason & D. E. Kiss (Eds.), *Proceedings of the Association for Financial Counseling and Planning Education 2015 Annual Research and Training Symposium* (pp. 68–71). Jacksonville, FL.

JumpStart Coalition for Personal Financial Literacy. (2015). *National standards in K-12 personal finance education.* Retrieved from http://www.jumpstart.org/assets/files/2015_NationalStandardsBook.pdf

Klapper, L., Lusardi, A., & van Oudheusden, P. (2014). *Financial literacy around the world: Insights from the Standard & Poor's ratings services global financial literacy survey.* Retrieved from http://gflec.org/wp-content/uploads/2015/11/3313-Finlit_Report_FINAL-5.11.16.pdf?x87657

Klapper, L., Lusardi, A., & van Oudheusden, P. (2015). Financial literacy around the world: Insights from the Standard & Poor's ratings services global financial literacy survey. Retrieved from http://gflec.org/wp-content/uploads/2015/11/3313-Finlit_Report_FINAL-5.11.16.pdf?x87657

McKibbon, K. A. (1998). Evidence-based practice. *Bulletin of the Medical Library Association, 86*(3). Retrieved from https://www.ncbi.nlm.nih.gov/pmc/articles/PMC226388/pdf/mlab00092-0108.pdf

Office of Community Services. (n.d.). *About financial capability services.* Retrieved from https://www.acf.hhs.gov/sites/default/files/ocs/financial_capability_services_0.pdf

Sackett, D. L., Rosenberg, W. M. C., Gray, J. A. M., Haynes, R. B., & Richardson, W. S. (1996). Evidence based medicine: What it is and what it isn't. *BMJ, (7023),* 312, 71–312. https://doi.org/10.1136/bmj.312.7023.71

Texas Council on Economic Education. (2012). *Mathematics TEKS on personal financial literacy.* Retrieved from http://smartertexas.org/?page_id=677

Whitebread, D. & Bingham, S. (2013). *Habit formation and learning in young children.* Retrieved from https://mascdn.azureedge.net/cms/the-money-advice-service-habit-formation-and-learning-in-young-children-may2013.pdf

AFC® Program Core Competencies

1. Set the Stage and Gather Client Information
   - Establish the counseling environment
   - Gather client information
   - Form a strategic counseling plan

2. Assist a Client in Creating an Action Plan
   - Assist a client in establishing goals
   - Assist a client in identifying strategies to attain goals

3. Develop Financial Statements, Ratios, and Spending Plans
   - Educate a client about a cash flow statement
   - Educate a client about a net worth statement
   - Educate a client about personal financial ratios
   - Educate a client about spending plans

4. Manage Money
   - Educate a client about financial services
   - Familiarize a client with basic tax management
   - Discuss employment considerations with a client

5. Manage Credit and Debt
   - Educate a client about uses of credit
   - Educate a client about credit reports and scores
   - Educate a client about credit products
   - Educate a client about debt management

6. Educate a Client about Consumer Protection
   - Educate a client about consumer rights and responsibilities
   - Educate a client about identity theft
   - Educate a client about investor protection

7. Educate a Client about Major Acquisitions
   - Acquire property
   - Educate a client about renting a home
   - Educate a client about purchasing a home
   - Educate a client about selling a home

8. Manage Financial Risks
   - Educate a client about financial risk
   - Educate a client about insurance products

© Springer Nature Switzerland AG 2019
D. B. Durband et al. (eds.), *Financial Counseling*,
https://doi.org/10.1007/978-3-319-72586-4

9. Discuss Investment Basics with a Client
   - Educate a client about investment fundamentals
   - Educate a client about investment choices

10. Educate a Client about the Financial Aspects of Retirement and Estate Planning
    - Educate a client about retirement planning
    - Educate a client about estate planning

Adapted from http://www.afcpe.org/certification-and-training/accredited-financial-counselor/afc-core-competencies

Sample Financial Counseling Forms and Worksheets

A description of how each form or worksheet may be used is provided below.

Action Plan
This worksheet offers a means to provide clients with a personalized checklist at the completion of a financial counseling session.

Client Consent and Release
This consent and release is provided as a sample that may be modified for use in providing financial counseling.

Client Information (Intake)
For the financial counseling process, it is important to know the factors associated with the financial situation for the individual or family. These include: income sources, income amounts, family structure, employment status, debts owed, due dates, interest rates, months delinquent, monthly living expenses, and periodic expenses.

Debt Payment Worksheet
This worksheet is to allow clients to create a list of creditors owed, including the types of debt, due dates, balances, monthly payments, and interest rates.

Goal Planning Worksheet
This worksheet helps clients create S.M.A.R.T. goals and track their planned goals.

Identifying Income Worksheet
This worksheet is designed to encourage clients to determine all sources of income sources.

Monthly Spending Plan Worksheet
There are three columns on this worksheet. The "your estimate" column is what the client completes with the assistance of the financial counselor. The "actual" column can be used to record actual spending for a month. After the client has completed the estimate and the actual columns, the financial counselor can assist the client in completing the "budget" column. Total monthly net income is totaled from the Identifying Income Worksheet. Total monthly obligations to creditors are totaled from the Debt Payment Worksheet.

Planning Periodic Expenses Worksheet
This worksheet is used to identify periodic expenses such as back to school shopping, insurance, or any other expense that does not occur every month, but still occurs on a regular basis.

Action Plan

Client(s) name: Date:		
Goals:		
1.		
2.		
3.		
Actions required:	Planned date of completion:	Actual date of completion:
Modification required:		
Next appointment date:		

Sample Client Consent and Release

I voluntarily consent to receive financial counseling services from the [INSERT NAME HERE]. I understand that the financial counselor providing financial information cannot recommend any investments, insurance, or provide legal advice.

In the course of financial counseling, it may be necessary for my financial counselor to discuss my financial information with his or her supervisor and with creditors to whom I owe money.

By my acceptance of these terms and conditions, I do hereby release, indemnify, and hold harmless [INSERT NAME HERE] agents and employees from any and all liability of any type whatsoever arising from any acts or omissions, negligent or otherwise, by said agents, employees, or volunteers, relating to [INSERT NAME HERE].

Signature: _____   Date: _____

Client Information Sheet

Client: **Last Name:** _____   **First Name:** _____

                Date of Birth: _____   **Gender:** _____

Relationship Status: ☐ Single   ☐ Married   ☐ Separated   ☐ Divorced   ☐ Widowed

Highest Educational Level: ☐   Some High School ☐   High School/GED ☐ College
☐ Graduate School

Race/Ethnicity: ☐ White   ☐ Hispanic or Latino ☐ Native American ☐ Black/African American
☐ Hawaiian/Pacific Islander   ☐ Other (please specify) _____

Employment Status: ☐ Full-time ☐ Part-time ☐ Seasonal ☐ Retired ☐ Unemployed ☐ Student
Occupation: _____
Payment Frequency: ☐ Weekly ☐ Bi-Weekly   ☐ Monthly ☐ Semi-Monthly

Veterans/Active Duty/Reserves   ☐ Yes   ☐ No
If yes, in which branch did you serve? _____

Contact Information:

Local Street Address: _____

Phone # _____ **Cell Phone #** _____

E-mail Address: _____

Number of child dependents (under 18): _____   **Number of adult dependents:** _____

Financial Information:

Household Monthly Take-Home Pre-Tax Pay: $_____

After Tax-Pay: $_____/**Month**

Housing Status   ☐ Buying   ☐ Renting ☐ Room & Board ☐ Shelter ☐ Other _____

Current rent/house payment? $_____/**Month**

Please indicate the area(s) you are most concerned with today (Check all that apply):

Money Management/Budgeting _____   Start Building Credit _____

Credit Report Questions _____   Unexpected Crisis _____

Behind in Monthly Payments _____   Rent/Mortgage Questions _____

Student Loan Questions _____   Pay Down Debt _____

Medical Expenses _____   Unemployment _____

Repayment of Loans _____   Set up Savings Plan _____

Other (Please specify) _____

Please indicate how you heard about us:

_____

What questions would you like to have answered during your session?

_____

_____

_____

Debt Payment Worksheet

Creditor's name	Type of debt	Balance owed	Monthly payment amount	Monthly payment currently being paid	Current or past due?	Interest rate (APR)	Credit limit

Goal Planning Worksheet

Date: _____   Name: _____

Use the following to help you create your **SMART goal(s)**:
S – Specific- Who, what, where, why, and how of the goal?
M – Measurable – How will you measure your progress? What are the key items to accomplish?
A – Achievable – What attitudes, skills, and abilities will you need to accomplish your goal?
R – Realistic – Explain how this goal is realistic for you at this time.
T – Timely – When will you start/finish your goal? What is the timeframe of your goal?

Goal # 1 _____   Goal # 2 _____

Specific: _____   Specific: _____
_____   _____
_____   _____
_____   _____

Measurable: _____   Measurable: _____
_____   _____
_____   _____

Achievable: _____   Achievable: _____
_____   _____
_____   _____

Realistic: _____   Realistic: _____
_____   _____
_____   _____

Timely: _____   Timely: _____
_____   _____
_____   _____

Identifying Income Worksheet

Date:_____

Client's
Name:_____

Sources of income	Monthly	Yearly
ACTIVE EMPLOYMENT		
Wages, tips, or commissions		
Spouse or partner wages, tips, or commissions		
Part-time employment		
Unemployment		
DISABILITY		
Social security disability		
Disability insurance		
RETIREMENT		
Pension		
Social security		
Retirement distributions		
ADDITIONAL ASSISTANCE		
Child support		
Veterans' benefits		
Alimony		
Student loans or grants		
Scholarships		
Income tax refund		
PUBLIC ASSISTANCE		
Housing		
Medical		
Food		
Other:		
Other:		
Other:		
Notes:		

Monthly Spending Plan Worksheet

Expenses	Your estimate	Actual	Budget
Saving/investing			
Rent or mortgage payment			
Life/health insurance			
Auto/home insurance			
Utilities			
Water/sewer/garbage			
Child support			
Child care and babysitting			
Food at home			
Meals eaten away from home			
Auto payment(s)			
Gas and fuel			
Parking			
Diapers, formula, baby supplies			
Children's allowance, school expenses			
Hairdresser			
Health and fitness			
Doctor/dentist/pharmacy			
Clothing/uniforms			
Dry cleaning/laundromat			
Tobacco/alcohol			
Entertainment			
Personal care toiletries			
Pets			
Gifts			
Charities			
Auto maintenance			
Auto tags and registration			
Property taxes			
Out of town travel/vacation			
For reserve account (total periodic expenses/12)			
Other			
Total monthly net income			
Total living expenses			
Total monthly obligations to creditors			
Balance			

Worksheet for Planning Periodic Expenses

Expense	Jan	Feb	March	April	May	June	July	Aug	Sept	Oct	Nov	Dec	Total	Monthly avg.

Date: _____

Client's Name: _____

NOTES: _____

How to Read Research Articles: A Guide for Practitioners[1]

1. What's the research question?
   Identifies the purpose of the study. It is typically found in the introduction section and/or abstract.

2. What do we already know?
   The literature review tells us what is currently known regarding the research question and should summarize knowledge gaps to justify the research purpose.

3. What's the conceptual framework?
   The conceptual (or theoretical) framework is the lens the researcher uses to investigate the research question and explain the results. It guides the research design and informs the expected findings (i.e., the hypothesis).

4. Who is in the study?
   The composition of the sample is critical to understanding the relatability of the results to your clients. Sample specifics (e.g., age, gender, marital status) can typically be found in the method and results section.

5. What method was used?
   This section will outline the source of data and statistical techniques to other researchers can judge and replicate results. Peer-reviewed journals help to ensure credibility, allowing you to focus on results.

6. What's the variable of interest?
   This is the key factor the researcher is trying to explain variation of (dependent variable). It is important to understand how it's measured and how the explanatory factors (independent variables) are hypothesized to impact variation in the dependent variable.

7. What are the findings and implications?
   The results section presents the raw findings while the discussion/conclusion section interprets the results within the context of the conceptual framework—identifying why the results matter and who these results are useful for.

8. How can this enhance my practice?
   Ideally, findings will be translated into specific tools/suggestions for practitioners—if not, you will have to get creative! Still have questions? Reach out to the authors—most are happy to chat with you! (Contact information will be included in the article.)

---

[1] Source: www.afcpe.org

Index

© Springer Nature Switzerland AG 2019
D. B. Durband et al. (eds.), *Financial Counseling*,
https://doi.org/10.1007/978-3-319-72586-4

Financial literacy
  definition, 18
  vs. financial knowledge, 19
  life and financial contexts, 19
  macro-economic life, 21
  motivation and confidence, 19
  OECD, 18
  principles, 21
  societal well-being and participation in
    economic life, 19
Financial Planning Association (FPA), 28
Financial Remedies, 183, 184
Financial Therapy Association (FTA), 28
Five-D cycle, 106
Ford Financial Empowerment Model (FFEM),
  57–58
Formal education, 53
Free Application for Federal Student Aid
  (FAFSA), 144
Free association, 79, 80
Freud's model, 77
Front-end ratio, 23
Furniture arrangement, 121
Future-time reference (FTR), 138

G
Gambling disorder, 158
Gender, 50
Generalizable model, 128
General systems theory, 48, 87–88
Genograms, 70
Gestalt therapy, 82–84
Goal planning worksheet, 209

H
Heuristics, 137
High-touch interventions, 148–150
Hoarding disorder (HD), 157, 158
Housing and Urban Development (HUD), 11
Housing expense ratio, 23
Hypnosis, 79

I
Implicit Association Test (IAT), 59
InCharge Financial Distress/Financial
  Well-Being Scale, 133
Income worksheet, 209, 221
Informal education, 53
Insight/action-focused theories, 35
Integrated Evidence-Based Financial
  Counseling, 203

J
Just-in-time education, 146

K
K-12 environment, 197
Klontz-Britt Financial Health Scale
  (K-BFHS), 163
Klontz Money Behavior Inventory (KMBI),
  162
Klontz Money Script Inventory (KMSI), 163
Klontz Money Script Inventory-Revised
  (KMSI-R), 163
Kolbe A™ Index, 69

L
Land-grant institution, 6
Leading, 115
Libertarian paternalism, 145
Life evaluation, 129
Lifestyle/style of life, 81
Lighting, 122
Liquidity ratio, 23

M
Macrosystem, 49, 54
Marginal utility of wealth, 128
Mental health, 53
Mental health professionals, 80
Mental health professions, 92
Mental Research Institute (MRI),
  87, 97–98
Mesosystem, 48, 54
Microsystem, 48
Millennials/Generation Y, 203
Milwaukee-based Brief Family Therapy
  Center (BFTC), 97
Mindfulness, 60
Mindfulness-based stress reduction, 73
Mint, 184, 185
MONEY 2000™, 189
Money disorders, 160–165
  assessment
    FAS, 163, 164
    K-BFHS, 163
    KMBI, 162
    KMSI, 163
  avoidance, 154, 155
  client's financial stress, 153
  compulsive buying, 158, 159
  counseling techniques, 154
  definition, 157

CPSIA information can be obtained
at www.ICGtesting.com
Printed in the USA
LVHW08*2351211018
594347LV00004B/149/P